The Future of Finance

Adjiedj Bakas
Roger Peverelli

For Herman Wiegerinck
and Jo-Anne Raming-van Dongen

Copyright © Adjiedj Bakas and Roger Peverelli, 2009

The right of Adjiedj Bakas and Roger Peverelli to be identified as the authors of this book has been asserted in accordance with the Copyright, Designs and Patents Act 1988.

First published in 2009 by
Infinite Ideas Limited
36 St Giles
Oxford, OX1 3LD
United Kingdom
www.infideas.com

A CIP catalogue record for this book is available from the British Library

ISBN 978-1-906821-01-2

Research by Trend Office Bakas, VODW Marketing, Minne Buwalda
Editors: Minne Buwalda, in cooperation with Helen Berliner and Hein de Boorder
Designed by Wentelwereld Grafische Vormgeving, Westkapelle
Cover by Baseline Arts Ltd, Oxford
Printed and bound in Malta

www.thefutureoffinance.com

Contents

foreword

At the time of publication, the financial industry is experiencing a worldwide crisis, which I believe has resulted from a casual approach to risk-taking. Previous bubbles, such as tulipomania in the seventeenth century, were caused by private investors getting carried away by their eagerness to invest in something new, and subsequently losing their money. Now we see professionals failing. We have already seen this in the past during the Asian crisis and the crisis in Latin American countries such as Argentina and Brazil. I believe this to be the result of the remuneration systems that have become fashionable in the industry. Let's focus on the blind spot of risk managers for the effects of financial incentives on behavior. Huge and advanced risk-management departments did not prevent large write-offs and big losses at a great number of very respected financial institutions. It may be an exaggeration to say, "the bigger and more advanced risk-management departments were, the bigger the write-offs and losses," but it is close to the truth. It is not an exaggeration to say that risk-management failed in a lot of places. The risk-management profession has been very active in developing statistical analysis, stress-tests, guarding procedures and scenario analysis. The number of identified risks has grown over the years. Nowadays in the financial industry we distinguish macro-economic risk, credit risk, interest-rate risk, liquidity risk, business risk, operational risk, concentration risk, counter-party risk and reputational risk. And there is even more. It would appear that at present, the risks that remuneration schemes and financial incentives pose are not on the agenda of risk managers. But I think they should be. Normally the organization which originated the loans also kept the credit risk, the loans staying on their own books. That was an incentive for making careful decisions. The creation of the securitization market made the split possible between origination and credit risk. What was overlooked by investors and risk managers was that all the statistics of the past become irrelevant if such a regime change occurs. Shedding the credit risk leads to a greater appetite for risky behavior with the originator, especially in a country with weak public supervision. And many people with expertise in number-crunching missed the crucial notion that institutional changes and regime changes make all the old numbers irrelevant.

Suppose you have money, you are good at statistics but you are not a good poker player. But you know a good poker player. You have analyzed his results statistically and hire him to work for you. You pay him a fixed wage, accept occasional losses (all part of the game) and as an incentive for playing well, you offer him 20% of the profits he makes for you. According to your analysis of his past results, this is a profitable contract for you. It is not difficult, though, into understand that the expert poker player will play differently under this contract than he used to play. He will take more risks in the hope of large profits and he won't be concerned about big losses because he will shift those to you. He will have his fixed salary and possibly a big profit share, which will not be recouped in the event that a big loss is incurred. You don't have to be a trained economist or an experienced risk manager to understand this. Nevertheless, incentive schemes in the financial sector are very much like this poker contract.

The standard remuneration contract for a hedge-fund manager is almost an exact copy: a fixed fee plus 20% of the profit and no loss-sharing. The same goes for traders at banks. If they have a profitable year they gain a lot; if they have a year with losses they still have their salary. Less extreme but still following the same principles are the incentive schemes of the highest management. They also have elements of the poker-player contract. Volatility in profits creates better rewards than less volatile profits, even if these profits are, on average, the same. And if, after having made large profits – only made possible by taking risks – the tables turn and losses mount up, the employee gets away with it without having to

repay bonuses he or she received in the past, while the employer is left to pay the bill. In some cases, employees are even given an extra amount of money just to leave.

An example from everyday practice with the same mechanism is the way "deal-makers" at banks get special deal-related fees. When a stock-listed company goes to the bank to ask for a loan, their account manager will explain that the bank cannot go any further than a loan within the boundaries of 1:3 in terms of equity to debt. This employee has the credit risk for the bank in mind and knows that it will be bad for his career if he is too friendly. But then a private-equity fund turns up at the very same bank, to finance the takeover of the very same company. The private-equity investor has contacts with a different department of the bank. The personal incomes of the bankers in this department depend to a large extent on the on the number (and the size) of deals they make. And their proposal for financing this takeover will be based on a 1:9 equity to debt relation. This example is not an invention, it's an example from real life. It is not difficult to understand that officials who are paid based on the number and size of deals are eager to make as many and as sizeable deals as possible. And they get their personal fee not when the money is safely returned to the bank, but as soon as the money is transferred out of the bank.

Suppose you want to buy a house. The seller of the house explains to you that you are lucky, because he has already hired and paid an expert, who made an assessment of the house and its value. Would you be happy to be so lucky, and accept everything that is stated in this expert's report? Or would you think, "I am not so sure whether the opinion of an expert hired and paid by the seller, is also a good guidance for me as a buyer." In his personal life, no economist or risk-manager would, as a buyer, rely on an expert who is selected, appointed and paid by a seller. In the financial sector, however, this is common practice. Investors rely on rating agencies which are hired and paid by the very same organizations that they are to rate, and whose products they are to judge.

What can we conclude? That risk-management is too important to leave to professional risk managers. Statistical analysis is useful, but without common sense it is dangerous. Risk managers should be more assertive in addressing the behavioral effects of incentive schemes within their firms, even if management doesn't like it. They must have an eye for the effects of financial incentives in the broader perspective of the outside world.

Financial incentive schemes should be corrected in such a way that only long-term results are paying off. Deal-makers in the financing of private-equity should be rewarded only when the loan is repaid, not when the loan is going out. Traders should be rewarded according to their long-term result instead of a yearly – perhaps lucky – result. Management schemes should be amended in such a way that short-term bonuses are abolished. Short-term bonuses are an incentive for irresponsible behavior. Long-term bonuses are sensible but it should be ensured that the official who is getting a bonus cannot have any influence on the reporting of the result to which this bonus is related. He or she should even be out of office before the bonus is granted. Risk managers should see it as their job to analyze the potential effects of financial incentives on risk-taking behavior, both inside and outside the firm. Shareholders should ask for such an analysis, critically judge it, and actively use their powers to set the guidelines for a remuneration policy. In order to prevent misunderstandings, I want to stress that my criticism is not based on the idea that many people in the financial industry are being payed excessively. People positioned at the top of many other industries, such as sports or entertainment, often have a higher income than those in top positions in the financial industry. My criticism is that there is a lack of thorough analysis of the effect of financial incentives on behavior in the financial sector. This is the real worry and an urgent issue to resolve.

The global economy achieved its current size thanks to the invention of money and the creation and expansion of the worldwide financial sector. How will the financial sector develop in the coming decades and lift itself out of its current crisis? There are various "unmistakable trends," such as continuing technological developments, demographics, miniaturization and the prices of oil and raw materials. I am pleased to see that these trends are described in this book. It is also good to see these trends being transposed into future scenarios. The authors further place their trends in a historical perspective, which is very useful. History often repeats itself, but in different guises. If you take a historical perspective, you are not that put out by, for example, the failure of a single World Trade Organization negotiation round. This book has become exciting and readable thanks to the combination of history, trends, scenario techniques, the valuable contributions of many industry insiders, and the connection of all of that to trends and information from outside the industry.

Gerrit Zalm

Gerrit Zalm is Chief Financial Officer of DSB Bank, Chairman of the International Accounting Standards Committee Foundation (IASCF) and an adviser to the private-equity fund Permira. He spent twelve years as Minister of Finance of the Netherlands.

preface

In the summer of 2007, we met at a congress where we were both giving speeches on social and financial trends. We complemented each other on our content, and hit it off immediately because we, among other things, share a passion for art, history, and modernization.

While brainstorming, we found we had very similar ideas about financial services for consumers, an area that is expecting to see drastic changes in the future. These changes will bring providers of financial services back to their roots. Back to why money was invented: to promote trade by barter. Back to why banks, insurance companies, and pension funds were established: to stimulate entrepreneurship, to limit and share risks, to help people with their savings, and to make more money with money through reinvesting. Capitalism, according to Karl Marx, is the circulation of debt. As long as that goes well, there is nothing to worry about, except for the occasional bubble. These upward and downward movements have been part of the continuous process that led to the fully developed financial industry of the twenty-first century. In this book we will consider the future of this industry.

We have written this book primarily for the financial community, particularly those who work in banks, insurance companies, and pension funds. Other stakeholders in the field, such as accountants, credit card companies, lease companies, hedge-funds, and tax authorities are mentioned indirectly.

Our focus does not lie on information technology, forms of organization or cost efficiency. We focus on growth strategies and the business development of B2C (business-to-consumer) markets in three continents: Asia, America, and Europe. Africa and the Pacific are mentioned in passing.

Understandably, the many professionals in the financial industry have all hands on deck just to survive the current turmoil. However, in doing so, they run the risk of developing tunnel vision at a time when finding new direction is crucial. This is why we thought it important to write this book at this particular time. We wanted to look above and beyond the current crisis and to help the financial industry define new strategies and "leap over its own shadow." The aim of this book is – beyond the day-to-day struggle – to inspire, to be thought – and discussion provoking and to spark new ideas and innovation.

It may sound like a cliché, but every cloud has a silver lining: a financial crisis marks the transition from one era to another, and after a crisis, there will always be another Golden age. The fact that history has cyclical patterns, is also emphasized by scientists. Carlota Perez of Sussex University for example states that over the past 200 years we have seen 5 technological cycles that show remarkable similarities. During the 'installation period' of such an age, companies can integrate new technologies to their businesses relatively cheaply. Later on in this phase, 'technological euphoria', as Perez calls it, appears, creating a bubble on the financial markets. After this bubble has burst, a recession or a depression follows, in which financial markets calm down. That is the turning point in a technological age. This is when the time of 'deployment' sets in, in which society adapts to the new techno-macro economic paradigm and the full potential of the technological revolution develops. This period ends when the power of the new technology fades and the world is waiting for the next revolution. The 5 cycles we have seen in the past 200 years – interrupted each and every time by a financial crisis during the installation period – were: the industrial revolution, the age of steam power and railroads, the age of electricity, of steel and heavy machine building, the age of the car and mass production, and today's age of information and telecommunication. According to Perez the current financial crisis is the turning point in the technological era of today, necessary to fully develop the potential of today's information- and telecommunication technology.

In the coming years banks, insurance companies and pension funds will streamline their organizations and renew financial products drastically, making them much more transparent by using technology, the autonomy of the consumer, and the opportunities of globalization. The current remuneration structure in the industry will radically change and will go back to basics. There's simply no alternative. Risk assessment will be more strict and the 'me too' sentiment, that has reigned for a long time within the macho leadership climate, will be put to its grave. This sentiment was responsible for rewarding ever bigger risks with ever bigger bonuses. If you weren't in this game, you would quickly be seen as a loser. Now that this machismo is bankrupt and the bonus culture will be scrapped, there will be more room for feminization in the industry. Not a bad thing, considering the growing importance of female consumers.

This book was created on the basis of sessions with think-tanks within VODW Marketing, interviews with experts from the financial industry, and also research at the knowledge bases of Trend Office Bakas and VODW Marketing.

The people who participated in the think-tanks of VODW are: Margot van Beusekom, Marcel van Brenk, Beate van Dongen-Crombags, Charlotte Buys, Lucas Goossens, Jan Heuvel (Onna Onna), Marloes Jansen, Dries Laurs, Marinde van Leeuwen-Fontein, Carlotte Mos, Danielle Nieuwenhuis, Jos Nederpel, Isolde Schram, Maton Sonnemans, Albert Spijkman, Thijs Out, Wouter in 't Velt, Herman Wiegerinck, Derk van Wingerden and Suzanne IJsebaert.

We want to give special thanks to Lilian Alibux, Hong-May Cheng, Reggy de Feniks, Irene van den Brink and Valborg Korthals Altes, for their important contributions.

For this book we used an enormous number of sources. Because we wanted to keep it easy to read, we refrained from using footnotes. Instead a list of our sources is given in the back of the book, and is also published on the website for this book. We have tried our utmost to be as careful as possible in naming our sources. If, however, a source is not included, or not correctly listed, we offer our apologies in advance. If and when we are made aware of any such omissions, we will correct this in the next printing of the book and on the website.

Many experts from the industry were kind enough to cooperate through interviews and comments on our views. In alphabetical order they are: Jeremy Alwyn (Head of Bank Distribution Europe, Zurich Financial Services); Steve Austen, Kimberly Bastoni (Senior Vice President of Custom Marketing and Development, TNS United States), Theo Bouts (Chief Operating Officer of Global Life, Zurich Financial Services), Lans Bovenberg (Professor of Economics at University of Tilburg), Bertina Bus (Marketing Manager Global Finance Sector, TNS Global), Frits Bussemaker (Consultant at Ordina), Hugo Caballero Albiñana (Market consultant in Chili), Walter Capellmann (Partner of Capellmann Consulting, Germany), Ricardo Fakiera (Vice President Merrill Lynch International in the Netherlands), Raquel Goshima (Marketing Research

Expert Financial Services in Brazil), Tilman Hengevoss (Chief of Marketing Officer and Head of Corporate Development, Zurich Financial Services Switzerland), Robert Hovenier (Managing Director, Fortis Intertrust Switzerland), Guido Lanzoni (Head of Credit, UniCredit Banca di Roma, London), Bob Neuhaus (Executive Vice President of Financial Services, TNS North America), Annette Nijs (Managing Director europa China Institute at Nijenrode Business University), Pim Mol (Director of Private Banking Rabobank), Frans van der Reep (Senior Strategist of KPN), Ravi Sankaranarayanan (Chief Executive of Retail and Commercial Banking, Europe and Middle East, Royal Bank of Scotland), Harry Smorenberg (independant consultant), Graham Tocher (Regional Director for Asia Pacific, Latin America, Middle East and Africa, TNS Finance, Singapore), and Gerrit Zalm (Chief Financial Officer of DSB Bank, and Chairman of the International Accounting Standards Committee Foundation).

The Future of Finance contains columns by: Peter Blom (CEO, Triodos Bank), Arturo Bris (Professor of Finance, IMD Lausanne), José Manuel Campa (Grupo Santander Professor of Finance at IESE Business School), Sir Ronald Cohen (Founder of Apax Partners), Ray Davis (CEO, Umpqua Bank), Jo van Engelen and Roderick Munsters (Chief Marketing Officer and Chief Investment Officer, APG), Ricardo Fakiera (Vice President, Merrill Lynch International in the Netherlands), Paul van de Geijn (Member of the Group Executive Committee, Zurich Financial Services), Nick Jue (CEO, ING Retail Netherlands), Jean-Noël Kapferer (Professor of Marketing at HEC School of Management, Paris), Wim Kok (Member of the Board of Directors ING Group), HRH Princess Máxima of the Netherlands (Member of the United Nations Advisors Group on Inclusive Financial Sectors), Joseph Pine II (author of *Authenticity*), Isidoro Unda (CEO, Atradius), Richard Wacker (CEO, Korea Exchange Bank), Joop Wijn (Director, SME Rabobank) and Michiel Wielhouwer and Arie van Dusseldorp (Country Manager of Visa Europe and Marketing Director of LaSer Nederland). We thank all of them for their contribution.

In particular we would like to express our gratitude to Nout Wellink for his extensive cooperation. As President of the Dutch National Bank (DNB), Member of the Board of the European Central Bank (ECB), President of the Basel Committee on Bank Supervision, and Governor of the

International Monetary Fund (IMF), he is an extremely busy man. Mr Wellink nevertheless managed to find the time in his schedule to make a great contribution to this book. The support of this highly esteemed opinion leader also made it possible to present this book at the head office of DNB. Tobias Oudejans, a spokesman for Nout Wellink, went to great lengths to make this presentation a success.

Michel Noordermeer (NVB), Jan Lodewijk Roebroek (Fortis Investments), Willy Linssen and Meg Kang (Heartware Korea), Els van Weering (IMD Lausanne), Rebecca Kemsley (Portland Capital), Hadewych Kuiper (Triodos Bank), and Jan Willem Stapel (Fortis Intertrust USA) were kind enough to introduce us to various interesting contacts in the industry.

And last, but not least, our editor Minne Buwalda helped us to turn all of this into prose. Thank you all. Many, many thanks.

We wish you many moments of recognition and lots of inspiration reading this book.

Amsterdam, Barcelona, Beijing, Frankfurt, Hong Kong, London, Madrid, Maldives, Milan, Moscow, Mumbai, New York, Paramaribo, Paris, Reykjavik, Rome, Santa Agnes de Corona, Santa Teresa di Gallura, Santiago de Chile, São Paolo, Singapore, Tel Aviv, Tokyo, Zurich.

Adjiedj Bakas & Roger Peverelli

part 1

Financial Services
Past, Present and Future Scenarios

When you haven't any coal in the stove and you freeze in the winter
And you curse to the wind at your fate;
When you haven't any shoes on your feet and your coat's thin as paper
And you look thirty pounds underweight,
When you go to get a word of advice from the fat little pastor,
He will tell you to love evermore.
But when hunger comes to rap, rat-a-tat, rat-a-tat, at the window;
See how love flies out the door.

For money makes the world go around,
The world go around, the world go around.
Money makes the world go around,
The clinking, clanking sound of
Money, money, money, money,
Get a little, get a little,
Money, money, money, money,
A Mark, a yen, a buck or a pound,
That clinking, clanking clunking sound
Is all that makes the world go round,
It makes the world go round.

(from the musical *Cabaret*, lyrics by Clifford Bradshaw)

Money Makes the World go Round:
a Bit of History

Many people know the song "Money, money" from the musical *Cabaret*. The best-known sentence from the song is: "Money makes the world go round." The meaning is clear: there is nothing as important as money.

You can think about money any way you want, but it's obvious that it has played an important role in the way people have organized the world. Money made possible the existence of urban cultures and the difference between peasants, artisans, rulers, and soldiers. Money has broadened the horizon beyond the places where we happened to be born.

The First banks, Insurance Companies, and Pension Funds
The earliest banks, insurance companies, and pension funds made us begin to save and invest, and to work more than we strictly needed to in order to cover our cost of living at that moment. Money and the financial services that emerged from it brought us prosperity, and at the same time security, safety, and peace of mind. Money offers the prospect of better times, and the feeling that we can contribute to that. It is difficult to imagine what a world without money would look like, but that world would certainly be far less developed.

What is Money?
Historically, money could be anything, as long as it was generally accepted as a means of payment and as a monetary unit to record debts and credits. In the long history of mankind many things have had the status of money: cows, cowry shells, whales' teeth, eggs, feathers, ivory, jade, rice, salt, and vodka, to name just a few.

Cowry shells were accepted as money in many places, for example in Africa, India, and China. In West Africa, they were used as a currency until the twentieth century. In China, the cowry was so important that the Chinese

character for money is derived from the pictogram of a shell. Among the most ancient metal coins found in China are copies of cowry shells cast in bronze or copper.

Horse Trading and The First Banks
Before money made its appearance, people had to make do with barter. This could be very awkward. Imagine that you and your friends went hunting and killed a mammoth. One dead mammoth means a lot of steaks, too many to munch away in a short time, and refrigerators did not yet exist. So it was wise to invite all the neighbors in for a big party or to exchange part of your meat supply for other products. But there wasn't much time to bargain because the meat would soon go bad, and moreover there weren't many products for exchange. The woman in the cave down the road might have an extra pottery bowl or a few animal hides to offer, but that would be about it.

Goods From Hand to Hand
Money was useful, not only for moving scarce goods from hand to hand more smoothly, but also for settling conflicts. Since the traditional principle of "an eye for an eye and a tooth for a tooth" repeatedly led to bloodshed, human beings had to find a more civilized solution. The payment of compensation for a crime was a more peaceful and therefore more attractive solution. Interestingly, the English verb "to pay" was derived from the Latin *pacare* meaning "to pacify," or "make peace."

Other recurring transactions provided incentives to introduce money: the payment of dowries to in-laws, the payment of taxes to rulers, and the payment of offerings to gods and ancestors. But it would be necessary to standardize these recurring payments, in order to be able to treat everyone equally. Imagine if one person paid with cows, while the other had only pigs or apples to offer in return.

Payments to Bearer
Even before real coins were struck, there was already mention of some kind of banking institution. In both ancient Mesopotamia and Egypt, a system developed in which cereals and fruits were stored in central,

government-guarded warehouses. After some time, receipts for similar batches of goods would pass into the hands of third parties, giving those receipts the status of an official currency. There were also written orders for the payment of certain amounts of cereal to their bearers, which were used to settle debts to tax collectors, priests, and merchants.

Even after struck coins were introduced in Egypt, these cereal bank papers remained in use as currency. During the reign of the Ptolemies, a dynasty of Greek pharaohs (323 to 30 BC), the banking system of the cereal warehouses became further sophisticated. The administration of the warehouses, which had spread all over Egypt, became centralized in a sort of central bank located in Alexandria. Here, transfers were made on paper, without a coin or grain of cereal changing hands.

A New Development: Struck Coins

A transitional form between barter and the use of struck coins was payment with weighed quantities of metal: iron, copper, bronze, tin, silver, or gold. (Like the English word "pound," the verb "to spend" derives from the Latin word *expendere* which means "to weigh.") Of all of these metals, gold was of course the favorite, not only because it was so rare, but also because of its beauty and the fact that it doesn't rust. The disadvantage of payments in weighed metal was that you always had to carry your balance around, and you couldn't just count sums out in coins.

After a while, however, these metals began to be cast into molds. We already mentioned the metal cowry shells made by the Chinese, who also used molds of miniature spades, shovels, and knives for their coins. Completely independent of China, the use of such "tool coins" also developed in Europe. In ancient Greece, for example, metal nails were used as coins.

Standardization of Coins

The striking of coins developed in earnest in Asia Minor (in modern-day Turkey) where the Lydians invented a way to cast precious metals in small round molds, obtaining uniform shapes and weights. To signify this standardization, they impressed a stamp in the metal.

The first real coins date from 640 to 630 BC, and their use was quickly adopted by the Greeks and Persians. These coins not only had an important economic function, but they often served a political purpose as well. In ancient Greece, with its many small city-states, the striking of coins with a city's coat of arms was a sign of political independence. Roman emperors had their images struck on coins to demonstrate their far-reaching influence and as a form of propaganda. It enabled their subjects in the provinces to know their names and what they looked like. The use of coins quickly spread all over the world, due to their ease of use. Instead of always having to weigh goods or metal, one could simply count out coins.

Paper Money

The first paper money originated in China in the tenth century, where it was used from the year 960. The reason for this development was a shortage of copper, which was used to make coins. Around 1020, however, the great number of banknotes in circulation led to inflation. In following centuries, frequent periods of super-inflation even led to the abolishment

of banknotes in 1455, after more than 500 years of use.

In Europe, paper money didn't make its appearance until the seventeenth century. During the English Civil War from 1642 to 1649, many people took their jewelry, gold nuggets, and coins to the vaults of goldsmiths, for fear that they would be stolen at home. By 1660 the goldsmiths' receipts and payment orders for certain sums of money to their bearers had developed into banknotes.

The Gold Standard

Although paper money has no intrinsic value, it became accepted because the value was covered by goods – mostly precious metals. In the beginning this was mostly silver; the British pound was originally the equivalent of one pound of silver. But by the nineteenth century, silver had become increasingly replaced by gold and the "gold standard."

Gold is sometimes used directly as currency – gold circulation. A second system is to issue paper money that can be exchanged for gold at any time, as the total value of that money equals the total amount of gold in the central bank. In a third possible system, the possibility to exchange paper money for precious metal is limited, because the amount of paper money issued is greater than the value of gold stocks in the central bank.

By 1900 the gold standard was in use in most countries. However, it was suspended in times of crisis: during the First World War and the years of the Great Depression in the 1930s. After the Second World War, the United States was the only country left with a currency still related to gold, which led the dollar to replace the pound as the most important currency in the world. From that moment on, exchange rates were expressed in dollars, until the early 1970s when the dollar lost its direct relation to gold and this system began to disintegrate.

Credit Cards, E-money, and M-banking

The credit card was invented in 1950 by Ralph Schneider and Frank McNamara. Diners Club was the first company to issue credit cards. It soon joined a network of companies including American Express, Visa, and MasterCard to create a worldwide system that enabled people to pay with their cards almost everywhere. Everybody wanted to start "paying with plastic."

At the moment, new generations of credit cards are being developed: cards that can be used by new cash registry systems. They enable you, for example, simply to swipe your card through a scanner, and the amount would be debited before you even got home.

Visa is the world's largest credit card company. In 2006 its subsidiary, Visa Europe, processed €1,200 billion worth of transactions. CEO Peter Ayliffe expects that many consumers won't be using cash in the future.

However, we are still a long way from becoming a cashless society in Europe, 80% of payments are still made in cash or by check. Nout Wellink doesn't believe in the disappearance of cash in the first place, because "the anonymity of physical money can't be replaced." Technology always leaves traces and trails, even when you try to destroy them. People like the anonymity of the banknote; this doesn't necessarily mean their money is "dirty," it just means that people will always have reasons for wishing to pass on money without leaving a trail.

Virtual Money and Central Banks

Wellink doesn't deny that the role of physical money has to a large extent been taken over by non-physical money. This has consequences for central banks, which traditionally have had the monopoly on printing banknotes. As Wellink says, "As a result the future income of central banks could decrease, compared to that of the overall financial sector and the risks it takes. This could have consequences for the independence of central banks because, in the long-term, they could become dependent on government financing. They are so independent now because they have the banknote monopoly. Every now and then they worry about how they will secure that independence when banknotes become less used."

Changes to Come in The Near Future

The trend towards virtual money over the past half-century was initiated by the rise of the credit card. Other developments are now influencing

The Future of Finance

this trend: the rise of many different forms of Internet banking and electronic money (e-money) since the 1990s and since 2000 the rise of cell phone banking, or "m-banking."

As cell phone use increases – Nokia anticipates more than three billion users worldwide in 2009 – m-banking will become more popular. Even PayPal, which we will discuss later in this book, is an example of the virtualization of money.

Monetary experts Douglas Wood and Ismael Erturk of the Manchester Business School state: "Technical innovations, the massive scale on which transactions now occur and irreversible trends to financial deregulation and commercial globalization, mean the current decade will see more change in international payment systems than the preceding millennium."

Early Insurance Companies and Pension Funds

The principles of insurance can be traced back to Babylonia, where merchants were encouraged to assume the risk of caravan trade by providing loans to be repaid (with interest) only after the merchandise had safely arrived. This custom became law in the Code of Hammurabi (c. 2100 BC). The Phoenicians and Greeks used a similar system for maritime trade. And the Romans used funeral associations as a form of life insurance, paying funeral costs for members and later also making payments to survivors.

The Achaemenian monarchs, a dynasty in the old Persian empire, were the first to insure their people and to make the insurance process official by having it recorded by government notaries. The process originated from the tradition of

the leaders of various ethnic groups offering gifts to their monarch at the beginning of the Iranian New Year. Their presents were assessed by court confidants and duly recorded in a register. When the value of a gift exceeded 10,000 Derrik (Achaemenian gold coin), it was recorded in a special register – which had advantages for those making such gifts.

The Registration of Gifts

The purpose of gift registration was to identify generous donors, who would then be helped by the monarch and the court should they get into trouble. The historian and author Jahez writes in one of his books on ancient Iran: "...and when the owner of the gift got into trouble or wanted to construct a building, throw a party, marry off his children, etc., the responsible person at the court would review the registration. If the recorded amount was more than 10,000 Derrik, the donor would receive an amount twice as high."

Insurance and Trade Growth

Independent insurance contracts (insurance policies not bound by loans or any other type of contract) were invented in Genoa in the fourteenth century. This new form of insurance contract made it possible to separate

insurance from investments, a separation that turned out to be useful for the first time in maritime insurance. After the Renaissance, insurance in Europe became more refined as more specialized variants developed.

As European cities and trade grew, the medieval guilds took responsibility for protecting their members against losses from fire and shipwreck, and would to bail them out of captivity by pirates for example. They would support them during sickness and poverty, and provide for a decent funeral if necessary.

In London, Edward Lloyd's Coffee House established in 1688, was a place where merchants, ship owners, and insurers met to conduct their business. By the end of the eighteenth century, Lloyd's had developed into one of the first modern insurance companies.

In 1693 the astronomer Edmond Halley recorded the first table of mortality rates based on statistical laws of mortality and compound interest. This table allowed for the scaling of premiums based on age, whereas previously these rates were the same for all ages.

Insurance developed rapidly with the growth of British trade in the seventeenth and eighteenth centuries. Companies were formed that completely focused on the insurance sector, and policies were signed by a number of individuals, who would sign their names and the amount of risk they would assume under the contract – hence the English expression "underwriter," used for insurers.

Great Fires and Other Calamities

Insurance as we now know it can be traced back to the Great Fire of London, which destroyed 13,200 houses in 1666. In the aftermath of this disaster, Nicholas Barbon opened an office to insure buildings. In 1680 he founded Britain's first fire insurance company, "The Fire Office," to insure brick and wooden houses.

The Great Fire of New York in 1835 made people there realize the necessity of having adequate reserves to meet unexpected big losses. Massachusetts was the first American state to assert that companies were obliged by law to maintain sufficient reserves.

The Great Fire of Chicago in 1871 emphasized the costly consequence of fires in densely built modern cities. To cope with such situations, reinsurance was introduced to share losses across many companies – now a common practice in other types of insurance.

In Great Britain, the Workmen's Compensation Act of 1897 obliged employers to insure their employees against industrial accidents. Insurance against liability, encouraged by law, made its appearance around 1880 and proved to be of great importance by the time the era of the automobile began to take hold.

Benefit Associations and Government Intervention

In the nineteenth century, many benefit associations were founded to insure the life and health of their members, and many fraternal orders were created to provide their members with cheap insurance. Nowadays, many fraternal orders, such as employee organizations, still offer insurance. Many employers also offer group insurance policies to their employees; frequently this includes not only life insurance but also accident and medical care insurance, as well as retirement programs.

From the end of the nineteenth century, governments gradually entered into the insurance arena, focusing especially on health, disability and unemployment insurance, and retirement benefits.

The Three Financial Pillars of Retirement

In most countries the retirement system is supported by three pillars. The first pillar is a basic retirement program, usually arranged by the government. Its objective is to supply some basic provision to prevent dire poverty among the elderly. In some countries this first pillar is more than just a basic income which decreases the role of the second pillar.

The second pillar is a fringe benefit (postponed salary) that provides an additional retirement benefit, usually within tax limits. These retirement benefits are always created within the employer-employee relationship. The purpose of the second pillar, combined with the first, is to provide a reasonable income to the beneficiary, which is related to the salary earned during their working life.

The third pillar is voluntary and is intended to enable people to endure the financial consequences of old age, of work interruptions and some other financial gaps that may arise (for example when changing jobs, residing abroad, or during unemployment). It consists of commercial savings or insurance products with or without an insurance element, and with tax concessions and limits.

The Relative Importance of Each Pillar
In developing countries, generally only the first pillar exists. Some countries even prohibit employers and employees from making arrangements that would form a second pillar – for example Poland, Hungary, and the Czech Republic. In the remaining European countries, all three pillars exist, with varying degrees of relative importance. Many countries place 50% importance on the first two pillars together.

The importance of the first pillar is a political choice. In countries with a communist history, the first pillar has often a marginal existence. In southern Europe, however, the first pillar is usually dominant (70–90%), while in northern Europe the first pillar weighs in at about 40%. The importance of the second pillar is determined by law, tradition, and the way employers and employees arrange matters between them. Because the third pillar is the least economically efficient way to build retirement benefits, it constitutes a separate category.

The First Pension Fund
Retirement income, as we all know, is income for the time when we no longer work due to age or disability. Often, pension schemes include an allowance for a remaining partner and children. They may also contain provisions that enable an employee to continue saving for his or her retirement during special periods of time, such as (compulsory) military service, pregnancy, and short-term unemployment.

The first pension fund was created at the end of the nineteenth century, when German men were allowed to retire at the age of seventy – the average life expectancy at the time being 72. Later, the retirement age dropped to 65 years. Even lower retirement ages were agreed upon for groups of people with physically demanding jobs, for example road workers, construction workers, and miners.

Until now, on average, most retirement programs are based on a retirement age of 65. However, since people in general live much longer than in the past, the economic sustainability of retirement at 65 is currently being re-evaluated.

The Booming Financial Industry After 1990

In 1989 the Berlin Wall came tumbling down. This event was symbolic for the melting away of the major, worldwide political division between East and West and sparked the beginning of the globalization of economies all around the world. Since then, the financial industry has become ever larger and ever more powerful.

New economies of scale, facilitated by the information revolution, global financial integration, US regulatory changes allowing commercial banks to engage in investment banking and other previously restricted activities, and the emergence of hedge-funds and private-equity – have all resulted in a dominant financial sector. In the US of the early 1980s, the financial sector accounted for 6% of both total corporate added value and total corporate profits. Since then, the industry's share in added value steadily increased, reaching close to 10% in 2006–2007. The industry's share of profits, however, skyrocketed to an extraordinary 40% in 2007. Fortune 500, the list of the 500 biggest enterprises, contains 123 financial companies in 2008. That is a staggering 25% – especially for a sector which doesn't actually produce automobiles, clothing, or machinery, but merely serves as an "intermediary and organizer" of those production resources.

In many countries, the super-bankers, hedge-fund managers, and owners of private-equity firms have, like the oil barons, become the new nobility of twenty-first-century capitalism.

Hedge-funds and Private-Equity Firms

Also of great importance is the advent of hedge-funds and private-equity. A hedge-fund is a private investment fund with broad possibilities to generate yield, independent of what the stock market does or what market tendencies are. Hedge-funds deal with large investments, usually from a limited number of mainly institutional investors. This is because by limiting access for private investors, hedge-funds have to comply with far fewer regulations.

A hedge-fund invests usually for a prearranged term. An important difference between hedge-funds and regular (mutual) investment funds and shares is that they make money by using the imbalances in the market – and so it doesn't matter if the market goes up or down.

The problem with hedge-funds is often a lack of supervision. There is generally much less control than there is for banks, insurance companies, and retirement funds, while the opportunities for supervisors to intervene in hedge-funds are considerably fewer.

Commercial Investment Banks and Hedge-funds

Commercial banks and investment banks have also discovered the hedge-fund business. In 2007 on the Alpha's Hedge-fund 100, a yearly top 100 list of the world's largest hedge-funds, the banks JPMorgan Chase and Goldman Sachs came first and second, with $33 billion respectively and $32.5 billion in hedge-fund assets.

The hedge-fund business is growing fast. In 1994 the total amount of assets under management by hedge-funds was about $300 billion. Attracted by high returns, by the spring of 2007, this market had grown to a total of $2,000 billion. The expectation is that in the coming years this growth will continue.

Many believe that the greatly increased role of the financial sector works in favor of greater efficiency, forcing out lethargic managers, encouraging a relentless search for greater productivity, and allowing for a constant restructuring that increases innovation throughout the economy.

Private-Equity and Venture Capital

The term "private-equity" is used for investments in companies that aren't listed on the stock market. Venture capital, which invests in high-risk companies such as start-up enterprises, is often considered part of the private-equity sector. In most cases, this concerns "leveraged buyouts": buyouts of companies with borrowed money that must be repaid later on by the bought-out company. As a result, immediate profits become a more important driver than long-term considerations.

This type of takeover incurs little risk for the investor, while the bought-out company is stuck with enormous debt. And after the buyout, the private-equity firm starts a thorough reorganization of its acquisition, often selling off parts of it to repay and make a profit. More often than not, private-equity firms buy healthy companies, strip them of their assets, load them up with an enormous amount of debt and, in the end, have the taxpayer pick up the tab. It's everyday practice and governments as well as the public are getting fed up with it.

Hedge-funds and the Gold Rush

A day doesn't go by when hedge-funds aren't mentioned in the papers. The name is now synonymous with a group of savvy investors who are trying to enrich themselves through short-term transactions on any market. Among professionals this strategy is known as Global Macro: investing in global macro-economic trends and profiting from them. Besides this strategy, there are a dozen other strategies that hedge-funds use to their advantage. From Long/Short to Event Driven, all these strategies differ from those of the traditional fund manager, who invests in any asset class and waits for a profit to accrue when his investment goes up in price.

The mutual fund industry is growing, but the growth of the hedge-fund industry is staggering. The sociologist, author and financial journalist Alfred Winslow Jones is credited with setting up the first hedge-fund in 1949. Jones was followed by people like Soros, Steinhardt, Robertson and many other historic names. Whereas there were only a couple of hedge-funds in the 1960s, there are now around 10,000, with estimated assets under management of approximately $3 trillion and with new funds hitting the markets every day.

Analysts state that the main reason for this popularity is the difference in fee structure. Where normal mutual funds, depending on the asset class they invest in, charge a fee of 1–2%, hedge-funds go by the golden rule of 2/20, which stands for a management fee of 2% and a performance fee of 20%. The performance fee means that, from any given goal upwards the hedge-fund manager is entitled to 20% of this upside profit.

According to many portfolio managers, money has no loyalty and it flows to where it will get the highest return. In today's world, investors have become more opportunistic and they seem to be chasing short-term gains. The stellar growth of hedge-funds and the attention they receive from private and institutional investors is a result of some exceptional examples.

James Simons' hedge-fund, Renaissance Technologies, even charges a management fee of 5% and a performance fee of 44%. Expensive, you say? The fund has approximately $30 billion of mainly institutional assets under management. For this cost structure, investors receive probably the most advanced black boxes in investing around today. The total capacity of Renaissance is said to be $100 billion. Yes, that is $100,000,000,000.

Renaissance uses computer-based models to predict price changes in easily traded financial instruments. The predecessor to Renaissance was a hedge-fund called Medallion. This fund managed to return an unbelievable 35% annual rate of return (after fees) from 1989 and is viewed by many as the most successful hedge-fund in the world. Unfortunately, it is closed to outside investors and nowadays Medallion manages only the money of Renaissance employees.

It is no surprise that James Simons ranks among the highest-paid hedge-fund CEOs, with an estimated net worth of $6 billion. It was only in 2007, after three years in the lead, that he had to accept being second best, as the first place was taken by John Paulson. The latter made his fortune by betting against the sub-prime market in 2006 through to 2008. From 2006 to 2007 one of his funds managed to return almost 600% to its investors. Of course, his investors were not the only ones to benefit. Paulson earned a staggering $3.7 billion in 2007 and was the top-earning hedge-fund manager.

This world is not filled with success. For every success story there are however ten failures. Permal Investment Management, one of the largest and most respected fund-of-fund hedge-fund managers in the world, says they are looking at only 1–2% of the hedge-fund industry in which to invest their money. As hedge-fund managers, they invest only in other hedge-funds – and with over 35 years of experience they have seen more failures than success stories. Among the biggest failures was the Long-term

Capital Management collapse of 1998, supervised by Nobel Prize winners Myron Scholes and Robert Merton, who lost $4.8 billion. More recently, in 2006, Brain Hunter from Amaranth lost around $6 billion from investors by betting on commodities. Even the brightest minds from Goldman Sachs lost billions of dollars in the 2007 market slump. Given the unregulated environment of hedge-funds and the black boxes they sometimes operate, risks are always looming.

Harry Kat of the Cass Business School in London has been the biggest hedge-fund critic. He argues that many of the high fees cannot be justified by the simple composition of certain portfolios and their performances. By using low-cost products that are highly traded and transparent, Kat has proved that many hedge-funds overcharge their clients and that the returns they generate do not relate to the high fees charged. Kat is one of the most read business authors on the Internet and, at www.fundcreator. com, people can replicate their own hedge-fund returns by certain given parameters. The model developed by Kat creates synthetic hedge-fund returns at much lower costs. This new phenomenon is seen by many as the next stage in the evolution of this industry.

Although many hedge-fund managers will claim that their investment process is unique, which is possible, future returns remain uncertain. Even inferior investment processes can do well when marketed the right way. Like everything else, this world has also changed from being all about investing to being all about marketing. For the future, it is likely that more money will be concentrated among the top hedge-funds, alongside which there will exist a large pool of smaller hedge-funds.

Undoubtedly, this industry is dealing with the latest Gold Rush, one bigger than has ever been seen before. We shall probably read a lot more about hedge-funds in the years to come…

This column is the personal opion of Ricardo Fakiera. In daily life he is Vice President of Merrill Lynch International Bank in the Netherlands.

Money makes the world slow down: the present crisis

Bubbles and Other Financial Crises

Money has steered the development of our world considerably. Without money we would not be where we are now. We would never have worked so hard, and there would never have been such prosperity. Our economic system has, over the centuries, become more and more efficient and effective. However, it has some intrinsic problems – one of which is the "bubble."

A financial bubble is the massive trade of a certain kind of product against prices that usually deviate a great deal from the intrinsic value of that product. Financial bubbles are most often linked with great optimism: an unrestrained or naive belief in streets of gold, in fast and easy profits, or in a new technology. In a financial bubble, there are probably some experts who know just how fragile the bubble is, While the general public, however, oblivious to the danger, simply allow it to expand until, inevitably, it bursts.

Collective Insanity

A very early example of such a bubble is the tulipomania in the Netherlands during the seventeenth century, when the cost of a tulip bulb could equal the price of a mansion along an Amsterdam canal.

In the past, people in large numbers have put their faith and savings in technologies such as railroads (1840-50), cars and radio (both in the 1920s), transistor electronics (in the 1950s), and computers and biotechnology (early 1980s).

The latest bubble of this kind was the introduction of the Internet, roughly between 1995 and 2000. Suddenly, investors were inflamed with some sort of collective insanity, causing stock prices of Internet companies, or "dot-coms," to lose all touch with reality. But every bubble is bound to burst, and

after the initial euphoria came the inevitable shock. When the dot-com bubble eventually burst in 2000, it left many investors disappointed – or even bankrupt. In the spring of 2000, the plummeting stock prices of Internet companies had serious consequences for many investors.

A large number of "dot coms" went bankrupt. The then famous fashion retailer Boo.com was the first in what became a long line of bankruptcies. When the web-grocer Webvan went belly up, a staggering $1.2 billion evaporated, an unbelievable amount of money considering Webvan was a "start-up". Although the bursting of the bubble caused stock prices to plummet, it was the long list of bankruptcies that had the most profound effect on investors and on the economy as a whole. Nasdaq darlings such as Yahoo and Amazon saw their values drop 80% in no time. In the second half of 2000 and the year that followed, hundreds of thousands of employees lost their jobs at American Internet companies.

Stocks in this booming industry proved to be not such a good investment after all. Many new investors left the stock market to start investing in real estate – a supposedly safe investment. Since then, of course, we have seen housing prices in many countries rise disproportianately, without any relation to salaries and rents.

Ethical Blunders

The credit crunch that has plagued the financial sector since 2007 was primarily caused by poor risk-management and a variety of ethical blunders. Regarding ethics, one may expect to find many more skeletons in bank closets.

An example of this phenomenon is "life settlement" investments: investments in second-hand life insurance policies, which have become very popular in recent years. "Death bonds," as they became known, were invented in the 1980s in the US, when terminal AIDS patients began selling their life insurance policies to secure money for medical care. This worked fine until AIDS inhibitors became available – they were a blessing for AIDS patients of course, but investors found themselves confronted with large losses.

Nowadays it is not only the terminally ill who sell their policies; the policies of American senior citizens have generated a huge industry. The fair market value of these policies is higher than the price that policyholders would receive (the cash surrender value) if they were bought out by insurers. The principle is simple: speculators pay the premiums and then collect on the life insurance when the original policyholder dies. In 2006 the value of the insured amount of these traded policies was $12 billion; one year later, by 2007, their value had already grown to $30 billion.

Another area that will receive much attention in coming years – and within ten years will lead to the next financial bubble – is green energy and environmental technology.

Bubbles, credit-crunch phenomena, and other crises will continue to be part of the financial sector's future, because *homo economicus* is a stubborn creature who wants to believe in streets of gold and instant profits.

The Road to (Self-)Protection

Macro-economist Lans Bovenberg expects that in the future people will be better protected against themselves and their own weaknesses that can lead to bubbles.

He says: "The worldwide economic integration of countries and regions makes economic cycles, such as Kondratieff cycles, more synchronized. Within trade blocks like the EU this already shows: economies develop more uniformly than before. Capital becomes more mobile and risks are being spread worldwide. This is an excellent principle, which will only continue in the future. You can see this, for example, with the credit crisis in the US. Risks were so widely spread – also to Europe and Asia – that American banks suffered fewer losses than they would have earlier on, when all the risk would have been spread only within the US. This system obviously has one big disadvantage: too many risks are now being traded too far from the spot where these risks originate. Whereas a local banker can determine if a local citizen can obtain and repay a mortgage, when such a risk is sold several times over, overseeing of the system becomes blurred. These relatively new risks for the financial industry should be kept under control."

Bovenbergt continues "I expect that in the future there will be institutions which improve supervision of this sort of phenomenon. Since people remain strange risk-takers, they need such institutions to protect them from themselves. These institutions will supervise new types of contracts in the industry in order to control the risks that come with them. An additional task will be the matching of individual and collective interests. These institutions will be rooted in local central banks already existing in the hearts of the local societies. While they are needed to gather decentralized information, they must be supranational themselves and have their tasks delegated to them by local central banks."

The Credit Crunch

Since the summer of 2007 there has been a crisis in the international financial markets, the "credit crunch." American banks had loaned people more than was justified by the value of the collateral – for example to finance the decoration of a house or to pay the real estate agent. Often they used a so-called "step-up loan": a loan with a very low initial interest rate (in 2001 it was 1%), which would automatically increase over time. In this way, many Americans were able to borrow large amounts of money, far beyond their actual spending power.

With a step-up loan, the new house would have to be sold before "normal" interest rates kicked in. But when increasingly high prices caused the homes demand to drop, many step-up borrowers could not sell their houses in time. They then had to deal with interest rates they couldn't possibly afford. When normal interest rates subsequently rose, many American homeowners with large mortgages couldn't carry their interest burden, and in 2006 and 2007 many were forced to sell or foreclose on their homes. In some cases, they simply sent their keys to the bank (so-called "jingle mail") and left the bank with real estate that was rapidly dropping in value.

Sub-prime Lending

The phenomenon that worsened this crisis was "sub-prime lending." Accustomed to decades of rising home prices, mortgage providers started lending money to people who were actually not creditworthy.

How do you determine someone's creditworthiness? The credit history of all mortgage applicants in the US is checked through a credit-rating system. If their credit history is poor, the applicant is considered to be not entirely credit worthy. Nevertheless, even if eventually they would be unable to pay their interest – so the reasoning went – the increased value of the collateral would make up for the loss.

From 2002 many financial institutions knowingly and willingly provided mortgages to this category of applicants, often when it was completely clear that doing so would cause problems to the mortgagee. Short-term profiteering won over decent advice. When the collateral no longer covered the losses, reality finally caught up with this practice. Selling a mortgage product like this, knowing full well that the customer will get into serious trouble, makes it an immoral act. And with this type of financing, several banks threw away their reputations.

In the summer of 2007, the real estate bubble burst and caused a crisis in the interbanking monetary market. When banks and other financial institutions had to report a drop in the value of their investments, they experienced huge losses. Many large banks had to write off billions due to this crisis.

The Swiss bank UBS beats them all, with a financial loss of $32 billion and the end of the crisis nowhere in sight. Some banks got into such problems they were threatened with collapse, due to customers' complete loss of confidence. You may remember the images of the "run on the bank," with people lining up in front of the British bank Northern Rock to cash in their savings. Bear Stearns was the first of the Wall Street investment banks to get into real trouble, and mortgage banks Indy Mac, Fannie Mae and Freddie Mac soon followed. The last two, now nationalized North American mortgage giants, have supplied and guarantee around $5.2 trillion worth of mortgages. This amounts to about half of all North American mortgages. You can imagine the possible damage.

Time and again, the credit crisis seems to be retreating, until somewhere on the globe another skeleton drops out of someone's closet. Every time optimism starts to return, a new round of write-offs is announced, even causing write-offs in other, neighbouring industries.

In early August 2008, the number of people with a normal credit rating who were behind on the payments on their non-sub-prime mortgages, turned out to be four times as high as the year before. The largest group of mortgage clients, the so-called "prime segment," shows a doubling in defaults. There just doesn't seem to be an end to this crisis.

The ordinary consumer will interpret the current crisis as the financial industry's lack of insight into their own businesses. How can a large company get caught by surprise like this every time? The fact that one minute the end of the crisis is announced, then the next minute a major financial company has to take more write-offs or is even nationalized, suggests a complete lack of direction. This of course makes it harder and harder for the financial industry to win back the confidence and trust of the public. In July 2008, one year after the credit crisis began, the total damage caused by the crisis was estimated at €500 billion.

Help From Central Banks

Ultimately, banks in trouble will get help from central banks, because not doing so could initiate a snowball effect that could put the entire financial system at risk of collapse. But such interventions are not without drawbacks.

From a moral point of view, such rescue operations are barely justifiable. As Henry Kissinger said, "There is an inherent contradiction when financial entities are permitted to reap extraordinary profits and manage vast assets and then, when conditions change, are declared too large to be permitted to fail, requiring taxpayer bailouts. Financial institutions, whether investment banks or hedge-funds, need supervision in a way that protects the taxpayer's interests."

A principle of capitalism is: he who takes the profits must also suffer the pain in less prosperous times. Mortgage giants Fannie Mae and Freddie Mac experienced quite the opposite. In the period from 1998 to 2003, the five most important members of the board raked up $199 million between them. Their shareholders also profited massively. But when things went very wrong, it wasn't them who had to pay. Instead, the taxpayer was left to pick up the bill. "Profits are privatized, the risks are socialized."

And now, thanks to the Housing Bill, which was approved during the writing of this book, troubled American homeowners are also being bailed out by the state, which means that yet again the American taxpayer is made to pay for the (excessive) risks that other people took, and would have benefited from, were it not for the drop in housing prices.

Financial Injections

On several occasions, central banks had to provide liquidity support as well as lower interest rates to prevent a serious disruption of the financial system.

Central banks have taken drastic measures. In 2007, to prevent the interbanking money market from tipping over, the European Central

Bank (ECB) injected into it a stunning extra €1.322 billion of short-term loans. The prognosis indicates that the ECB intervention in 2008 will be even larger, since an additional €414 billion was already injected in the first quarter. By comparison, in 2005 and 2006 such additional interventions for each year were only €53 billion and €109 billion respectively.

"The Spanish Central Bank took a different approach," says Reggy de Feniks, managing consultant for VODW in Spain. "Years of consistent, traditional policy and strict regulation made sure that Spanish banks steered clear of risky business such as credit derivatives and repackaged credit risks. This is why Spanish banks are sailing through the current credit crunch with relative ease. Stronger still, thanks to its strong cash position, Banco Santander can afford to go on a shopping spree in the UK, a country that is obviously being much harder hit by the current turmoil in the financial markets."

These money market problems have caused stock prices to plummet. Fortis Bank stocks dropped so much that the already heavily leveraged acquisition of ABN-Amro proved too much; the governments of Belgium, the Netherlands and Luxembourg had to step in. In Germany, Iceland, and the United Kingdom, banks were nationalized. In the US, the financial hurricane meant the end of many high-profile investment banks. Bear Stearns, previously traded at over $150 per share was sold for $10 per share to JPMorgan Chase; it was a shotgun wedding arranged largely by the Federal Reserve (FED), as a total collapse of Bear Stearns was deemed too harmful for the financial system. Lehman Brothers, however, in the eyes of the FED, wasn't pivotal for the financial system and was allowed to go under. Merrill Lynch was bought by Bank of America; Morgan Stanley greeted Mitsubishi UFJ Financial Group as its new main shareholder, and Warren Buffett invested $7.5 billion in Goldman Sachs, doing a very sweet deal for himself once again. With credit very hard to come by, even the last Wall Street investment banks, Goldman Sachs and Morgan Stanley, were forced to become "normal" commercial banks. This means they have to comply with tougher legislation, but it also means easier funding for them. Now the ultimate financial injection is being given by the American taxpayer: a $700 billion (seven hundred billion dollars!) bailout, taking the "toxic" bad loans off the banks' books.

Trust Betrayed

Guido Lanzoni, Head of Credit at UniCredit Banca di Roma in London, says: "It remains to be seen if the lowering of interest rates by the FED, combined with the liquidity injections of the central banks around the world, will succeed in resurrecting the credit markets. Especially with the growing threat of inflation looming everywhere."

Money markets are struggling, due to lack of trust between banks. Until illiquid assets are revalued and trust is restored, cash will be tight. According to Bloomberg, from the spring of 2007, the industry was faced with a staggering sum of $500 billion in write-offs and almost $1 billion in losses. Until then, companies will have to struggle just to survive, irrespective of the monetary easing measures introduced to stimulate aggregate demand.

Lanzoni continues: "In order to restore a shaken confidence, it will be crucial to re-assess counterparty risk and re-establish trust. Once confidence is restored and – in parallel – the painful deleveraging process completed, new rules in accounting (setting new frameworks on topics such as off-balance sheet items and stock-options) and Corporate Governance could prevent the same mistakes from happening again. More than ever, quality of earnings is needed to restore credibility, and attract key investors. Whether the regulators' actions to kickstart the access to capital, and allow exiting its vicious circle of weakening balance sheet and credit tightening are successful, is way too early to be judged." "In the long run" predicts Lanzoni, "a new generation of leveraged products will be inevitably invented to artificially boost shareholders' value, compress taxes, and reduce capital requirements. Let's hope that – this time – buyers, rating agencies, auditors, will look at them differently, not under estimating any macro effects."

A Shadow Banking Sector

There are many examples of financial institutions venturing into shadow banking. Mortgage banks Fannie Mae and Freddie Mac were originally founded with a social function in mind and a clear goal. President Roosevelt wanted to stimulate house ownership among Americans – and his initiative was successful. Over 50 million households from the less prosperous classes were able to become the home owners.

But Fannie Mae and Freddie Mac strayed from their original course: both mortgage banks became involved in the trade of financial derivatives. Although this can be very profitable, it is very hard to oversee the risks of these complicated instruments. Moreover, there's no regulation in place that really covers such diversification.

When asked about the ultimate cause of the crisis, Willem Buiter, professor of Economics at the London School of Economics, said: "Ultimately, the cause lies in the exaggerated triumph of transaction-based financial capitalism. There has been a tremendous shift from the traditional banking model, which was based on savings and the best possible safekeeping of these savings, towards a transaction model in which savings and securities were used in various ways for the construction of financial products. And this was encouraged by naive and inefficient regulation."

Buiter has in mind not only the Special Investment Vehicles (SIVs), in which banks had placed their mortgage bonds, and which remained outside of traditional regulation; he also has in his sights the barely transparent, barely regulated activities of hedge-funds and private-equity when he claims: "A complete shadow banking sector has been created."

The Future of Hedge-Funds

Within the last decade, hedge-funds have overtaken private-equity in assets under management. They have established a more attractive fee structure for their managers by taking their performance fees on a yearly basis rather than from realized capital gains, and have begun to encroach on transactions that private-equity would have considered its preserve.

The focus of hedge-funds has been mainly liquid instruments and derivatives, but their spectrum of activity has covered almost every investment area, including macroeconomic, event-driven, currencies, commodities and statistical arbitrage investment. Hedge-funds' ability to sell short was their key differentiating feature, since it potentially enabled them to make returns in all markets conditions. It was always clear that, as in every other financial market, a serious worsening of market conditions would sooner or later test performance and sort players into those who knew what they were doing and those who had simply been long-only investors benefiting from a strong bull market.

Since mid-July 2007, we have experienced this testing period, including the worst June month in the equity markets (MSCI World Index – 8.1%) since the 1930s. During the first eight months of 2008, the average hedge-fund lost 4.83% (according to Hedge-fund Research) against a fall in global equity markets of about three times that. What can we learn from this performance about the future of the industry?

The first lesson is that the ability to engage in short-selling, which was felt to give hedge-funds a strategic advantage, has been harder to exploit than most hedge-fund managers expected. Borrowing shares has now become competitive, expensive and is in some cases impossible. The very high volatility of the past twelve months has made it difficult for hedge-funds to hold onto their short positions without incurring steep month-end losses, which they are obviously extremely keen to avoid. The very activities of other hedge-funds in both the taking and the covering of short positions have amplified market movements in unpredictable directions. So the jury is still out on short-selling as a way of making money in a down market.

The second lesson is that hedge-funds as a whole did indeed enhance returns to their investors through the use of leverage as markets rose, and then did provide a hedge against the recent stock market decline. As a group, though, they have been unable to deliver positive returns in a falling market and only the top performers have provided attractive returns. In this respect, the depression of performance figures may make the choice of manager as crucial as in private-equity. You need to pick a top quartile manager to do well.

A tiering of hedge-fund managers by performance has now begun and redemptions are likely to follow from under-performing hedge-funds. The ensuing liquidation of port-

folios is likely to depress market prices of specific stocks, which will test managers once again.

As with private-equity, we can expect the most sophisticated managers with rare skills in short-selling and the use of derivatives to survive the current downturn and then prosper in the upturn, which will eventually come. This will be their opportunity to show that their performance relative to long-only funds will justify the higher fees they charge. ☐

Sir Ronald Cohen, often called "the father of British venture capital," is the founder of Apax Partners.

Frauds

The poor ethical image of the financial industry was further tarnished by various events which indicated that the banks' internal control mechanism no longer worked. The banking world was dumbfounded when the French bank giant Société Générale (SocGen) announced in January 2008 that one of their Paris-based futures traders had succeeded in making a financial dent in their books to the tune of €4.9 billion. It is very embarrassing for prestigious financial institutions when frauds surface within their own ranks. Yet it is taking banks far too long to trace large-scale fraud by their own employees. Incidents like these have undermined confidence in the financial sector considerably.

Financial service providers have begun the twenty-first century with an image that can only be described as cumbersome, bureaucratic, and above all, unethical and corrupt.

Furthermore, the seemingly endless stream of reports of excessive remunerations for top management and top traders on Wall Street isn't doing the industry any good. And the end is not in sight just yet. The British Office of Fair Trading observes that so-called "free" bank accounts have become a bigger source of income for the banks than mortgages, credit cards, and savings accounts combined. The main reason for this is that banks pay out a very low interest rate on simple bank accounts (which are hidden charges, really) and yet charge an exorbitant rate when such accounts are overdrawn.

This leads to a high level of one product subsidizing another, but also of one client group subsidizing others: less affluent – often younger – clients overdraw their accounts considerably more often than richer (usually older and more cautious) clients. In doing so, it is they who pay for the "free" bank accounts of the richer customers. So for many consumers, "free" bank accounts aren't free at all. This is yet another example of intransparency that could cause trouble in the years to come – and not only in the UK.

In the meantime, a real estate bubble is looming in Spain. Reggy de Feniks says: "With house prices having risen by 190% between 1997 and 2007 and an overactivity in construction, price adjustments have also begun in Spain. Furthermore, with many households heavily in debt, a rise in 'bad loans' is inevitable – especially since unemployment is on the rise and the economy is cooling down. Spanish banks have financed this real estate bubble and will be confronted with – at the least – a decline in growth in the near future."

So it's a sector in which a collective memory seems to be missing. Reconsideration of its very essence is of the greatest importance for the financial industry.

Credit Insurance Stronger than Ever

Well into its second century, credit insurance continues to evolve and increase its value to businesses selling products to other business enterprises. In the twentieth century, credit insurance began to take root as companies, throughout Europe in particular, sought opportunities to sell their products to businesses in neighbouring countries. Companies such as Atradius, whose predecessor companies acquired more than fifteen businesses across the globe between 1990 and 2005 to more effectively meet the needs of these international traders, epitomized the industry's move to globalization.

Now more than ever, globalization is driving international trade, and the challenges of growing a business internationally will increase demand for protection of trade receivables. All businesses would like to be able to do business on a cash basis, but to gain a competitive advantage the ability to offer products and services on payment terms can give a company an edge. Trade receivables are an important asset and growing risk-management requirements such as the Sarbanes-Oxley Law highlight the importance of protecting them. The more flexible the terms, the higher the risk and the greater the need for protection.

The need for a global footprint means entrance barriers are high. We may see new local players entering the market, particularly in emerging markets, but building the required infrastructure to compete for business internationally requires long lead times and big investments. To compete effectively, these small players will need to become part of an international network. Only the top three credit insurers have these networks in place and antitrust laws make consolidation of these three players unlikely.

The need for protection against political risks has increased following changes in political environments in many countries. Though the post-cold war era has enjoyed twenty years of political stability, this is not expected to last. Competition is no longer primarily a local event. Fierce international competition will be brutal in determining who will and will not survive. The increasing complexity of global economies requires sophisticated global knowledge of buyers to predict who the winners and losers will be.

Companies have to operate efficiently at all levels to survive. That means credit insurance has to be cost efficient. A more complex risk environment and regulations like Solvency II will play a significant role in the future of credit insurance, driving the price of risk protection up. Alternative tools such as credit default swaps may be attractive for a small number of companies, but there are few effective substitutes for protecting against defaults stemming from commercial and political risk. Viable substitutes are unlikely and credit insurance will therefore remain the most valuable tool available to protect trade receivables. ☐

Isidoro Unda is CEO of Atradius.

Future scenarios

Where to Go From Here?

The financial industry is at a crossroads at this moment, although it doesn't seem to realize that. Right now, however, would be the perfect time for the financial industry to redefine its role.

To know how the credit crunch will develop further would be like looking into a crystal ball. The damage caused by the crisis has already reached hundreds of billions. People all around the world are nervous, because they actually believe the entire economic system could collapse completely.

Because the Federal Reserve pumped so much cheap money into the American economy during the last half of 2007, the dollar dropped further and further compared with, for example, the euro. This will cause European exporters to experience additional difficulties.

In Japan and Germany, the machine and automobile industries are especially hard hit by the weak dollar and the resulting drop in demand for their products in the US. When BMW CEO Norbert Reithofer had his company calculate the cost of every penny the dollar loses in comparison to the euro, the results were terrifying: BMW lost €80 million for every cent that the dollar dropped. In 2007 this led to losses of more than €500 million, and BMW decided to move part of their production to the US.

Commodity Countries and The Danger Zone

For countries with many natural resourses, such as the Arab Emirates, Australia, and Brazil, the effects of the crisis are less severe. They will continue to flourish because of the turbocharged growth of new economies like China and India, and their insatiable appetites for oil, steel, copper, and other commodities.

Countries that mainly export consumer products, in past years aimed mainly at the US market, will experience more problems from the credit crunch. Think about Asian countries such as Thailand, Malaysia, and China. China – which will eventually surpass the US as an economic superpower – is experiencing such growth that we can't speak of a crisis there, but its growth will nevertheless be slowed down by diminishing exports to the US.

The countries that may really get in trouble due to the credit crunch are those that borrowed heavily in recent years to finance their fast growth: countries like the Baltic States, Hungary, and Iceland.

Temporary Instability

While each economic crisis had a different trigger, their common features were lightheaded speculation and a systematic under appreciation of risk. With each passing decade, the role of speculative capital has increased, a development that will continue in coming years. Speed is a characteristic feature of speculative capital. Rushing in at the first sign of an opportunity and moving out again at the first sign of trouble, speculative capital has the tendency to inflate upswings into bubbles and downward cycles into crises. Worldwide regulation will eventually tackle this cause of financial and economic instability. But in coming years, we will still be confronted with the destabilizing effects of heavy speculation.

The Slowdown of Globalization

Certain current developments might indicate a temporary slowdown of the process of globalization, for example the higher prices of oil and food. In 1999 we paid $10 for a barrel of crude oil; in the summer of 2007, this was $70 a barrel. In the summer of 2008, prices even reached $147 a barrel, before coming down again to around $100. Nobody knows where the price of oil will go or in what time frame, as it is extremely volatile. At the time this book went into print, prices were below $75 a barrel. People in the oil business, however, don't rule out the possibility of prices reaching a stunning $200 a barrel in the years to come.

Oil drives such a large part of the global economy that it is almost impossible to really imagine a world in which a barrel of oil costs $200. Unquestionably, the shock would force nations to go much "greener" much faster, particularly by conserving energy and developing and adopting new non-fossil fuels. But none of this can be done in a time span of just one or two years.

So the predictions tend to be gloomy: some analysts see a shift toward regional trade, and even a major reversal of globalization itself, as the rising cost of transport makes it too expensive to ship goods over long

The Future of Finance

distances. No industry will be unaffected; any company that moves goods or people needs oil.

An oil price of $200 a barrel could bring about the long-predicted demise of the automobile industry. Airlines are also vulnerable. In the spring of 2008, Air France KLM warned that their 2008 profits were likely to fall by a third. CEO Jean-Cyril Spinetta suggested in *Newsweek* that an oil price of $200 a barrel would cause a far bigger shock than 9/11 or the SARS epidemic of 2003, which already sent the airline industry into a tailspin. "It's more than a change, it's a revolution, an entire new industry, in fact," Spinetta said. "We would have a lot of bankruptcies very quickly in Europe, the US, and Asia. There will be severe cutbacks in the number of destinations as well as in the number of flights.

The political ramifications of this – which already show a tendency towards protectionism – combined with the ever-rising costs of doing daily business, could force globalization to retreat. "It's a herald of the reversal of globalization," said Jeff Rubin, chief economist at CIBC World Markets, in *Newsweek*. "At $200 a barrel, you'll see transport costs rise to a level that will effectively reverse the trade liberalization of the last thirty years." He predicts that world trade will reorganize itself regionally, so while Japan may continue its trade with China, the United States will increasingly import its goods from Latin America.

Nevertheless, not everybody is convinced that globalization will grind to a halt, or even reverse, because of the high cost of transport. According to Gerrit Zalm, CFO of DSB Bank and former Minister of Finance in the Netherlands: "It is to be expected that physical production will take place closer to the area of sale, because of the increased cost of transportation. You can see this happening already in the US. But all this talk about globalization supposedly coming to a halt, I don't believe in that. I think, to an extent, globalization will waver in the coming years, but will ultimately continue and lead to more uniformity in taste, consumer behavior and more uniformity in cultures. In the end, we are moving towards a global way of doing business, based on price mechanisms and a free market economy."

Increasing Inflation Worldwide

Another danger lurking for many economies is inflation. For 2008, substantial inflation is already expected for many emerging markets. Countries especially at risk are those in which a strong middle class isn't yet fully developed, and which are therefore completely dependent on their exports – for example a country like Vietnam.

In past years, much of the Western production that was outsourced to China was later transferred to Vietnam because of its still very low labor costs. But due to the soaring prices of food and oil, inflation in Vietnam is rising quickly, while exports to the crisis-stricken US stagnate.

Meanwhile, leaders in Hanoi and elsewhere have been unable to raise interest rates, tighten the money supply, or adjust a dollar-pegged currency sufficiently to avert an inflation-induced meltdown. Instead, they imposed a rice-export ban and various domestic price controls. From Seoul to Jakarta to Islamabad, policymakers are making the same mistakes as the government in Hanoi. They favor haphazard administrative emergency measures such as price caps, based on the flawed logic that today's price surge is temporary. Their overreaction could undermine economic growth – which, truth be told, is already weakening, thanks to declining Western consumption and deteriorating terms of trade.

Economic Cycles and Scenarios

In many areas we can recognize fixed patterns of change, like high and low tides. Many cycles have a time span of sixty years between a peak and a dip. Arnold Toynbee described these cycles in terms of conflict: cycles of war and peace. Arthur Schlesinger described the wave patterns in terms of politics and ideology. Joseph Schumpeter described them in terms of innovation – technological and financial. Nikolai Kondratieff described the wave patterns in a more general economic sense.

Kondratieff Waves

Kondratieff's theory can be explained as an economy that has cycles, much like a year has seasons. It starts with a period of profitable inflation, which is spring. A subsequent period of "stagflation" (economic slowdown, or stagnation, combined with inflation) represents summer. The profitable deflation represents fall, and the final deflation is winter, after which the cycles start all over again. In 1949 the last Kondratieff cycle ended. We saw profitable inflation in the period from 1949 to 1966, stagflation from 1966 to 1982, profitable deflation from 1982 to 2000 – and after 2000 we should be in a winter deflation, leading to a depression.

Seasonal Differences as States of Mind

There are great differences in people's mental states during the various seasons of the Kondratieff cycle. Spring is a period of great zest for work, an urge to consume and a strong tendency for economic expansion. In summer, people want to enjoy their acquired wealth and consume more and more. In this period, differences of opinion start to rise to the surface. Apparently, summer in the Kondratieff cycle is also a favorite season to start a war. Fall characterizes itself with an "everyone for himself/herself" mentality. The expenditure policy becomes irresponsible, and there is a lack of commodities. Nevertheless, everyone wants to continue living at the same prosperity level. Many live "on credit." Apparently, however, in winter, debts made in the fall can no longer be supported, and the economic system collapses. Extremism and fundamentalism surge, and war is a common phenomenon.

In a conventional winter, there are three real depression years and fifteen recovery years, during which the economy stays flat to catch its breath, so a new spring can announce itself.

The Origin of Kondratieff Wave Patterns

The existence of the Kondratieff wave patterns is explained differently by economists. First, there is the psychological explanation we mentioned earlier: when the economy is bad, people know they have to work hard to revive the economy. But the better the economy, the less willing people are to participate in the collective; they start making demands without putting in the extra effort.

Other explanations for the Kondratieff cycles see great wars as the driving force behind the wave pattern. Still others see technical innovations as the pacesetters. Notably, after the Kondratieff cycle of prosperity that ended in the mid-1990s, an era of well-being started: the economy of happiness.

The Shell Scenarios

How the current politico-economic globalization will develop is uncertain. The role that emotions play in the economy is large. Much depends on the way citizens and governments react to uncertainty and insecurity. Do they leave economic development to the market? Will they expect to find solace in ever more control mechanisms and (sometimes conflicting) laws and regulations? Or will they seek shelter in protectionism?

The Energy company Shell is known worldwide as the company that develops the best future scenarios. In past decades, the Shell Scenario method has found many followers worldwide – and it has a proven track record. Shell proposes that a company has to make its own future independent of any scenario: the so-called TINA (There Is No Alternative) approach. A company develops its future strategy in a way that can deal with all scenarios.

According to Shell, there are three possible scenarios for the future of globalization.

1. The Low Trust Scenario

The absence of market solutions to the crisis of security and trust, rapid regulatory change, overlapping jurisdictions, and conflicting laws, lead to intrusive checks and controls, encouraging short-term portfolio optimization and vertical integration. Institutional discontinuities limit cross-border economic integration. Complying with fast-evolving rules and managing complex risks are key challenges.

Low Trust globalization is characterized by a combination of a very strong role for institutional investors, and a legalistic approach to rules and compliance. Mandatory standards and systematic rating and disclosure reflect – and further reinforce – an overall climate of distrust. Legal risk is very high, and insurance costs for directors and officers reach staggering heights.

2. The Open Doors Scenario

Clarity about security and compliance, regulatory harmonization, mutual recognition, independent media, the setting up and implementing of voluntary best-practice codes, and close links between investors and civil society: all these encourage cross-border integration and virtual value chains. Networking skills and superior reputation management are essential.

In the Open Doors scenario, stakeholders have a major voice as well, often working in cooperation with investors and regulators. The capacity to understand and evaluate different market cultures is high, and trust is reflected in comply-or-explain codes. Board evaluation is emphasized. Legal risk is moderate – and reputation risks matter a lot.

3. The Flags Scenario

In this scenario, dogmatic approaches, regulatory fragmentation, national preferences, and conflicts over values and religion give insiders an advantage – thus putting the brakes on globalization. Gated communities, patronage, and national standards exacerbate fragmentation and call for a great deal of attention for country risk-management.

The Flags scenario sees political considerations interfering with a patchwork of stringent national rules, further encouraging a "home bias" in investment portfolios. The risk of loss of control is very high, as groups with good connections and national champions can weaken the rule of law.

What About Trade Barriers?

Over the period 2005–2025, economic growth rates range from 2.6% per annum in the Flags scenario, 3% per annum in the Low Trust scenario, and 3.8% per annum in the Open Doors scenario. This means that by 2025, the level of global economic prosperity is 40% higher in the Open Doors scenario than in the Flags scenario.

In the Open Doors scenario, technological progress is rapid, thanks to substantial research and development efforts conducted in an international environment and within a uniform set of global intellectual property rules. With trade barriers gradually dismantled and the hurdle of institutional discontinuities diminishing, foreign trade expands rapidly. Financial markets are more integrated, fostering the efficient allocation of capital on a global scale.

In the Low Trust scenario, trade integration also increases, albeit along a flatter path due to security concerns and continuing institutional differences across borders. Intellectual property regimes differ, and the spreading of knowledge is hampered by legal and security considerations.

In the Flags scenario, national barriers undermine collaborative research efforts and impede the wider distribution of technological innovations. Markets remain fragmented and high domestic savings are required in order to finance investments.

Bovenberg on Future Scenarios

According to the economist Lans Bovenberg, "When you make future scenarios, you especially take into account uncertainties. You divide them in two dimensions in four quadrants. For the financial branch, an important uncertainty is the extent of internationalization. How will globalization continue, and how will local entities like nation states and regions relate to globalization? Will nation states erode? Will city states come back? Will there be a backlash because of nation states trying to regain the power they lost during globalization?"

"The second important uncertainty is the development of community spirit and individualism. Collectivities are important for this sector, especially because individual products are normally more expensive than collective ones. Collective retirement is cheaper than the retirement of an individual freelancer."

Future Scenarios for the Financial Branch

When Bovenberg's basic idea is connected with the Shell scenarios and Kondratieff wave cycles, we could envisage the following four scenarios for financial service providers:

1. A United World

Internationalization continues and citizens increasingly organize themselves into collectivities. In this case, we can expect an enormous growth for the industry. Because of continuous globalization, as described in Shell's Open Doors scenario, the financial sector grows. Risks can be spread worldwide and economies become harmonized. Because people operate in collectives, or "tribes," they buy financial services in groups – which, as we said earlier, is very attractive for the industry.

2. A World of "Atoms"

Internationalization continues – as does individualization. Citizens manage their affairs more individually, outside of any collectives. In this case, many financial products will become considerably more expensive than they are now, and we will see a moderate growth of the industry. In this scenario, we will see a fragmentation similar to a random collection of atoms.

3. 1914 Revisited

Internationalization collapses and collectivity increases. In this case, the industry stabilizes and gradually starts to shrink. In 1914, after a long period of globalization, that process ended because of rising nationalism and regionalism. This is when the predecessor of the EU, the Donau Monarchy, collapsed; and this is how the predecessor of the euro, the taler, came to an end. Crisis after crisis diminished the faith of citizens in public reign. And finally, after a series of incidents, World War I broke out. A repetition of 1914 is possible.

4. Small Worlds
Internationalization collapses and individualization continues. In this scenario the financial industry will shrink considerably, as products become too expensive and international risk-sharing diminishes. The collapse of internationalization has a considerable negative effect on the vitality of the financial sector and will induce a downward spiral.

Choosing our Future
We ourselves vote for the first scenario, a United World. We think that the institutions suggested by Lans Bovenberg will be able to guide the world economy into smoother waters. We also expect, and we agree with consultant Harry Smorenberg, that the financial industry will eventually know how to break through national and regional frontiers, in spite of rising nationalism and protectionism. We think people in this "people's century" will want to make as much use as possible of their individual talents. At the same time, though, we think that people fear solitude and that they will try to find safety in the numbers of the various collectives.

In the next part of this book, we will elaborate on four megatrends that will fundamentally change the financial industry.

part 2

Financial Services
in the Twenty-first Century

The Future of Finance

Megatrend 1

Globalization, a New Economic World Order,
and a Rapidly Changing Competitive Arena

CNN Portable News Service

Your personalized news for January 5, 2023, 8.30 a.m.

News Headlines:

- At the White House yesterday, Empress Cixi II of China offered prestigious membership in the CATA (Chinese Atlantic Treaty Organization) to both the European Union and the United States. She did this during a state dinner, in the presence of King William V, European Union President Tony Blair, and the American president Arnold Schwarzenegger.

- In London, the twentieth Women's Park was officially opened. This is a new milestone in the segregated facilities for men and women, such as trams, hospitals, and parks, which have been introduced in a number of European regions since 2007. The new park is in line with the directive of the European Sharia Commission, under the leadership of Ken Livingstone.

- Triple G bank – the new name for Google/Greenpeace/Grameen Bank – has been reporting excellent results for 84 weeks in a row, and is also today the darling of the Hang Seng, the most important stock exchange in the world. Veola Water Bank also prospers, as worldwide demand for waterinsurance skyrockets.

- ING Deutsche Bank is expected to take an active stance as shareholder in the shareholder meeting of Temasek, the Sovereign Wealth Fund from Singapore, which has had to get used to the worldwide regulations on transparency for a couple of years now. So, fireworks in Singapore, and not because of the Chinese New Year. (The start of the Year of the Rabbit).

- This afternoon, Russian Olicharchs Abramovich and Berezowski finalize the take over of CitiGroup. The conglomerate will probably proceed as ABC123, the letters obviously representing the names of the three parties, and the numbers standing for 'doing business in a simple and transparent way'.

Personalized Messages and Advice

Our news service – now synchronized to your financial, spare time and business diaries – offers you the following advice for today:

- You do not need to wear warm clothing for your 13.15 business lunch; you should, however, take an umbrella. Your lunch date is from India, from a city where a large university campus was completed last week. You are advised to mention this to him. You can obtain more information about him via his avatar.
- Select code 9595 during your 16.00 hairdresser appointment, for the trendiest, most up-to-the-moment hairstyle for men in your age category.
- Your investments have been automatically adjusted in line with developments in the most important markets around the world: China, India, Brazil, Russia and the US.

Background

Before writing this book, we spoke with dozens of board members and thought leaders in the financial community. Financial service companies have experienced tremendous international growth in recent years, and the end is not in sight. When asked what development has had the most impact on the industry, the answer was invariably "globalization" (at that point in time at least).

The Future of Finance therefore begins with globalization. In Megatrend 1 we will set the stage by introducing the twelve pillars of power that will shape the world. We will then look at the different appearances of globalization in the corporate world, and the globalization of taxes and regulation. In Megatrend 2, we will pay ample attention to the consumer side of globalization and the emergence of the "global citizen."

The Twelve Pillars of Power

For a long time, world economic, political, and military power relationships were clear. By end of the Second World War, there were only two superpowers, the United States and the Soviet Union. A "cold war" raged between these two superpowers, and other countries chose either one side or the other. Also after World War II, Japan emerged as the second-richest country in the world, although this did not translate into political, diplomatic, or military power.

The fall of the Berlin Wall in 1989 and the disintegration of the Soviet Union in 1991 radically changed this picture. At the start of the twenty-first century the United States, while still topping the league of the world order, is seeing its power reduced in various ways. Other countries are growing stronger, and a new economic order is emerging worldwide, which will overturn the current balance of power.

This is fueled in part by the awakening of Chinese ambition from a long period of hibernation. Historically a superpower, over time China repeatedly lost this status. In 1421, Gavin Menzies argues, China discovered America and Australia – but never pushed ahead to colonize the two continents. How different the world would be now if they had! Napoleon once called China a sleeping giant; the giant is now waking up.

Mark Steyn, author of *America Alone*, states that by the end of this century, America will be the only free Western power. Europe will no longer exist as we now know it. Decades of peace and prosperity will have made the continent lazy, weak, and ripe for the picking by new powers.

In this century, twelve groups will form along the way. They will become the pillars of the new economic world order:

1. The seven economic blocs
2. The six superpowers
3. The "tigers"
4. The mixed regions: power and stagnation in the same area
5. The lost regions
6. World-governing institutions

7. Peaceful networks and diasporas
8. Angry networks and tribes
9. Religious and moral groups
10. The multinationals
11. The technology industry
12. ... prepare for a surprise.

1. The Seven Economic Blocs

The first of the seven blocs is the European Union (EU), which was founded in 1951 as a voluntary union of nation states, currently numbering 27.

The EU constitutes a single market with a standardized system of laws that apply to all member states, guaranteeing freedom of movement of people, goods, services, and capital. The EU maintains a common trade policy, agricultural and fisheries policies, and a regional development policy. Fifteen member states have adopted a common currency, the euro. At the beginning of the twenty-first century, the EU is economically successful. With almost 500 million citizens, the EU generated an estimated 30% share of the world's nominal gross domestic product (US$16.6 trillion) in 2007.

Although the EU has a weak foreign policy, with its members disagreeing on many foreign policy issues, it has, however, developed a role in justice and home affairs, including the abolition of passport checks when travelling from one member state to another.

The EU operation is a hybrid of "inter-governmentalism" and "supra-nationalism." In certain areas it depends on agreement among member states. But it also has supranational bodies that can make decisions without the agreement of members. Despite its flaws, the EU model is currently being copied in many areas in the world. A bloc not only provides economic advantages, but also the benefit of making former rivals economically interdependent, so that it is no longer in their interest to pick a fight. An Asian Union, for example, uniting rivals such as Pakistan and India, could prove to be the most lasting investment in peace in Asia – and peace is good for business.

Examples of current and potential trade alliances based on the EU model are:

1. In North-America, Nafta was created in 1994, a trade bloc between the US, Canada, and Mexico.
2. In South America, three trade blocs currently exist: Caricom in the Caribbean, and Mercosur and Unasur on the South American continent. It is expected that these three will merge into one South American trade bloc in the future.
3. In Russia and the Caucasus, a new bloc is anticipated; let's call it Kremlin+.

In Northern Africa and the Middle East, we may see two blocs.

4. We might call the moderate bloc – including Turkey, the Emirates, and Israel – the Ottoman Union.
5. The more Islamic bloc might be called the Sharia Union, uniting the Islamic fundamentalist forces in the Middle East.
6. In Asia, trade blocs such as Asean, Saarc, Apec, and others already exist. It is expected that in the future these will merge into one Asian trade bloc, which we could call Asian+.

A New Power Structure

In recent years, growing Chinese clout combined with a sympathetic diplomatic posture has helped reorient the power structure of South-East Asia toward China. China has become the number one or number two trading partner of virtually every country in the region. Seeking strength in numbers, South-East Asian governments not only strive to tap into China's new wealth, but also to embed Beijing in a multitude of organizations and dialogues in the name of "community-building" and closer integration. Japan, South Korea, and to a lesser extent India, Australia, and New Zealand, also participate in this exercise.

Ellen Frost of the National Defense University argues that we are witnessing the rebirth of a "pre-colonial maritime Asia," formed by the string of coastal communities, port cities and towns, and waterways connecting North-East and South-East Asia, India, and Australia.

Maritime Asia is the place where Asian wealth and power is concentrated. Home to 60%–70% of all Asians, it has the largest cities, and globalization-driven investments. To take better advantage of this asset, Asian governments should explicitly make Maritime Asia a part of their vision on integration. They should work with local officials, business representatives and civil and social groups to remove the barriers that impede the natural flow of Maritime Asia. These include border taxes, tariffs, quotas, corruption, crime, outdated transport links, redundant security checks, and restrictions on labor mobility. For example, Asian governments should develop and introduce one single legal framework to facilitate a "one-stop shop" program within the trade bloc Asian+. This should aim to limit the cargo clearance of container ships in major ports to one thirty-minute stop and declare this legal framework mandatory for the entire region.

This process is already underway in Asia, and similar transitions in power structures can also be observed in Africa, South America, and other parts of the world.

2. The Six Superpowers

Goldman Sachs envisions six superpowers: the United States, Japan, and the so-called BRIC countries, namely Brazil, Russia, India, and China. Russia will be the smallest superpower, economically speaking. The Russian economy runs parallel to trade in oil and gas, which makes it extremely one-sided. The countries Russia exports to would also like to decrease their dependency on autocratic Russia over time. In addition, Russia is facing a serious decrease in population. Nevertheless, oil and gas reserves in this country are so large they will provide an attractive income for a consider-

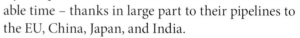

able time – thanks in large part to their pipelines to the EU, China, Japan, and India.

In 2007 a Russian submarine planted a flag on the bottom of the Arctic Ocean. Russia claims that a large part of the North Pole is a natural geological extension of their territory. This is something that most other countries, including the US, strongly disagree with. The North Pole is known not only for its melting ice caps, but also for its potentially large quantities of natural resources, among them gas and oil.

According to the same Goldman Sachs research, by 2032 India will occupy third place on the list of superpowers, having by then overtaken Japan. Prior to that, by 2016, China will seize second place, behind the United States – and by 2025, China may have surpassed the United States.

Actually, this isn't anything to be surprised about. Around 1800, China accounted for about a third of the world's economy. It is partly a matter of power due to the size of the Chinese population. The country is well aware of this and will demonstrate ever more dominant behavior on the world scene. Already we see that China has a very dominant presence in Africa, with promises of technical help and financial means.

According to *Jane's Defense Weekly*, China could also surpass the US in the military field by 2090, though at the moment, China doesn't seem to have any major military ambitions. The Chinese army is characterized by an entrepreneurial spirit. Their military personnel is involved in businesses, owns companies, and already forms China's largest multinational, according to the American trend-watcher John Naisbitt. Things are rather different in India, militarily speaking. For many decades at odds with its Islamic neighbor Pakistan, India's army has become the largest and most experienced in Asia at the start of the twenty-first century, making India the country best equipped to deal with terrorism.

Brazil, which occupied a modest fifteenth place in the world economy in 2003, follows a different strategy. Brazil is rich with raw materials – raw materials that other countries would very much like to have. Apart from that, Brazil has the largest concentration of Japanese outside Japan, as well as the largest concentration of Germans outside Germany. Both of these groups greatly stimulate Brazil's economy – an important pillar of which is industry.

Although Brazil as the eighth largest weapons exporter in the world, is involved in many of the world's problems, Brazilians are seen as harmless football players and happy party-goers. And they cherish this image. Moreover, they will probably maintain this image because they manage formally and politically to stay out of major conflicts themselves. They manage to do so because they use domestic hydro power and other forms of energy, such as biodiesels, and obtain their oil from their own backyard, South America.

Researchers at Goldman Sachs expect a lot from Brazil in the next fifteen years. The discovery in 2007 of some gigantic oil fields along the country's coast makes its future even brighter.

Japan has for decades had a place among the world's top economic countries, and will retain this position in coming decades. Despite the cost of an aging population – Japan is now the most graying country in the world – Goldman Sachs and other opinion leaders in the financial world expect Japan to retain its position in the world's economic top six.

This is due to Japan's highly industrialized capabilities and their entrance onto the robotics stage, their production of goods in various locations (Japanese cars are also made in the US, China, and Europe), their ongoing innovation (as in their robotics sector), and their work ethic and morality. Of course, economic strengths are subject to change: an aging population, for example, will cause the leisure sector to grow. But Japan remains an important power in Asia, where it has strong cooperative bonds with Russia and (despite occasional nationalistic quarrels) China. Japan has even outsourced work to a part of China which they occupied during the Second World War, because the people there still speak Japanese.

Less than ten years ago, Fortune 500 listed precisely one company from India and one from Russia. The list of 2008 already mentions seven companies from India and five Russian firms. China, meanwhile, has 29 Fortune 500 companies. These are still considerably lower numbers than those of the US and Japan (153 and 64 respectively), but it is about as many as France, Germany, and the UK (39, 37 and 34 respectively). Considering that five of the 29 Chinese Fortune 500 companies are new entries since 2007, this demonstrates a very rapid development. *Fortune* magazine itself speaks of a "powershift".

We also observe this shift of power in another field. The trade negotiations of the World Trade Organization (WTO) reached a deadlock in July 2008. India and China – grown into economic powers to be reckoned with – decided to stand their ground and to secure their own interests. So although an agreement on principles was already reached, India and China let the talks stall over details, much against the will of the US. This is very much a new stance on the part of China and India.

The growing pains of the Indian economy are also giving the Indian banks some more prosaic sorrows. While the country's ATM grid is growing rapidly, the Indian power grid, is unable to cope with the economic growth and the resulting demand for energy. On top of that, many people and small enterprises illegally tap electricity from the regular grid.

This causes many long or short power outages. Yogesh Sharma, relationship manager with Indian Axis Bank in Amritsar, says: "People who need cash from an ATM at night, for a night out, or to go shopping, often lose their cards when the power is cut off. The machine destroys these cards for security reasons. Applying for a new card costs time. Moreover, customers need their money immediately. That's why they went to the ATM in the first place. Most clients understand, and don't blame the banks. But we're trying to come up with solutions, because it isn't something that improves customer satisfaction. We already installed emergency batteries that take over the power supply at some ATMs, but by then the card is already blocked. We also have guards in place and there is a phone number people can call, but we're not able to return their card at that moment. However, building your own power infrastructure as a bank, simply to provide electricity for your own ATMs, isn't an option yet."

3. The "Tigers"

Then there are the smaller regions, nevertheless with strong economic foundations and efficient talent management. Although ambitious, well governed, full of confidence, and rich, they are simply too small in size to play the role of superpower. The question is in which direction they will move. These so-called "tigers" can be independent smaller countries or regions within countries. Tiger countries include Switzerland, Singapore, Chile, Taiwan, Vietnam, South Korea, and Canada. Some tiger regions within countries are Bavaria in Germany, southern China, the Punjab and Maharashtra in India, and southern Brazil.

4. The Mixed Regions: Power and Stagnation in the Same Areas

Some regions, countries, and cities have weak areas as well as strong ones. In most big cities, we already find rich sections where highly skilled people live and work – and these people are expected to become even richer in the future. Their skills will earn them more money to spend and invest. They have an open-minded, liberal lifestyle, and they like globalization and technology. For them, multiculturalism is simply a form of natural enrichment.

However, these same cities harbor large groups, or tribes, of what we might call "globalization losers." These angry groups are becoming poorer; they have no relevant skills for the new world order and technology is making them jobless. The fact that their neighborhoods are turning into ghettos is creating tension and reducing their ambition even more.

We can see the rise of mixed-power regions in several parts of the world. Keeping these powers in balance and managing their anger will become one of the major issues in these areas.

Several of these regions are seemingly dormant. Some, having reached considerable economic or cultural heights, have now gone into decline. Reasonably stable, with populations that are predominantly aging, they are not innovative and don't excel in any one area. Their performance is average. Living off investments made in better times, these are nations that have basically gone into "retirement." Their populations have few ambitions to turn their countries into world leaders. But while structures may have rusted to a standstill, for the well-to-do, it is quite pleasant in these regions, thanks to the peace and stability of the political climate.

In the 1920s, Argentina and Uruguay were among the eight richest countries in the world. In 1900 England was the sole superpower in the world...

Losing a leading position can happen overnight, but most often it happens gradually. If, let's say, every month you earn €5 less than the month before, you won't feel any urgent need to change things. This is what led to the decline of Argentina and England in the early 1900s – and will also lead to the decline of some mixed-power regions in the twenty-first century.

5. The Lost Regions

As we have said before, globalization has its "winners and losers." History has never been fair, and the future won't be either. Some regions and tribes will lose out in the future. In the lost regions, people will have little or nothing. For the most part, their populations will live in poverty, plagued by a permanent lack of water, (civil) wars, corrupt governments, extreme population growth, human rights violations, and so on. These are countries such as Chad, Pakistan, Afghanistan, Congo, Somalia, and Sudan. On the whole, their prospects are not very hopeful.

Paul Collier, Professor of Economics at Oxford University and Head of the Centre for the Study of African Economies, dubbed the population of these regions the "bottom billion", as this is the number of people we're talking about. They live in about fifty countries, mainly in Africa.

Some of these regions are chronically angry at themselves and the rest of the world – and it just doesn't seem to be possible to make them less angry. What they have in common is the offended mood in which they live their lives: a mixture of a perceived superiority and inferiority complex.

When the leaders of these countries behave angrily, they sometimes appear to have the support of the population. Since they are all dictatorships, it is difficult to estimate exactly how great this support is. Meanwhile, nationalistic arguments are often used to justify anger. Although these countries may have little or no economic importance, their anger can frighten the rest of the world and they can seriously blackmail other pillars of power.

6. World-Governing Institutions

A globalized world needs global institutions to regulate society. The current institutions trying to govern a fast-changing world are increasingly coming under attack and their legitimacy is eroding. The general feeling is that they are unable to cope with the challenges facing this world.

The United Nations, for example, is not able to prevent further growth of an already too-large world population. UN peacekeeping troops and NATO troops are fighting wars that can never be won (such as in Iraq and Afghanistan). And the UN Security Council does not represent new powers, such as the BRIC countries.

Financial institutions such as the World Bank and the IMF are not up to the task of governing this complex global economy and its new financial players. Henry Kissinger has said, "The International Monetary Fund as presently constituted is an anachronism. It has tried to adapt, but too slowly. It needs to be reformed."

Nout Wellink, who is among other things Governor of the IMF, adds: "The globalization of the financial world has had a great impact on the institutional setup of the international financial system. In earlier days, if countries had financial problems, they would go to the IMF, where they could borrow money under certain conditions. Nowadays they don't need

the IMF; they can go to many other sources [such as hedge-funds and Sovereign Wealth Funds] that don't usually have such difficult conditions. The relevance and role of organizations like the IMF and the World Bank is declining, because 'the market' is taking over. I expect this development to continue in the foreseeable future."

If the IMF is to play any significant role in the future, it might want to raise its ambition level. Gerrit Zalm, CFO at DSB Bank and former Minister of Finance of the Netherlands, says "Perhaps the IMF can take on the role of global authority for all aspects of the financial industry, using local executives. This, however, would mean the IMF would have to be drastically reformed, and I don't see that happening any time soon."

7. Peaceful Networks and Diasporas

Waves of migration have always changed the way we live. The Jewish Diaspora started after the first temple of the Jews in Jerusalem was destroyed by the Romans. This Diaspora grew and the Jews became powerful worldwide despite the fact that they had to make do without a homeland (before the founding of Israel in 1948).

Hispanics in the US manage to maintain their own way of life and their culture. For instance, they buy their food at their "own" shops and create all sorts of social networks on which they can fall back in times of need. All around the world, the closeness of Chinese Diaspora communities is remarkable. And so the list goes on.

Currently there are more people of Italian descent living outside of Italy than within the country. There are more than 60 million Chinese living outside of China; more than 35 million Indians living outside of India; and more than 7 million Americans outside of the US.

A diaspora of homosexual men and women has always taken place (5–10% of the world's people are homosexual). Thanks to globalization and the new media, they've been able to develop a global lifestyle and organize themselves into a powerful tribe.

New professional networks and virtual-friends networks (such as MySpace, CyWorld, and MSN) will also become more powerful. We will see more on this subject later on, in Megatrend 3.

In the new world, like-minded tribes and migrations of people with multiple loyalties will play an increasingly important role. Living with multiple loyalties is complicated. European security agencies reported in 2007 that some Europeans of Chinese descent were arrested for spying for Chinese companies. An Indian IT company, while working for the airline industry, reported several Muslim employees who tried to infil-

trate IT-programs for airplane builders Boeing and Airbus, in order to gather intelligence for future bomb attacks. On the other hand, double loyalties can also be used in a positive manner to smooth out differences and build bridges.

All in all, this pillar of power will influence the world in more ways than one.

8. Angry networks and tribes

Angry tribes are groups of people who are unhappy with the way the world is developing. Some are white Westerners who lost their jobs to immigrants. Some are immigrants who are disappointed in their new homelands. Some are activists wanting to protect the earth or animals (Earth Liberation Front, Animal Liberation Front). Some are groups with a separatist terrorist tradition, such as the IRA in the UK or ETA in Spain. Some have a political agenda, like the communists in India who attack multinationals; others have a more nationalistic or even xeno-phobic agenda. And all of them are against globalization.

Traditionally, one third of any population supports change, one third opposes change, and one third is indifferent – as long as their own inter-ests are not affected. Those who are against renewal and change are a varied bunch, voting extreme right, extreme left, or not voting at all.

9. Religious and moral groups

After a period of liberalization and secularization, there is now a loud call in the Western world for clear, compelling moral rules. Ethics are the center of attention. People feel the need to get a grip on things. In these hectic, insecure, and unsafe times, they long for an orderly world characterized by decency and respect.

As the Kondratieff wave pattern indicates, after a time of increasing prosperity, we now find ourselves focused on improved well-being – with ethics playing an increasingly important role. The moral views considered important here are often expressed by organizations such as Greenpeace and Amnesty International – worldwide organizations that are quite powerful because of their influence on public opinion.

Religious lines of demarcation are also sharper than they have been in decades, with people more conscious of their religious backgrounds and beliefs. While some may have thought religion would be seen as old-fashioned in the future, this is definitely not the case. Most parts of the world – including those that are the most technologically advanced – are still religious. And the quest for moral and ethical boundaries will make people increasingly religious, even in hi-tech regions such as Silicon Valley, where one whiz-kid recently stated, "I don't believe in God anymore, but I do miss Him." (We'll talk More about this in Megatrend 4.)

10. The Multinationals

Multinationals are more powerful than many countries. Exxon Mobile, for example, had revenues in 2007 greater than the GDP of Bahrain and Yemen combined. In today's world, more than 140 companies report annual sales in excess of $50 billion, whereas only about 60 countries can report an annual GDP in excess of $50 billion. Of course, sales and GDP cannot be taken as equivalents, but these figures show the economic power of some companies.

Multinationals may originate in specific countries, but national issues are far less important than international issues for these companies. Multinationals have become superpowers, with considerable influence on the life, work, economy, and society in the countries in which they operate. With investments that can bring greater prosperity and sustainability to their host country, the board of a multinational is often more powerful than the government.

11. The Technology Industry
Technology, past and present, has brought drastic changes to our lives. Think of electricity, the light bulb, cars, aircraft, radio, television, and computers. Nout Wellink is convinced that "the key driver of the financial industry is technology" – referring to the Internet, connectivity, mobility and flexibility. (We will elaborate on this in Megatrend 3.)

12 ...To Be Disclosed in the Next Section.

The Pillars of Power's Dynamics Will Define the Playing Field
The ways in which the twelve pillars of power reinforce and compete with each other will define the playing field of tomorrow's world. What this playing field will look like is not entirely clear.

Robert Kagan, columnist for the *Washington Post* and co-founder of the Project for the New American Century (PNAC), argues that an era of renewed competition among great powers is upon us. This competition is characterized by the tension between two main political traditions: the Western liberal democracies and the Eastern autocracies – primarily Russia and China.

What we do know for sure is that these twelve pillars of power will shape the future of mankind. And in this new economic world order, the financial industry will have a new place and play new roles, as we will explore in the following section.

The Three Corporate Faces of Globalization

Concerning companies, we see three different appearances of globalization. There may be more, but these are the forms we see as most important for the future of finance:

1. Globalization through outsourcing, offshoring, and "world-sourcing" – that is not yet concerned with mergers and takeovers.
2. Globalization through international growth and consolidation – where mergers and takeovers are pivotal.
3. Globalization through ownership by Sovereign Wealth Funds – participation in which makes ownership seriously global.

The word "globalization" has been used by economists since the beginning of the 1980s, but it only became popular from the latter half of the 1980s into the 1990s.

"Globalization" has different meanings. It can refer to the process by which people from all over the earth are becoming unified into a single society capable as functioning as a whole. However, it generally refers to economic globalization: the integration of national economies into an international economy through trade, foreign investment, capital flows, migration, and the spread of technology.

One of the most significant books on globalization is *The World is Flat*, by *New York Times* journalist Thomas Friedman. The world is "flat," Friedman suggests, in the sense that globalization has leveled the competitive playing field for industrial and emerging market countries. Friedman also argues that the pace of globalization is picking up – but not everyone agrees with him on that.

1. Globalization Through Outsourcing, Offshoring, and World-sourcing
Outsourcing refers to the transfer of in-house jobs to an outside supplier to reduce costs, take advantage of other companies' expertise, and to leave room for a company to concentrate on its own core business. It is not new and takes place all over the world. Back-office outsourcing began in the US in the 1960s – with payroll processing, among other things.

It gathered speed with the rapid advances in IT.

The last decade's revolution in telesales and customer support propelled outsourcing into a new dimension. In India it is thought that call centers alone now employ in excess of a million people – compared to just 300,000 at the start of this decade. Providers have sprung up at all levels of the outsourcing spectrum: from the lowest level of manufacturing and data processing, to levels requiring customer interaction (telemarketing, customer service, market research), web development, engineering, and the transfer of intellectual capital.

- Offshoring is the term for closing operations in one country and transferring them to another. Offshoring has typically been seen as a strategy to reduce labor costs. Some years ago, many Western companies had their products manufactured in China because of the low wages there. But when Chinese factory workers demanded more money and better working conditions, more and more companies transferred production to even cheaper countries such as Vietnam, Cambodia, Bangladesh, Indonesia, and India. Besides reducing labor costs, offshoring is also being used to get a foothold in emerging markets and to take advantage of centers of expertise, such as software development in India. Japan, for example, has regularly used offshoring to get into virtually closed US and European markets. Business functions that can be taken offshore today even include research and development. As with outsourcing, the offshoring enabled by technology is expected to move up from unskilled laborers to professional services. This growing shift of white-collar jobs to developing countries breeds fear in the West. Some Western business leaders even call it "a redistribution of the middle class" from the rich world to the poor. Others think these fears are exaggerated.

- World-sourcing taps into global diversity and resources, and distributes management, operations, processes, and production in such a way that they create the greatest efficiency, thus giving customers the best possible value. World-sourcing is based on the notion that a company's business model is its most valuable asset – rather than its location. By opening up to the world, looking for the best talent and ideas, a company improves its brand and shows itself to the world. Companies will be judged not by nationality, but by the quality of their goods, services, governance, transparency, environmental practices, degree of corporate social responsibility, and the actual value they deliver to customers worldwide.

- The world-sourcing logic dictates that companies focus on the best value and quality of products. All aspects of business (including materials, talent, innovation, logistics, infrastructure, and products) are sourced wherever they contribute the most value most efficiently.

Outsourcing of Patients

We all know about the outsourcing of call-center activities in the financial services. Now we're taking a giant step forward: like call centers and manufacturing facilities, health care is moving offshore.

As health-care costs continue rising in the industrialized world, medical travel will be part of the solution. Many Western insurers have already signed alliances with hospitals overseas. Patients may complain at first, because they don't trust foreign hospitals. Thailand may be an ideal destination for a holiday, but can a country that still has open sewers have clean, modern hospitals? This is the question that many people in Europe and the US are asking. And the answer is – yes!

India is a country with impressive credentials in several medical specializations. Their eye care, for example, is very sophisticated. With 10,000 eye specialists in India, the quality of medical care and surgery is extremely high. And in most areas of specialization, the cost of treatment in India is estimated to be on average one-eighth to one-fifth the cost in the West.

An Ernst & Young study showed that a cardiac procedure costing anywhere from $40,000 to $60,000 dollars in the US costs $30,000 in Singapore, $12,000 to $15,000 in Thailand, and only $3,000 to $6,000 dollars in India.

The cost of surgery is lower not only because Indian surgeons charge lower rates, but also because there is less litigation. Therefore the cost of malpractice insurance in India is about $4,000, compared to $100,000 in New York.

A different study by Ernst & Young projects that the medical tourism sector may earn as much as $2 billion annually by the year 2012, from $333 million in 2004.

Healthcare insurers will distinguish themselves more and more by offering treatment in distant foreign countries, with luxurious transportation to the hospital, and comfortable aftercare in locations similar to tropical beach-holiday resorts. Their coverage may come to include not only care that is strictly medical, but also more general aspects of healthcare.

Besides luxury, lower costs, and better service, there is yet another reason for Western insurers to turn to foreign hospitals: waiting lists. If you can't be helped immediately in your own country, a foreign hospital may well be a pleasant alternative. Especially in countries with long waiting lists for specific medical treatments (such as the Netherlands and Great Brittain), an insurer can offer its clients the option of treatment abroad.

Protests Against Outsourcing and Off-shoring

In the 2008 American presidential election, outsourcing and US job losses became a political issue.

The Communication Workers of America (CWA) union has been particularly active, seeking to influence the policies of individual states. At the start of 2008, politicians in Minnesota pushed for legislation to give customers an automatic right to request an alternative, American, callcenter if they were dealing with personal or financial information. Cleverly, the CWA campaign focused as much on the customer as the displaced worker.

Three issues were cited in the campaign: a very poor level of customer service, data fraud, and of course the risk of terrorism. Many US companies now pointedly refer to the use of American-only call centers in their advertising.

2. Globalization Through International Growth and Consolidation

Companies also expand their geographic area, not so much due to their philosophy of world-sourcing, but as the result of mergers and takeovers.

In the past decade, we have seen many national and international mergers and acquisitions (M&A) in the financial industry. As a result of the credit crisis, this process shifted into top gear. And although recent events render all lists outdated even before they are printed, here are a few examples:

National
- Monte dei Paschi di Siena buys Antonveneta from Banco Santander
- Bank of America buys LaSalle from ABN-Amro
- Wachovia takes over World Savings Bank
- Bank of New York buys Mellon Financial Corporation
- San Paolo di Torino merges with Banca Intesa
- UniCredit Group takes over Capitalia
- Allianz sells Dresdner Bank to Commerzbank
- Citi Chile and Banco de Chile merge
- Wells Fargo takes over Wachovia

International
- Dresdner Bank takes a stake in Gazprombank (Russia)
- Banco Santander buys Banco Real (Brazil) from ABN-Amro
- BNP Paribas buys Banca Nazionale di Lavorno (Italy)
- Sumitomo Mitsui (Japan) takes a stake in Barclays
- Ping An (China) takes a stake in Fortis
- UniCreditGroup (Italy) take over HypoVereinsbank (Germany)
- Société Générale (France) buys Banco Cacique (Brazil)
- Bank of America buys Merrill Lynch

The Future of Finance

Consolidation in the Financial World is Accelerating

We don't see this wave of consolidation and internationalization coming to an end any time soon; in fact, we see it accelerating. This conclusion comes from very different observations.

We can see that shareholders demand growth "no matter what." New emerging markets also offer enormous growth possibilities. Economies of scale are noticed and exploited better and more quickly. Successful international formulas inspire other players to develop similar strategies, and everyone wants to spread their risks.

There is a growing routine in outsourcing and offshoring, which makes solutions of this kind ever easier to implement. We also see parties become more experienced, too, with cross-border mergers and acquisitions, making even a country like Italy accessible.

We see the influx of new money from Sovereign Wealth Funds and new markets emerging, which will also lead to an increase of internationalization. Technology – especially the Internet – will be a tremendous accelerator of international ambitions.

However, in the European banking world, further international consolidation is still being hampered by some rational and emotional restrictions on cross-border mergers and takeovers. Regulation and supervision play important roles in this. Governments are often closely intertwined with their banking sector, be it in the form of government property or investment in public debt. Banks are often considered national symbols that should by no means fall in foreign hands.

Think for example of the soap opera that ensued when Dutch bank ABN-Amro announced it wanted to buy the Italian bank Antonveneta. In the end they succeeded, but not until they had first overcome fierce Italian national feelings. Another example of such an emotional and nationalistic reaction came from the French President Nicolas Sarkozy following a massive (€4.9 billion!) embezzlement at the French bank Société Générale. The French government approached their two largest banks, Crédit Agricole and BNP Paribas, to see if they would be prepared to launch a break-up bid for Société Générale, petrified that a weakened SocGen would fall to a "foreign predator" like Italy's UniCredit Group or Spain's Banco Santander.

On the other hand, the Dutch Minister of Finance, Wouter Bos, as good as actively cooperated in the sell-off of ABN-Amro.

Certainly worth mentioning in this context is that the European Union is taking active steps to stimulate the integration of the European banking world. The goal here is to create a single European market for financial services. In that market, financial institutions authorized to provide services in one member state could provide the same services throughout the EU, competing on a level playing field within a consistent regulatory environment. Such a single market in financial services would act as a catalyst for economic growth across all sectors of the economy, boost productivity, and provide lower-cost and better-quality financial products for consumers and enterprises.

European Integration Through Merges and Acquisitions

The process of European economic integration is ongoing project. What started as the creation of a single market for goods has evolved into a more integrated economic arena with a common monetary policy and higher levels of economic and financial integration than previously expected.

However, corporate integration and the restructuring of industrial activity are still in development. The next twenty years will determine the new landscape of European industrial structure, with corporations evolving from the "national champions" we observe today into truly European champions.

The rise of M&A activity in the 2000s has already been driven in part by the increasing legal and economic integration of European countries. M&As within European borders are moving from being primarily domestic, as industries follow a process of consolidation, to cross-border deals, as companies expand abroad to other EU countries. Although the number of domestic M&As remains steady at about 81% of all completed deals, the value of cross-border transactions has increased from 20% in 2001 to 34% in 2007. However, for this trend to continue, several structural changes must happen in the environment that European corporations face.

Firstly, government involvement and economic nationalism has to diminish. A large portion of economic activity is still handled directly by state-owned enterprises or has a high level of government involvement through explicit and implicit regulations. Industries as important as telecoms, utilities, finance, insurance, transport and high-tech manufacturing are directly linked to national and regional governments. These links will weaken as integration occurs and the rationale for government involvement should diminish. We have already seen positive progress in the last two years on this front.

Secondly, M&As have to move from being a friendly club atmosphere to foster a search for the most competent alternative to maximize value for the corporation. Up until now, the vast majority of completed deals in Europe are either friendly or neutral (97%). Hostile deals are extremely rare (1% of the completed deals). This percentage is considerably below the worldwide trend. M&As in Europe continue to be too much of a gentlemen's business. Competing bids, hostile bids, and more open discussion about strategic alternatives to maximize deal value should become more of the norm rather than the exception.

Thirdly, deals will involve more equity transactions and less debt financing. The time for cheap money has ended and is not likely to return any time soon. The majority of completed deals in Europe in the recent past were paid exclusively with cash. Although, on average, deals paid with cash only are smaller than deals paid with mixed forms of payment, the size of deals financed exclusively with cash has consistently increased.

Finally, the last two trends taken together imply that the role played by activist investors will increase. A more active market for corporate control, with less access to debt financing, implies that smart value investors and managers with the ability to restructure and bring forward innovations to extract value out of existing corporations will flourish. This group will include private-equity firms, activist funds, and exceptional managers.

The speed at which these trends will materialize depends primarily on European

citizens. These trends imply a dynamic business environment, with lots of opportunities driven by a rapid pace of corporate restructuring and change – a process of accelerated creative destruction. Such a process requires people to be well trained, as European citizens are, with the enthusiasm and ability to view change as a constant source of opportunity and not a threat to the status quo – something European citizens will need to develop.

José Manuel Campa is Grupo Santander Professor of Finance at IESE Business School.

3. Globalization through ownership by sovereign wealth funds

This type of globalization is all about making participation in ownership seriously global.

Sovereign Wealth Funds (SWFs) are similar to hedge-funds. But instead of being privately owned and managed, they are owned and managed by a national state. Large SWFs are often the result of income from natural resources, like oil revenues, or from other trade surpluses – such as China and Singapore are currently experiencing due to their tremendous export of goods and services.

The first SWFs were already founded in the 1950s and 60s. The oldest, the Kuwait Investment Authority (KIA), manages 10% of the annual oil revenues from this super-wealthy desert country. KIA is, among other things, a majority shareholder of British Petroleum (3% of the shares) and Daimler-Benz (7%).

Other government funds are very young. The SWFs of Taiwan, South Korea, China, Qatar, Russia, and Venezuela all date from after the year 2000. And recently, Western oil-producing countries such as Norway and the US have founded their own SWFs.

The Future of Finance

Investment bank Morgan Stanley estimated that in mid-2007 there was about €1,800 billion in SWFs worldwide – and that this figure would double around 2010, most likely reaching five times that amount by 2015. Morgan Stanley itself, by the way, got involved with an SWF when the Chinese SWF China Investment Corporation (CIC) bought a share of €3.17 billion in the investment bank in December 2007.

Deutsche Bank Research calculated in 2007 that in terms of capital, these funds would be about one-sixth of the size of the world's pension funds, and about one-fifth of the size of all insurance companies. APG, the third-largest pension fund in the world, has €216 billion in assets (in December 2007) – so it is still larger than the Chinese sovereign wealth fund CIC. Nevertheless, there is approximately one and a half times more capital in SWFs than in all hedge-funds put together.

Merrill Lynch, in its report "Sovereign Wealth Funds," makes an attempt to calculate the future size of SWFs. In an optimistic scenario, they calculate that by 2011, this amount will stand between €4,000 and €7,000 billion.

SWFs Gain Access to Western Financial Service Providers Due to The Credit Crunch

The credit crunch seems to know only losers, but it also has a few winners: Sovereign Wealth Funds. Previously, these funds had difficulty accessing American and European markets, because of the Western fear of foreign influence. But that has changed. When Western financial institutions were in desperate need of money, they welcomed with open arms the Asians, Russians, and Arabs with their mega-investments:

- DIFC Investment, Dubai: 2.2% of Deutsche Bank
- Istithmar, Dubai: 2.7% of Standard Chartered
- Dubai International Capital: a share in HSBC
- Kuwait Investment Authority: 6% of Citigroup
- Qatar Investment Authority: under 2% of Credit Suisse
- Libyan Investment Authority: a small share in Fortis
- Temasek from Singapore: 9% of UBS, 2.1% of Barclays, shares in Fortis Bank and Merrill Lynch
- China Development Bank: 3% of Barclays

The Chinese SWF, China Investment Corporation (CIC), is fairly aggressive. In spring 2008, CIC signed a deal with Christopher Flowers, a Goldman Sachs ex-banker, to start a $4 billion private-equity fund focusing on investments in financial institutions, especially smaller banks and brokerages. Indirect private-equity fund investments were deemed to cause fewer (political) tensions than direct Chinese investments in Western financial institutions. It also made the fund less vulnerable to domestic criticism. In case the investment didn't produce the expected

returns, the private-equity company that made them could take the blame.

Oligarchs in the Slipstream of SWFs

Besides SWFs we are also seeing the rich of this world – especially from the Middle East and Russia – investing in banks and insurance companies. For example, HSBC, the fifth-largest bank in the world, is now 3% owned by the Saudi tycoon Maan Abdul Wahed al-Sanea. The super-investor Warren Buffett became the "savior" of Goldman Sachs.

The billionaire Suleiman Kerimov, having made his fortune in the Russian business world of the 1990s, and whose capital in 2008 was worth approximately €19 billion, has shown great interest in bank investments. He possesses 7% of Russia's largest savings bank, Sberbank, and has shares in large business banks such as Morgan Stanley, Crédit Suisse, and Deutsche Bank. Through his Swiss investment vehicle Millennium Group – which already owned about 2% of Fortis – Kerimov invested an additional €400 million in Fortis.

Unknown and Unloved

Strategic investing by SWFs in vital sectors such as telecommunications, energy, media, and banks, is often seen as politically motivated. The fear is that SWFs from China, Russia, and the Middle East will exercise political influence through the companies they partly own. In this context we speak of geo-economic motives, aimed at controlling the economic activities within a particular area, without the use of military force. To obtain the desired political results, control over the wealth – and with it the socio-economic stability – of a population can be an effective alternative to military force.

It remains to be seen to what extent this current wave of SWF mega-investments from Asia, Russia, and the Middle East is inspired by such aggressive motives. However, the fact of the matter is that the national economies of these regions are simply unable to absorb their vast cash surpluses. This means they have no alternative but to invest abroad, in this case in the Western world.

An IMF report about SWFs published in February 2008 says that, at least until then, there was no proof that governments which own SWFs actively interfered with the investment decisions of those funds. As Nout Wellink points out, "A Sovereign Wealth Fund from Singapore doesn't want to take over the Netherlands. They just want a high return of investment."

A reason for the Arabs to invest through SWFs is to try and make their one-sided economies less oil-dependent. Nevertheless, their increasing financial influence is giving rise to some concern in the industrialized world.

Of course, governments can protect those sectors and industries concerned with national security. The question is how far that goes. Most countries already have legislation providing for prevention of foreign investments in strategic sectors. The US, for example, has the Committee on Foreign Investment (CFIUS). In 2007 this organization approved the Dubai Ports World Investment takeover of the transshipment company P&O. However, Dubai Ports World Investment abandoned the deal when American Congress went ballistic. Having the Arabs transferring goods in American harbors was, apparently, still a bridge too far.

The West appears to be having difficulties letting go of its economic supremacy. But to turn back the clock with protectionist measures would be unwise. The American Secretary of Commerce Carlos Gutiérrez and Governor of California Arnold Schwarzenegger argued in the *Wall Street Journal* against this kind of overreacting, encouraging cross-border trading. According to these two Republican gentlemen: "As immigrants, we're proud of America and the strength it derives from being uniquely open to trade, to investment, and to ideas and people. Recently, prominent voices in punditry and politics have questioned the benefits of America's openness and called for an isolationist U-turn that would choke off our innovation and prosperity."

Chinese in The Boardroom

Wealthy private investors more often come from non-Western countries, as Merrill Lynch quite rightly states in its World Wealth Report. Pim Mol, Director of Private Banking at Rabobank, predicts therefore that in Asia there will be many new private banks in the near future: "Nowadays wealthy Asians still bank in private Swiss and Western banks. But as far as the power of shareholders is concerned, UBS, for example, is more Asian than Swiss. And since Asians are quite capable of establishing and developing such banks themselves, you have to anticipate that happening."

The boards of UBS and Citibank will, according to Mol, most probably be headed by an Asian – and Asians do business differently from Westerners. This will show in the banking of tomorrow. Mol says, "Bottom-of-the-pyramid thinking is well established over there: inventing your products bottom-up and not top-down. Have a look at Tata Nano, the automobile for the "little man," which only costs €2,000. This invention started with the price, and from there it was developed and fabricated. This type of thinking is scarce in the West. From this perspective, micro-credit – which is actually based on this principle – has a bright future, as Harvard professor C.K. Prahalad has been saying for some time. The

financial industry will experience many changes in ownership over the next ten years, which will cause a profound shift of power among shareholders. This will subsequently have its effects on the formation of the various boards."

Financial institutions: potentially a twelfth pillar

In the previous section we described the three faces of globalization of companies: globalization through outsourcing, offshoring, and worldsourcing; through international growth and consolidation; and through ownership by Sovereign Wealth Funds.

No matter how you look at it, financial services are going to become even more global than they already are. The middle classes and the elite class are both expected to grow, according to the Merrill Lynch World Wealth Report. The world is expected to become richer, and even more money will be circulating through financial services.

With their investment policies, the financial industry effectively chooses the direction of the world's development. The decision to invest in sustainability and clean alternative sources of energy, for example, is vital to the development of a new energy economy. Traditional financial institutions, along with Sovereign Wealth Funds are also expected to play a major role in financing this new economic world order.

Globalization of Taxation and Regulation

To Portable Global Taxing

Globalization and the development of technology have resulted in unexpected new challenges for traditional tax systems. Take for example modern medicine: if a surgeon in the US operates on a patient in a Spanish hospital by video-line, who pays which taxes to whom?

In the coming years, portable, or international, taxation will be developed bit by bit. National taxes, however, will not disappear overnight. Harry Smorenberg, an independent consultant, does not believe a really universal tax will become a reality. However, he does believe that a combination of the Swiss and American models is possible.

In Switzerland, 80% of the tax is "local," meaning it benefits the region where you live, and only 20% of the tax is national. In the US, where every state is free to design its own tax system, there are many kinds of taxes. According to Smorenberg, a combination of both systems would benefit both the world economy and the trend toward globalization.

Tax Evasion and Tax Havens

With globally integrated financial markets and modern communication techniques, the creation of offshore financial accounts – the setting up of bogus companies, away from the prying eyes of the tax man – is a piece of cake. In these new times of "borderless banking," wealthy individuals can easily evade taxes in their home country by transferring capital abroad and channeling investments through offshore jurisdictions.

In Italy, a recent tax amnesty resulted in the disclosure of €75 billion in assets held offshore. In 2007 Ireland collected almost €840 million from about 15,000 Irish residents hiding undeclared income in offshore bank accounts. This amounts to about 8% of the total 2006 Irish income tax collected.

This type of tax evasion is facilitated by the existence of jurisdictions that have strict bank secrecy rules which prevent information exchange with the customer's country of residence. The increased flight into offshore finance and bogus companies with unclear structures, based

in preferably sunny financial centers, can make life very difficult for domestic tax authorities.

Some of the most important tax havens are Switzerland, Luxembourg, Singapore, the Cayman Islands, the Maldives and the Bahamas. Data from the BIS, IMF, and OECD suggests that a total of $5–7 trillion is held offshore.

Offshore tax evasion undermines the fairness and integrity of national tax systems, and adversely affects the willingness of the vast majority of law-abiding taxpayers to voluntarily comply with their tax obligations. Tax evasion also hinders healthy economic development, since decisions on where to locate funds are driven by the possibility of easy tax evasion and not by the true economic return on capital.

Moreover, strict bank secrecy and the reluctance of tax havens to cooperate in countering tax abuse undermine the national fiscal sovereignty of other countries. International regulation is needed since globalization and technology will make it even easier to evade national tax rules.

The Future of the Rich

The growth in market capitalization in the emerging markets has caused the wealth of the seriously rich, the high-net-worth individuals (HNWIs are persons who own a minimum of $1 million assets, not including their homes and other assets for personal use), to rise by 9.4% to $40.7 billion in 2007. This is stated in the twelfth annual World Wealth Report, issued by Merrill Lynch and Capgemini. The number of HNWIs in the world rose in that same year by 6% to 10.1 million, and the number of super-rich (ultra-HNWIs are persons who own a minimum of at least $30 million in assets, not including their homes and other assets for personal use) rose 8.8%. For the first time since these reports were issued, the average assets of HNWIs now surpass $4 million. In 2007 India lead the way with a growth of 22.7% of the HNWI population; China came second with 20.3%; and Brazil followed closely with an increase of 19%.

Transition to Safer, Trusted Investments

Due to the increasing turmoil in the financial markets and economic uncertainties, HNWIs have repositioned their assets from high-risk investments into safer, less-volatile asset classes. According to the World Wealth Report, 44% of the financial assets of HNWIs consists of cash deposits and bonds with a fixed coupon. This is an increase of 9 percentage points, compared with 2006. In general, HNWIs lowered their exposure to the US and demonstrated more interest in domestic markets.

"Green Investments" Are Becoming Popular

The increased attention everywhere to the environment causes "green investments" to rise in popularity across the globe. They promise investors high returns and simultaneously they give the investor the opportunity to be socially involved. The Middle East and Europe harbor the most environmentally friendly HNWIs and ultra-HNWIs with 17% and 21% respectively in 2007. In the US, a mere 5% of HNWIs and 7% of ultra-HNWIs have green investments in their portfolios. Internationally, 50% of HNWIs stated that financial returns were their main reason for allocating a part of their portfolio in environmentally friendly assets. Considering future sustainability, the World Wealth Report expects a continuing growth in green investments.

A Look into the Future

Despite the great uncertainties about short-term prospects, positive developments in the emerging markets still seem able to provide robust growth.

The balance between the power of the emerging markets and the fully developed markets will probably continue throughout 2008. The short-term perspectives will be volatile, as certain risks remain to be assessed. Generally speaking, the global economy has two clearly defined challenges to overcome: taking away the obstacles that are obstructing growth in the developed markets, and keeping inflation in check in the emerging markets. The way these challenges are faced will be decisive for the growth of the international HNWI population. On the basis of the results of 2007, taking into account the recent developments in the world markets, the World Wealth Report predicts that total HNWI wealth will increase at a rate of 7% per year to $59.1 billion by 2012. ☐

Source: World Wealth Report 2007, Merrill Lynch/Capgemini

Checks and Balances for Super-Elites

In today's world, the 1,100 richest people's net worth is almost twice the net worth of the 2.5 billion people earning the least. The free-market principles that drive the global trade of goods, services, and ideas gave rise to a super-class of elites whose actions effect millions of lives. Global elites get their power in a new way, using international, institutional connections, forming an in-crowd network that often runs deeper than national loyalties. This new super-class can afford to operate with a freedom that is impossible in nation-states, where the checks and balances of government help to counteract a disproportionate concentration of power in the hands of a few.

Without international organizations capable of ensuring such measures, the world is possibly more unequal than ever before – and this inequality may pose a danger to international stability. But despite this, national governments remain wary of giving up authority to international governing institutions.

New Regulation of SWFs

The International Monetary Fund (IMF) established a work group in May 2008 to formulate guidelines for SWFs, representing altogether as much as $3,000 billion in capital. The group is formed from representatives of the 25 IMF countries, Saudi Arabia, the Organization for Economic Cooperation and Development (OECD), and the World Bank. José Barroso, President of the European Commission, threatened to impose binding rules within the EU if the Sovereign Wealth Funds don't come up with their own code of conduct.

These guidelines will most likely target the need for transparency of the funds. For example, the world's largest Sovereign Wealth Fund, that of the United Arab Emirates, valued at approximately $875 billion, is like a black box to the outside world. No one knows where the Arabs invest nor do they know the purpose of these investments. Moreover, with rising oil prices, the power of oil-producing countries will increase. At $200 a barrel, the proven oil reserves of the six Gulf nations alone would rise in value to $95 trillion, about twice the size of the public-equity markets,

according to Morgan Stanley's Managing Director, Stephen Jen.

German Chancellor Angela Merkel has called for an EU-wide investment-screening mechanism. The Canadian government has also indicated it will consider the creation of a national security review process for foreign investments. The G8 countries have called for the IMF and the World Bank to identify the best practices in transparency and accountability to adopt for Sovereign Wealth Funds. At the same time, the G8 called on the OECD to promote the best practices for investment-receiving countries to adopt, to ensure that their SWF policies are transparent and non-protectionist.

Regulations for Fair and Transparent Financial Services
In the Netherlands in 2007 there was a big riot about insurance policies that combined life insurance with investments. Being a complicated product, the costs weren't clear to many people. In some instances, these "hidden costs" amounted to up to 40% of the deposit.

It is not only the regular consumer, but also experts who often have a hard time determining the fee structures of these policies. Such a lack of clarity, which has received an immense amount of press coverage, is extremely harmful for the perceived trustworthiness of the entire financial industry.

The Dutch government has commissioned the supervisory institution, Autoriteit Financiële Markten (AFM) to investigate these policies, and it is expected that legislation will be adjusted accordingly. In the European arena, regulations for investment companies and financial markets were already adjusted in 2007, when the so-called MiFID was enforced.MiFID stands for Markets in Financial Instruments Directive. This European guideline, according to the AFM website, aims for "the stimulation of fair, transparent, efficient, and integrated financial markets," and "to provide regulations for intermediaries" in order to protect the European individual private investor.

The need for more transparency could also lead to more specialization in banks and insurance companies. Pim Mol, the Director of Private Banking at Rabobank, expects that "there will be a separation in the financial industry between investment banks, savings banks, and retail banks. They will each operate according to different regulations and a different supervision regime. There will also be a separation among insurance companies. This untwining and specialization has become inevitable and will cause a lot more pain, but all of this is necessary to reach optimal transparency."

Reliable Corporate Management

In the US, ever since the credit crunch broke out, we have seen a similar call for more supervision of the financial sector and more emphasis on corporate governance. This call for more checks and balances resulted earlier in the Sarbanes-Oxley (SOX) law. Passed in 2002 by the American Senate, the SOX law for corporate management was the result of financial scandals of previously unknown proportions in corporations such as Enron, WorldCom, and AOL, due to failing internal control.

One of the stipulations of the SOX law is that there must be a section in the company's annual report that evaluates internal control of the correctness of the numbers stated in annual financial reports. The Chief Executive Officer and the Chief Financial Officer must sign a statement that their procedures are airtight. The accountant must, in addition to his regular financial reporting tasks, add an explicit statement in which he agrees with the statements of the CFO and CEO. In particular, the Sarbanes-Oxley dictates that corporate directors can be fined and even sent to jail for not complying with the rules for reliable corporate management. Non-American corporations that are quoted on the American Stock Exchange must also comply with the SOX law.

Towards Global Supervision

With regards to the supervision of financial markets and institutions, while every country will still have its own system, the globalization of the financial industry will induce a tendency towards uniformity – although internationally this may take a few years.

Gerrit Zalm says: "A worldwide authority for the financial industry would be ideal, but I don't see it happening any time soon. What we do get are more international agreements, such as the Basel agreements for banks and insurance companies. Stock market authorities, united in IOSCO, are also joining their efforts, and IFRS accountancy standards are regulated worldwide. Efforts like these can, in most cases, cover systemic risks, such as banks going belly up. There are simply too many authorities in the financial industry."

Within Europe, much still needs to be done to integrate the supervision of financial markets. In the area of European banking regulations

alone, there are as many as 41 national authorities for the current 27 EU member states. These national supervisors – as members of the European Committee for Bank Supervisors – are responsible for the prudential supervision of banks. Their varying interpretations of European rules often result in additional national regulations and additional costs for banks already under supervision in multiple countries.

In the United States, the Federal Reserve (the central bank of the US) is a joint venture of a number of privately owned banks and is less independent than it may seem at first sight. "In fact it is just a commercial bank," says Ron Abdoelhafiezkhan, who is among other things financial advisor to the royal families of the Emirates. "But it is one that has an enormous stature, even though it's eroding somewhat at the moment. It is not really an independent supervisor like the European Central Bank. It is, in fact, an institute for the self-regulation of American financial institutions. The problem with self-regulation is that it often sounds better than it actually is. That is what we have already seen several times. A true independent supervisor would be better for the United States."

Pim Mol adds: "The fact that the FED is not really independent is beginning to take its toll. Over the past years, it has lowered interest rates too fast and too much. That's over now. That is why I expect that there will be a call for a truly independent FED." The lack of the FED's real independence probably also led to a wrong approach to the current real estate bubble.

In 2007 the US Treasury Secretary Henry Paulson praised the new Dutch supervision model, devised by Jeroen Kremers, a former top-level official at the IMF and former top-level official at the Dutch Ministry of Finance. Paulson used the Kremers model as a starting point for his plan to improve the scattered and failing American supervision system. This model is flexible, and with some adjustments could be applicable in many countries.

Previously, financial supervision was organized according to the sectors of banking, insurance, and stock companies. But in the market, these clear divisions between sectors had faded because of the many mergers and complex products. And so Kremers deemed it better to divide the supervision functionally into prudential supervision and behavioral supervision.

Prudential supervision, for instance by a central bank, focuses on the solidity of financial companies and contributes to the stability of the financial sector. Behavioral supervision focuses on "orderly and transparent market procedures, clear relationships between market parties, and careful treatment of consumers by financial corporations".

If the industry is to avoid another bubble, it must learn from the current one and previous bubbles, and supervision should be organized more strictly and internationally. The best solution would in fact be a world-wide central bank. This will, however, have an impact on the freedom of banks and insurers to offer certain products, as well as affecting their options to invest in sectors that are already overvalued.

Self-Regulation and International Agreement

Nout Wellink doesn't anticipate some kind of worldwide financial regulation, but considers self-regulation to be the ultimate authority: "What you want is to develop various self-regulating systems. These systems would also be good buffers, because from time to time, things are bound to go wrong. People's inevitable irrational behavior – such as overspending even in times of abundance – needs to be compensated for and corrected by the system, the market itself." Nevertheless, an international financial-economic consultative body will be needed.

Perhaps the seven economic blocs we mentioned earlier will create such an institution. This institution could become the platform for negotiations on trade, world financial and economic issues, on moral and political issues, the distribution of natural resources (for instance how to deal with resources under the North Pole), and on the organization of space travel. With only seven parties taking part, such an institution would be able reach agreements much more easily than the current UN, which has more than 140 parties to consider – a lost cause from the start.

Dramatic Changes in the Game, the Arena, the Players, and the Rules

The twelve pillars of power, and the various forms of globalization taking place at the moment – especially consolidation, mergers and acquisitions, as well as the rise of Sovereign Wealth Funds – will, combined, have an enormous impact on the way financial service providers will compete.

An Entirely Different Ball Game
New and greater "gaps" arise because consolidation doesn't only bring economies of scale – it also brings diseconomies of scale. New imperfections arise from a larger scale which makes it harder to attend to more specific customer needs and wishes.

More Consolidation Introduces New Opportunities for Third Parties

1. The Bigger the Strategic Focus, the More Will Fall off the Plate

In industries that have been truly global for some time, for example consumer electronics, we have seen the increasing centralization of corporate strategies. This results in large multinational players like Samsung and Sony, who are focused on a limited number of key countries.

The adage here is "go where the money is." This generally means countries that are attractive because they have a mix of volume, growth, and prosperity. It is in these countries that large budgets will be invested, and where the return on investment will be biggest. The countries usually labeled as "key" in any corporate strategy are: the large European countries (the UK, France, Italy, Spain, and Germany), the USA, Japan, Korea, and the emerging markets (Brazil, Russia, India, China, and Turkey). To this list is normally added a home market, where a strong position has long been held.

Within financial services – parallel to ongoing consolidation and internationalization – we also see more centralization of strategy and more hard choices to be made, not only with respect to a country's given priority to conquer a market share, but also with respect to specific consumer segments, products, and channels.

2. The More International the Aim, the More Distance from the Final Consumer

The bigger and more international the player is, the greater the chance their output will become more generic. Not being close enough to the individual market, propositions to consumers become an "average" of what people want in twenty different countries – and average never wins.

This phenomenon can be found on all levels: in product offers, in service concepts and the types of services offered, and in the way the various customer touch points are filled in (including advertising, the orientation of the sales force to marketing materials, and the organization of regular service).

This poses an important challenge for the large multinational players. Theo Bouts, COO of Global Life Zurich, says: "the scale on which you work is very important. We aim at selling universal products through local propositions. Local packaging is the key to success in the struggle to conquer the local markets. The fact that products are manufactured worldwide brings a reduction in costs. To be able to deal with the ambiguity of this standardization on one hand, and local wishes of consumers on the other, will become the dominant competence of globally operating financial service providers. Global players must, much like the automotive industry, 'set up their production' globally. Local marketing and sales departments subsequently have to bring the propositions to the consumer. All of this will have a profound impact on the way the insurance business is structured and on employment. There will be little room for local players."

According to Ravi Sankaranarayanan, Chief Executive of Retail and Commercial Banking, Europe and Middle East, at the Royal Bank of Scotland, the distance to the consumer is ultimately determined by "the DNA of the company, the level of competition in market developments," rather than its international or local scope. In the Fast Moving Consumer Goods (FMCG) sector, there are many examples of successfully standardized worldwide propositions that appeal to a broad public, whatever their cultural or geographical background may be. Coca Cola, for example, is just as successful in Thailand as it is in the US.

In the financial industry, you see the same happening, for example with the universal formats for the mass affluent (including Citi, HSBC, Standard Chartered, and RBS). This involves a balance between standardization on one hand, so that best practices can be shared and worldwide talent pools can be set up, and on the other hand, maintaining enough room for local adaptations and customization. The secret is to start with in-depth client insight, subsequently building your proposition around it, so that everybody who has to communicate it to the client can understand it, but to still leave enough room for local marketing departments to adapt the proposition to local needs, values, customs, and other soft or emotional factors.

3. The More Colors You Mix in, the More Likely You'll Get Brown

Consolidation, by definition, means an increase in complexity. Try to merge a part of ABN-Amro with RBS. With all their corporate and marketing positions, that would be a very complicated operation. One common way to solve this is by far-reaching standardization. In this way, complexity is kept under control. But the effect is that all the players tend to start looking alike. Mix random colors together and you'll get muddy brown, no matter how clear your original colors are. The challenge is to retain distinguishing features, even after consolidation.

These three dangers of far-reaching consolidation and internationalization indicate immediately where "gaps between spheres" have become too large – large enough to jump into with a new proposition or gain territory with an existing one. We can characterize these "gaps" as:

- Specific countries and product market combinations (PMCs), in non-key countries. Specific combinations of country and product category, or consumer segment and product category.
- Too much distance between supply and real demand – products that are not relevant enough, or not enough response to consumers' true motivations and insights.
- Not enough "face" and distinguishing characteristics with the current (big) players.

Managing Complexity in the Financial Services Industry

Today, financial services companies find themselves serving a large set of customer segments, in different markets, all over the world and under different legal regimes. Needless to say, they operate in quite a complex world. Financial services companies play an essential role in shaping the increasing international interest of both firms seeking foreign capital and investors looking for diversification opportunities overseas. As their international outlook expands, so does the complexity that financial services companies have to deal with.

The first factor that drives complexity is diversity. Procedures in financial services companies as well as in the entire financial sector tend to be heavily regulated and very diverse at the same time. Simple transactions are subject to several legal regimes and you can only imagine the legal hardships foreign financial services firms face when they want to do business in China. Secondly, because the performance of financial services companies depends on both suppliers and creditors, a shock on either side has an immediate effect. In terms of ambiguity, the third complexity driver, financial services companies operate on such a large scale that it proves difficult to send a uniform message from top to bottom. However, as companies grow, this becomes more crucial.

So how do financial services firms manage and grow their international business in this complex environment? There is only one answer to this question: standardization, which has resulted in convergence. In the last decade, financial services firms have become larger and fewer and they are behaving more and more alike.

Firstly, there is convergence in risk policies. To calculate the required capital and to support decisions about what business lines or transactions to pursue, financial services firms have developed economic capital methodologies. These economic capital systems have contributed to a more market-oriented approach to risk-management. This, in turn, has increased financial stability and reduced complexity in transactions due to a higher level of transparency and efficiency.

Secondly, convergence in legal regimes has led toward a search for a unique legal system. Indeed, this may contribute to improvements of corporate governance as companies can benefit from a different approach. However, before converging to one system, it is very important to consider elements such as importance of ownership concentration in corporations and the role of institutional investors.

Thirdly, standardized norms and values in corporate sustainability have contributed to convergence as well as competition. Common principles are established and implemented and in their annual reports, banks compete for all the sustainability awards available.

Lastly, standards in KPIs (Key Performance Indicators) are among the best strategies financial firms have envisaged to reduce their complexity. They give investors a clear view of the company's objectives, they help employees by standardizing corporate activity in the firm, and they contribute to more efficient competition among firms.

Thus, when setting off to explore across borders, know the challenges you are facing and how to manage the complexity of your international business. □

Arturo Bris is Professor of Finance at IMD, Lausanne.

Adapted from Bris, A. "Managing Complexity in the Financial Services Industry," in *Managing Complexity in Global Organizations*, 2007.
At this moment we are seeing all sorts of players beginning to fill in the blanks between the spheres – players of all sorts and stripes.

International Competition: the Big League

A class of international players is emerging, competing with each other in the most "attractive" places on the planet. Their most important competitive features are: the exploitation of economies of scale – not only with respect to costs but also regarding access to knowledge – and knowing how to make these economies of scale translate into distinctive value propositions and supply. The credit crisis has added another dimension: the less a company has had to write off, the better it can focus on the market, and the more positive consumer confidence will be; and with it, of course, its distinctive competitive advantage.

This international competition is simply a given fact in some segments. Theo Bouts says: "Some markets no longer have a local variant. A segment such as the 10 million richest people on earth for many industries (airplanes, super yachts, investment banking) is already a global segment. Insurance is going the same way. Local players will have more and more difficulties catering to these segments." He continues, "that said, I think there is an increasingly important role for business networks in which local as well as global players will have their specific roles and where the alignment of specific local and global parts of the value chain will generate a competitive advantage."

Simultaneously, two alliances are being formed in Spain that fit into the picture Bouts draws. Insurer AEGON has started a joint venture with Caixa Terrassa, and insurer Zurich has started an alliance with Banco Sabadell. In both cases, the local player's input is his distribution network, as well as insight into what drives the local consumer. Multinationals AEGON and Zurich contribute their international expertise and their economies of scale concerning products and service. The outcome is obviously a win-win situation: the local banks can provide best-in-class insurance to their customers, thus reinforcing their relationship with their customers, while the multinationals realize an important growth in their share of the attractive Spanish market.

Strong National Players Arise

On the national level we see, next to the international players, a few national players who are deeply rooted in local society, strong enough and possessing enough critical mass to remain standing in the struggle with international players.

Consumers who don't live in key countries are often deprived of the advanced financial services that only large international players can provide. The space this leaves in these countries is taken by strong national players, with clear national ambition and focus, and limited international attention.

This, however, is not as easy as it seems. A strong national position like that has to be fought for. In Spain, for example, the so-called *cajas*, or savings banks, have to fight off strong Spanish international players trying to secure their home territories, such as BBVA and Banco Santander. Also, these savings banks are being hit relatively hard by the current crisis in Spanish construction and real estate.

Niche Players Make Their Move

Private banks are currently investing more in marketing because of the growth of other players due to consolidation; in the eyes of consumers, this growth and consolidation may well seem to go hand in hand with less attention to their individual needs. The same is true for other product or segment specialists, for example in personal finances or mortgages.

Such niche players have a rosy future ahead of them – if they are better able than the big players to sense what consumer needs really are, and can compensate for their lack of economic scale with flexibility and decisiveness.

More New Entrants

These new entrants have three different "blood types." The first can be described as international players who anticipate local imperfections:

ING Direct, for example, does this very successfully. According to Dick Harryvan, a member of the board of ING Group and CEO of ING Direct, the traditional Canadian savings products were complex and not very competitive; this created the ideal situation for a "foreign" bank to conquer Canadian market share fast.

Sofía Rodríguez-Sahagún, Director of Cuenta Naranja for ING Direct Spain, says that in her market, other kinds of "conventional industry wisdom" is used. In Spain, the number of bank offices per resident is very high. Traditional banks believed that growth could be realized simply by opening up more offices, while in fact, Spanish consumers were already very familiar with the use of direct channels. In short, it was the perfect setting to launch ING Direct.

In some countries, bank customers are burdened with high costs: opening and maintaining bank accounts, withdrawing money, you name it, it's all very expensive. And then there are the tariffs for investing, which differ considerably from country to country. These are yet more imperfections to be exploited.

Sofía Rodríguez-Sahagún says: "We found out that an important section of our clients would like us to be their principal bank and do all their daily banking operations with us." Most banks charge very high commissions for every operation. "So we introduced the Cuenta Nomina, a current account with a proposition that is both very simple and attractive: we charge our clients no commissions in contrast to all other banks. On top of that we even return money to our clients: when they pay their bills for water, electricity, Internet, etcetera, via our Cuenta Nomina, we return 2% of the value of their bills. It is a proposition that has proved successful."

A third imperfection is formed by the enormous differences in service levels. The new entrant who changes offerings in this area alone is actually changing the rules of the market – not only by changing the standard for consumer expectations, but also by the effect this has on the profitability of existing players. After all, they will have to bend, too, to a certain degree.

The second "blood type" of new entrants is coming from other industries: Virgin Money, easyMoney, GE Money, and GMAC are some examples. Their core strategy is cherry-picking, capitalizing on a specific imperfection and then leveraging their own assets. But it is also possible that they just smell blood: the credit crunch offers them the opportunity to move into the attractive financial industry at a time when the traditional players are vulnerable. Nevertheless, it is also a necessity: the harder it becomes to fund their businesses on the capital markets, the sooner the decision is made to tap into consumer markets. Usually, the new entrants choose product categories where loyalty and the consumers' threshold for change are low, for example savings, mortgages, car insurance, and loans.

Virgin is playing David-against-Goliath in every industry they operate in. In financial services, they capitalize on the sentiment that the known traditional players are all unwieldy and bureaucratic. The new entrant easy-Money offers basic financial services, without any extras. This approach is rooted in their original easyJet airline business and now continues in their financial services. Google, Apple or Veolia may be the next new entrants.

"In several countries in South America, we see that store chains, mobile telephone operators, and utility companies are far more effective in reaching the upcoming social classes than traditional banks and insurance companies," says Hugo Caballero Albiñana, a market consultant in Chile. Examples of innovation are on-the-spot credit approval at the time of purchase, and mortgages based on a client's ability to save instead of his income.

In Chile, there are three retailers that hold more than 70% of the market: Ripley, Falabella and Paris. They were small players in the 1980s but by the end of the 1990s they had all adopted the same strategy to accelerate growth. They had been catering only for the higher consumer segments and wanted to expand their client base by giving the lower segments the financial tools they need to gain access to their products by themselves. This meant giving them credit they might not otherwise find in traditional banks. Their first step was to bring their own credit cards on to the market, and their next step was to open their own banks. These retailers went even further and opened their own insurance companies, offering car insurance among other services. They now also run travel agencies and the trend will probably extend to car sales. In the last few years they have expanded to other markets such as Peru and Argentina with the same business model.

The "third blood type" is made up of new players from emerging markets, new superpowers, and rich countries with large quantities of natural resources. As indicated earlier, the large Sovereign Wealth Funds of Asia and the Middle East play an ever-increasing role in the financial industry, due to their participation in high-profile Western banks and insurance companies. We also find financial companies that, like GMAC and GE, evolved from other industries such as Gazprombank, which is now the second bank of Russia (and was originally the business bank of the energy giant Gazprom).

The same goes for the oligarchs, the billionaires from regions rich with natural resources. Although they now limit themselves to investment in Western financial service providers, we expect that the moment will come when their entrepreneurial mentality and unrestrained ambitions will translate into a more active role than investment. They can become more active as shareholders, for example by taking a critical stance at shareholder meetings, but buying and building aggressively may well be the next step.

More Partnerships

The back office of easyMoney is catered for by Zurich Financial Services. We will be seeing more and more such partnerships, as companies from other industries find financial services increasingly attractive. Here is an industry in which they can use their own assets (their distribution channels, brands, and customer base), and realize new revenue streams with margins not possible in their own industries.

In Japan, Sony markets insurance and annuity products, together with insurance company AEGON on a 50/50 joint-venture basis, to users of the Playstation platform. Such partnerships accelerate international growth strategies – in this case, of AEGON. Through such partnerships, you avoid the investment in building a brand in a new country, and you have your own "channel" without competition, where you can even create your own distinctive proposition.

"Embedded products in 'unrelated' propositions will have their share in the market of the future", also anticipates Theo Bouts, "We have seen more and more car manufacturers take products like car insurance into their sales process, and other manufacturers and service providers will recognize the extra margin possibilities in that. I am convinced that for customers, easiness in such propositions counts, and that if the partners in a business network can provide that, these propositions have huge potential."

International Concepts Take Off

The economies of scale of the large international players don't only come from efficiency, but also from knowledge, products, and access to financial markets. We expect to see more and more concepts from the players leveraging their international scale (whether product- or target-group specific) and capitalizing on local imperfections. Direct Line of RBS, Zurich Connect, and ING Direct are forerunners in this area.

Already we see various international formulas directed at the mass market of affluent consumers (the almost rich): for example Priority Banking of Standard Chartered, CitiGold, and Premium Banking of Barclays (more about this in Megatrend 2). With limited local adaptation they can utilize economies of scale, while offering a locally relevant supply in the market. Through globalization, many things become possible.

Theo Bouts says: "Global players can react rather quickly with adequate scale and skill advantages on global and local market imperfections. Especially when trans-national legal entities are in play (like in the EU), that will happen more and more. Economies of skill are getting more important than economies of scale. Rapidly applying skills in local imperfect markets creates opportunities. In that respect, life and pension insurance give more opportunities than general insurance where, with claims management, more local presence is required."

Besides such really global concepts, we also expect the development of international concepts aimed at specific groups of countries, such as Eastern Europe, Nordic countries, or the oil-rich countries of the former Soviet Union. By aggregating like this, the necessary scale will be reached.

Competing on Innovation, Entrepreneurship and Consumer Connection

In these new concepts, established players have found a good way to keep the competition at bay and themselves fill in the open spaces around them caused by their huge scale.

Companies across industries are using the principle of "brand frontiers" to achieve this: using precisely those most special products to revitalize the parent brand. Thus, Prius tells us something about Toyota, just as the iPod tells us something about Apple. The inventiveness of Prius makes the Toyota brand seem more innovative, vital, and relevant – a very successful strategy indeed. The brand-frontier strategy is also used in the examples above, and it's the sensible thing to do: you become less "muddy brown."

For large international players, innovation – more than communication – is the proven tool for remaining relevant and distinctive in the eyes of consumers.

New entrants from other industries and emerging markets all bring their own ideas, including pioneer spirit and thinking outside the box. In short, they are pushing the boundaries with their entrepreneurship and all-out ambition – instead of a 5%-growth-again mentality. Each of them changes consumer expectations of financial service providers. And the bar is raised for traditional players, who need to keep up no matter how small the competing new entrant is. Competition therefore is about innovation, entrepreneurship and consumer connection.

The Future of Finance

Seizing the Opportunities in a Changing Pension Environment

It may be superfluous to say that the world of the pension system is on the move: large pension structures are splitting into separate pension schemes and pension-delivery organizations. This is how All Pensions Group (APG), one of the largest pension-delivery systems worldwide, was created.

In the coming ten years, pension asset growth is expected to rise significantly in Europe following a recent OECD forecast. At the same time, many small pension funds are merging with larger ones and obsolescence keeps increasing. These inter-related developments cause an interesting momentum in the competition between pension funds and insurance companies. Both compete for the same pensions to manage. However, we believe that pension-delivery organizations are the better-equipped party in this matter.

In our home market (the Netherlands), we are already familiar with capital-based pension systems. Hence the projected pension-asset growth here is significantly less than in other EU countries. However, we think APG offers an attractive value proposition for employers and other pension-plan sponsors right across Europe.

Due to cost pressures and regulatory "best practice" requirements, the number of pension funds serving workers and the retired has been shrinking. We are convinced that this process of consolidation is not over yet. So while the overall growth of pension funds may be slowing, the movement of those assets to large pension-delivery organizations such as APG will continue for some time to come.

Of course, we are not the only company trying to step into this growth opportunity; insurance companies also want their share. Nonetheless, there are two elementary differences between these two kinds of organizations, which in our opinion intrinsically argue in favor of pension-delivery systems for the best "pension deal".

Firstly, we are organized as a not-for-profit co-operative as opposed to insurers who must generate profits for their shareholders. Our legal structure is consistent with the "solidarity" principle, which has served it well in the past.

Secondly, because we solely manage pension assets, we are able to concentrate on a long-term strategy. Insurers need to focus on both long and short-term asset management. Because of our expertise with long-term investments of pension-delivery systems, we are able to create more value for our clients. In particular, we expect to excel in finding the right mix of hedging our long-term real liabilities while optimizing the return of our investment portfolio.

The described growth opportunities offer interesting management questions. We will

continue to design our organization to be prepared to fully attract and absorb these chances.

To be continued...

Jo van Engelen (photo) is Chief Marketing Officer, and Roderick Munsters is Chief Investment Officer, of APG.

A New Look at Outsourcing and Offshoring

Relevance and distinctiveness will become increasingly important – as knowing exactly what drives consumers will. What are they thinking? How can they be served? It will be important to be close to the market.

This sheds new light on outsourcing and offshoring. Originally, cost advantages played an important role in decisions regarding outsourcing and offshoring. This led to some customer-centered corporate functions – such as the actual delivery of products or services – being carried out by third parties or at great geographical distance.

In these matters, customer-related criteria such as securing customer knowledge, being close to the customer, being a good listener, a fast learner, and able to react to new data – become increasingly important and can result in new decisions or the overturning of previous ones. From this point of view, we see consumer-centered business functions at the core of any market where they have to make a difference.

According to Theo Bouts: "Customer centricity will demand closer governance on the service-delivery processes, so outtasking will become far more important than outsourcing. Giving a part of your customer-important governance away to another partner in your business network will become rare. The smart orchestrator of a business network who can quickly couple and uncouple partners is the winner of the future."

Balancing Business and Marketing Decisions

International consolidation confronts individual players with a new challenge. On the one hand, the economies of scale, made possible by internationalization, must be capitalized upon. On the other hand, money is, in the end, made where the consumer is. The first consideration leads to strictly orchestrated formulas and alignment; the second leads to maximum capitalization of the specific characteristics of a local market.

What do we do centrally, and what do we decentralize? How do we structure the organization to realize both ends? Which tools do we use for alignment? How do we utilize the innovative power of the entire organization? And how do we shorten the cycle of learning, sharing what we have learned, and subsequently applying that?

Financial service providers are currently facing this challenge with various solutions. In the coming years we will see how these practices work out.

The Fight for Talent

As a result of the credit crunch, thousands of bankers have lost their jobs. Nevertheless, in the long run, talent remains one of the most important assets of the financial industry.

International competition doesn't only occur in the marketplace. We see a similar battle in the labor market. International operations are done by international people: people with an international background in their education, training, upbringing and work experience. These are people who move in different cultures with ease and actually thrive on the differences.

Add to this the extra requirements of entrepreneurship – a feeling for customers, and innovative abilities – and you are looking for a rare breed. To attract and keep such talent, financial services providers compete not only with each other, but also with multinationals in other industries. Building a strong employer brand and company reputation is essential for success in the international labor market – especially when that labor market is becoming ever tighter. More about this in Megatrend 2.

Megatrend 2

Dramatic Demographic Changes, New Identities
and New Perspectives on Compelling Value Propositions

July 8, 2038

George and Frank are enjoying their tea. They are celebrating George's 76th birthday. This year the retirement age in the US has been raised to 80; ten years ago it was 75. George had been expecting to retire earlier, but he is happy to continue working until he's 80. Frank, at 97, sits at home most days, bored. Since George's VirtualMe says that his life expectancy is 112 years, he will have to deal with boredom for quite a while before he can enter heaven.

Last year George's wife bought him a soundproof Yamaha portable studio. (Since its invention in Japan in 2009, the Yamaha box has become a best-seller all over Britain.) She expected he would spend most of his days in the studio, using his computer, playing with his toy train, and communicating with people around the world. She bought the soundproof studio because she concluded that George was suffering from Retired Husband Syndrome. (George had taken to complaining about the quality of her omelets, which he had always eaten without complaint before.)

Now Frank has decided to coach young George, who is decidedly suffering from stress. The almost total lack of privacy in this day and age makes it more and more difficult for him to see his 78-years-young girlfriend, since his wife can track his every step. He enjoys working, so overtime was a good excuse – but his wife's VirtualMe could usually find him. And so Frank went to George's web community to see if anyone could help George give his jealous wife's avatar the slip – thus allowing him to enjoy his extramarital affair. One web community member, Mr. Grace, a spritely 115-year-old, found an ingenious way to foil the hi-tech avatar, and George's stress level was reduced to an all-time low.

The two friends smile and enjoy listening to the birds singing in the wind. Technology is great – but nothing beats human naughtiness.

Massive Shifts in World Demographics

Not only will globalization have a huge influence on developments in the financial sector; demographic developments will also have an enormous impact. Population surpluses in one place and shortages in another, migration flows, aging populations, newly emerging tribes, and generations with their own loyalties and desires – all will have the financial industry shaking on its very foundations. Megatrend 2 looks at the most important consequences of this coming demographic landslide.

A Rapidly Aging World

In 2005, we were about 6.5 billion strong on planet Earth. According to the predictions of the United Nations Population Division, we will number approximately 9.2 billion people by 2050. While the total number of inhabitants in the "developed world" (Europe, the US, Canada, Australia, New Zealand, and Japan) will remain at around 1.2 billion, the population of the rest of the world will increase from 5.3 to 8 billion. That is a lot of mouths to feed – but also a lot of new customers.

The world population is expected to reach its peak around 2050, after which we will see a declining trend. One of the most important demographic developments is the aging of the world population. This aging trend is currently strongest in Europe and Japan. In Europe, in 1995 there were already more seniors (aged over 60) than youngsters (under 15), and by 2050 there will be twice as many seniors as youngsters on the continent.

In North America, there are still more youngsters than seniors, and there will be enthusiastic procreating in coming decades. There will also be more youngsters than seniors in Africa; the UN predicts the number of children there to triple by 2050. But Asia, Latin America, and the Caribbean will, like Europe, suffer from aging.

The Rise of Demographic Politics

The aging of the largest part of the world's population will be closely related to the world's economic, technological, and medical progress. Improved living conditions – through technical and medical developments, hygiene, and economic prosperity – will lead to a lower death rate. People will live longer. In the developed world, it will become more important to make careers for women as well as men, and so there will be less time available for the care of many children. As the number of children decreases and the population ages, and becomes too old to be productive, the world becomes imbalanced.

To reestablish this balance, politicians think up various methods for getting people to reproduce. In the Netherlands, families receive many tax advantages, and so founding families is stimulated. In Ulyvanovsk, the Russian region where Vladimir Ilich Ulyanovsk Lenin was born, September 12 was declared the "Day of Conception" in 2005, and couples are given half a day off to reproduce. September 12 was chosen because it is exactly nine months before June 12, the Russian national holiday. Parents who give the light of life to their child on this festive day win a prize; the first prize is an off-road vehicle. The policy seems to be effective, because on the national holiday three times as many children are born than on normal days.

Forty Million Workers Missing in Europe

A decline in population has a number of advantages. With fewer people, there is less strain on the environment, and lower energy and water use. There is more space per person, which is a blessing. But there are also negative aspects to population decline.

In the West, population aging will also result in a large group of elderly "inactives," and an explosion in the demand for medical care. Meanwhile, due to the shrinking population, there won't be enough workers to take care of all those seniors. The Founda-tion for Economic Research (Stichting Econo-misch Onderzoek or SEO) of the University of Amsterdam calculated that in Europe we will have to deal with a shortfall of 40 million youngsters. While technical developments haven't yet been taken into account to offset this number, even if many future care tasks could be carried out by robots and people could go abroad for their medical operations, the expected lack of workers is still alarming.

Tilman Hengevoss, CMO and Head of Corporate Development at Zurich Switzerland, adds: "The demographic change also implies the risk of political instability: the 'inactives' will represent a large majority in the political decision processes. They will be able to defend their political interests against the interests of the 'actives' in elections and referendums. This will cause heavy counter reactions from the 'actives' as they will have to carry the burdens without enjoying the profits."

More and More Working Women

The number of working women in the US, Europe, and Asia is growing steadily, especially in urban populations. In Africa, women have already been the main supporters of the family for ages. The number of working women will keep increasing because, among other reasons, the aging population will put great pressure on the labor market.

In urban cultures, highly educated women often stay single; this is one more reason for women to take good care of their finances, since there's no husband for back-up. Exemplary of this phenomenon are the adventures of Carrie and her friends in the television series *Sex and the City*.

From another perspective, women are becoming more important than they already are. "Women are taking control over family cash, new research reveals," says Robert Hovenier, Managing Director of Fortis Intertrust Switzerland in Geneva. "When it comes to managing money, gone are the days when men took sole control of the family finances, and their influence on money matters is likely only to diminish. More women than men will make the big household financial decisions by the middle of this century, according to a new report by the Future Foundation for NS&I."

Raquel Goshima, a marketing research expert at a leading bank in Brazil says: "The number of women as family head in Brazil is growing from 25% to 35% of total families (an increase of 79% in the past ten years). This is happening across all socio-economic levels. It demands the careful attention of financial institutions on two levels: Firstly, these women need to work and have higher career expectations as opposed to being house-wives after their kids are born, which could be considered the standard some decades ago. Secondly, women as family heads create a new chal-lenge for financial products and services designed for a traditional family with two parents, kids and the father as the head. In Brazil, we're not only talking about women business executives, but mainly about the most basic professions, from housemaids to manicurists, from salesclerks to call-center agents."

So for financial service providers, women are becoming an increas-ingly important target-group. Yet this is hardly recognized in the Western world. Here is a short introduction to some forerunners in this area.

Raiffeisen Bank launched Austria's first bank for women. The concept is based on extensive studies of women and finances, and the way women interact with banks. The aim of these in-depth studies was to learn about the details of women's banking behavior and needs, and to answer ques-tions related to their lifestyles, attitudes, objectives, and financial needs. The conclusion was that women approach finances differently from men, and that a dedicated bank for women would better serve Raiffeisen's female customers. Consequently, they developed a successful feminine banking concept, perfectly aligned with women's needs.

The current bank setup includes an inviting lounge-like interior in warm, bright colors, with round soft shapes and relaxing chairs, a coffee bar, and even a children's play area. These elements combined create an environ-ment in which female customers feel comfort-able making important decisions. Female employees assist customers, taking the time to explain products thoroughly, and to build strong relationships with their customers.

Sumitomo Mitsui Banking Corporation (SMBC) of Japan also developed specific target-group concepts, among them Club Women. Club Women targets women across all stages of life, but with an emphasis on younger, working women with a higher education. Its advisors are strictly female and especially trained in a "feminine" way of banking. They are, for the most part, friendly, plain girl-next-door types rather than super-models. The banking products are specifically tailored for women. In addition, customers also have access to a range of non-bank privileges such as travel arrangements, or discounts in spas, beauty salons, and gyms. PR is an important communication instrument, and free publicity articles appear in Japanese women's magazines similar to *Cosmopolitan*.

In car insurance, for example, we see Sheila's Wheels in the UK, 1st for women in South Africa, LadyCarOnline in Germany, and Segurisima in Spain. A key success factor for this kind of initiative is not only to "paint their brand pink," but to present real functional benefits with relevance to the target-group, in line with women's distinctive needs. In most of these cases, significant lower premiums are offered to the target-group because of their better driving skills: "Why should women subsidize the car premiums of men any longer?" Sheila's Wheels started with additional coverage for handbags and their contents, up to £300, if stolen or damaged while in the car, taking into account the increase in thefts from people in cars waiting at traffic lights in big cities.

Leading the way, however, are the banks for women in Islamic countries. In Pakistan the First Women Bank, founded in 1989, strives for the economic empowerment of women. In Saudi Arabia, though women are not allowed to vote or drive, they do have the right to manage their own finances. Saudi banks have invested extensively in "ladies' banking" over the past few years. For example, separate entrances to banks were made, dedicated products were developed, and the staff are female only.

The Masrafy Bank in Bahrain launched the first Islamic investment bank for women, targeting women with high net worth across the Gulf region. The venture may prove very lucrative. Studies by Abu Dhabi Investment House, who backs this initiative financially, show that women

in the Gulf region have funds worth $38 billion at their disposal, without there being any credible infrastructures available to them for investing those funds privately or professionally.

The Silver Economy

Now, a gray population should not automatically be branded as problematic. Of course the elderly in general need more care, but these care consumers are also considerably wealthy. Abbey National, a bank in the UK, reports that Britons of fifty years and older possess as much as three-quarters of the country's wealth. So the silver economy of the UK has a golden lining.

Worldwide, most millionaires – those with at least 1 million in liquid assets, excluding their primary residence – are over the age of 55. Not only do the elderly have value as consumers, but they should not be immediately discarded as members of the working population. More and more investments are targeted at keeping people working for as long as possible, especially in the industrialized world. And while nowadays employees in many Western countries can't get any education after the age of 45, this will change. Senior citizens will be increasingly deployed as sources of knowledge, and they will be educating and coaching the young – maybe through the Internet, maybe in classical mentoring relationships. The currently ruling motto "young, active, and sexy" will be replaced by "old, wise, and experienced."

What's true for women is also true for senior citizens: they are currently being ignored by financial service providers. We think this is because young marketeers still believe in the cliché that senior citizens are uninteresting, sedate, and no fun to work for.

But fortunately, we can also see the first exceptions.

The previously mentioned Japanese bank SMBC developed a specific concept targeting middle-aged citizens, the "Over 50 Club." The concept features, among other things, a monthly subscription magazine. People even pay €50 a year for this subscription. Articles cover various areas of interest for this target-group, demonstrating that SMBC understands the world of the over-fifties.

The Future of Europe

Europe's position and influence in the world will certainly not remain unchanged in the decades to come, both economically and politically. It would be wise if we Europeans would take this very seriously by reforming and actively restructuring our economies and by converting from less profitable to more competitive, knowledge-based economic activities. The urgency of this is still underestimated, both by ordinary citizens and by too many policy makers – partially because politicians quite often do not want to run the risk of losing popularity by advocating painful reforms, and simply because people do not like to be confronted with the need for change, especially if this threatens to affect their personal life, including their perceived level of security or protection.

But it is also because there is still a lack of real insight into the magnitude of challenges Europe will be facing in future decades.

International competition is rapidly intensifying and this is not going to end soon: Europe is facing a twin challenge from both the US and Asia. Of course, the rapid growth of economies like China and India not only creates new competitors to Europe but also vast and growing markets, offering new opportunities for co-operation, investment and trade. China, industrializing with a large and growing stock of foreign direct investment together with its own scientific base, has begun to compete not only in low but also in high value-added goods. And although Chinese wages are only a fraction of those in Europe, it is clear that the difference in quality of a growing number of products and goods produced in China or the EU is already small or non-existent. India's challenge is no less real – notably in the service sector where it is the single biggest beneficiary of the "offshoring" or "outsourcing" of service sector functions with an enormous and rapidly growing pool of well-educated, cheap, English-speaking workers. Undoubtedly, both China and India will be facing external or internal frictions in the future that might have a negative impact on their annual growth rates. It would be wrong, however, to use this as an argument to deny the reality of an already strong and rapidly growing relevance of these countries in the world economy. This trend is irreversible.

In the meantime. Europe is facing a second challenge: its aging population. Two forces – declining birth rates and rising life expectancies – are interacting to produce a dramatic change in the size and age structure of Europe's population. These are two separate but interconnected trends. The total population size in the European Union is projected to fall already by around 2020; in some countries, this decline will start even earlier. As a consequence, the average ratio of persons in retirement compared with those of the present working age in Europe will double from 24% today via 30% in 2015 to almost 50% in 2050. All this will have serious repercussions for public finances, healthcare, and pensions, but also for the labor market and our economic growth potential in coming years. As a consequence, a much better utilization of labor is desperately needed, both by increasing employment through increased labor-market participation and by working more hours on a lifetime basis. People will inevitably have to work longer before they retire, preferably on a flexible, tailor-made basis, taking their individual capabilities and preferences into account. And they must be better enabled to do so; they will have to be provided with up-to-date employability skills which are in demand. Modern, properly functioning educational systems, including life-long learning, must ensure that this is possible. Education, training, and work experience are key prerequisites for a healthy future – both for economic and for social reasons.

I have experienced myself, both as a union leader and as a political leader and prime minister in the Netherlands, how complicated it is to communicate all this and to convince people that the status quo is not an option. One of the underlying problems is that every reform or restructuring process, both internationally and domestically, counts winners and losers.

The first category (containing the winners) is much more abstract, silent, and invisible than the second one. Losers are those people who run the risk of losing their jobs or those who are affected by a reduction of their perceived or actual level of protection and security. And each of these losers has a face and a voice, quite often even a loud voice. Also in view of this consideration, sufficient job opportunities, an active labor-market policy, a genuine social dialogue and a high level of education aiming at empowerment and employability, are essential prerequisites for a smooth social and economic transformation process in European countries. If we want to remain competitive in this globalizing economy we must focus on innovation and modernization instead of taking a defensive stand. Confidence is the key word in my view. Europe can not afford to become a mainly passive, inward-looking continent – simply because the world is not going to wait for us.

Wim Kok is a member of the supervisory board of ING Group, of TNT, of KLM and non-executive director of Royal Dutch Shell. He was Prime Minister and Minister of Finance of the Netherlands and leader of the labour union FNV.

This column is a summary of a speech Wim Kok gave in January 2007 for Microsoft.

The Pension Population: a Time Bomb

In coming decades the financial consequences of an aging population will be one of the most important matters on the political and social agenda. In every country, a struggle over pensions will erupt – a struggle between generations.

Take the UK, where a time bomb is ticking under the pension system. A commission under the leadership of Adair Turner, former chairman of the CBI, a UK employers' association, advised that this time bomb can only be disarmed by decisive and politically controversial measures. According to this report, 12 million UK citizens (40% of the working population) are saving far too little for their old age. Over the next three decades, pensions will drop by an average of 30% if no hard choices are made. These choices concern raising taxes and national insurance contributions, obligatory additional saving, and raising the retirement age. Turner says that for many years, UK citizens have imagined they would retire in luxury, partly because many pension funds are linked to the stock exchange index. "Irrational behavior" on the stock exchange, and a lagging acknowledgement that society was becoming grayer, meant that many pension funds didn't take measures until the end of the 1990s. This was at least twenty years too late and the measures taken were still inadequate, according to Turner.

Later Retirement or a Considerably Bigger National Piggy Bank?

In most European countries, people are slowly getting used to the fact that the age of retirement will be raised to 67 or even 70. Because most of us seem to be healthier as we age, this is not such a strange idea after all.

Another solution might be to lower the allowance that the elderly receive from the state (as the German government did in 2006), or to start putting large amounts of money into national piggy banks like Sovereign Wealth Funds.

Oil-rich Norway has one of the biggest Sovereign Wealth Funds in the world; but the oil fund is not limitless. The Norwegian central bank, manager of this fund, recently reported it cannot pay more than a quarter of the Norwegian pension bill. Taxpayers will have to take care of the rest themselves. The Norwegian government has announced radical reforms to the state pension system. This includes raising the pension age from 62 to 67.

China will also use its Sovereign Wealth Funds to tackle the threat of an aging population and pension problem. Meanwhile, they are establishing structurally large buffers. Chinese citizens actually save a lot, but inflation has also been increasing rapidly.

Under the pressure of diminishing pensions, it becomes increasingly less likely that pensioners leave their houses to their children. They will have to consume the value that is tied up in their homes. There are already financial service products that capitalize on this trend – and there will certainly be more.

Norwich Union's Home Reversion Plan gives the customer a cash lump sum in return for selling part or all of their property to a "home reversion provider." The (former) home owner may continue living in the property rent free for the rest of his life, or until they must leave the property because they need long-term care. When this occurs, the property is sold by the reversion provider and, after deducting the selling costs, the equivalent percentage of ownership is taken from the proceeds of the sale. In this way, homeowners can unlock the money tied up in their property, and continue to live in their own homes.

Gray Emigration

Despite problems with pensions and the fact that many people will have to work to an older age, demographers expect that gray emigration will persist. An increasing number of senior citizens will choose to live, full- or part-time, in regions or countries other than where they were born and raised. Sometimes they make this choice individually, but often they choose to live in groups. More and more people have already purchased a second home before reaching retirement age; once they stop working they will move there for good. As so often happens, the first to do so will act as an example which many others will follow. The growth of "two-pension households," where both partners enjoy a pension, will ensure enough money to undertake such a step.

Floridazation, YEEPIES and Part-Time Residing

Every category of people has a preferred lifestyle, which gives rise to new trends: for example, the phenomenon that could be called "Floridazation." Named after the migration of American seniors to the state of Florida, it refers to those people who want to relocate when they retire – preferably to somewhere warm and pleasant, with good facilities, and where they can enjoy themselves.

Western baby-boomers, who were born soon after the Second World War, are approaching the age of retirement. They are generally well educated, have (had) good jobs, good health, and money. What's more, they are adventurous and certainly not aiming to spend the rest of their lives at home listening to their arthritis. They are enjoying a "second life." They still engage in new friendships; and online dating sites targeting those aged 55 and older – like Seniordate in Denmark, Ulteem in France, and Seniormatch in the US – are booming. It's a lot like an after-party.

YEEPIE stands for Young Energetic Elderly People Into Everything. Although members of this tribe will retain their roots in their homelands, they will increasingly spend long or short periods abroad. Seniors from northwest-Europe will settle en masse in Europe's "Sun-belt" – southern France, Spain, and Portugal – but also in more distant locations such as Thailand, Uruguay, Argentina, and South Africa. These seniors are creating a trend that is being picked up on by young people: "part-time living."

This entails a lifestyle we could call "five-star living": luxurious living in an urban environment, near to shops and facilities. It may be combined with a house in the countryside, where people can enjoy rural life and tend their gardens, giving them the best of both worlds. Many people have already become accustomed to this "part-time" lifestyle, by spending holidays in less-expensive countries such as Turkey or Mexico.

The Rise of Gated Communities

Real estate developers are experiencing a growing market for various forms of gated communities. These are protected housing estates or flats, where people can live with "those of their own kind." Ethnic or socio-economic diversity is not desirable, for this only causes unrest. There is maximum security in the area, including surveillance cameras, alarm installations, and guards supplied by security companies. Within their own gated communities, people do not have to worry about their safety or that of their children and property. Theft, burglary, muggings, and possible attacks are things of the past.

The part-time living we discribed earlier also results in a rise of security issues. Because people live in several places at once, it is important that their houses and possessions are safe when they are elsewhere.

The enthusiasm for gated communities is especially large among the prosperous classes. In Turkey, in particular religious affluent Muslims are creating communities of this kind so that, at least there, they aren't confronted with Western habits that don't go well with their beliefs.

Little can happen to people at home in their own fortress, and all that security equipment brings a feeling of safety. A good example of this is the "panic room," a room in the house where residents can go in the event of a break-in. Thieves cannot get to them in there. They can use a dedicated telephone to call for help, and make use of emergency food rations and lighting in the event of an extended stay.

Seniors, who are traditionally more fearful than the young, will stimulate the demand for new security concepts and equipment. Security-conscious seniors can form virtual communities and warn each other of problems: a form of "gray power."

An Ever-Growing Security Industry

Partly because of feelings of insecurity, cash money is becoming less and less common. In countries where it isn't safe on the streets, like Brazil, you can even pay $1 for your toothpaste with a credit card. In Brazil, but also in India, Indonesia, and South Africa cash dispensers (ATMs) are frequently guarded by armed security officers hired by the banks. In Chile, there are drive-through cash dispensers, so you don't have to leave the relative safety of your car. The role of private security will become increasingly important, while the role of the police will diminish. A transformation of European countries into police states would be very expensive and also very labor intensive. Although the number of working people is dropping, technology offers new forms of security that require fewer people. In the very near future, new ways of scaring off criminals will be brought on the market. Cell phones can also be used when people find themselves in threatened situations.

In several European countries, more people are employed by private security firms than by the police force. The same goes for India. In the upper social classes the demand for bodyguards will rise.

Fewer Savings, Fewer Investments

Savings are influenced by many macro-economic factors, including growth, interest rates, inflation, borrowing constraints, fiscal policy, pension systems, and income distribution.

Besides these economic factors, demographics have a big impact on savings. The life-cycle theory of consumption argues that people save less during adulthood, simply because they are providing for their children. Savings normally start to grow when the children become adults and parents begin saving for retirement. They fall again as retirees begin living off their accumulated assets. But this is not a hard and fast rule, as individuals may also save to provide bequests for their children, or to maintain a source of wealth for dealing with financial headwind.

However, in conjunction with demographic trends set off by the baby boom after the Second World War and the impressive increases in longevity in the developing world, the life-cycle influence on savings can have major implications for the global economy. For Europe, Japan, and East Asia, which have relatively high saving rates, a considerable decline in savings can be expected through 2030 as the elderly make up an increasingly larg part of the population. By contrast, sub-Saharan Africa, the Middle East, and North Africa have relatively young populations and should see increasing labor-force participation and savings through 2030. Overall, the forecast drop in global saving is quite substantial: from 21.6% of income in the first half-decade of this century, to 19.9% by 2030, according to the World bank's Global Economic Prospects 2007. Demographic influences also imply a decline in demand for investment, as fewer workers are available for each unit of investment. On balance, it is likely that investment will decline in regions where elderly dependency ratios are rising, albeit not by as much as savings. In these countries, this will lead to a decline in their current account surplus (or a rise in their deficit), and to a rise in global interest rates.

Generation Y: Individualism and the Collective
Marketeers in the industrialized world will have to deal in coming decades with Generation Y, also called "Millenials." Born between 1980 and 2000, Generation Y will be the generation in power in twenty years, as management as well as customers.

The inherent characteristic of this generational group is their great diversity. Prevalent subcultures, such as punks in the 1980s, no longer exist. That people enjoy listening to the same music doesn't mean they automatically wear the same clothes or view life in the same way – which makes them seem even more inscrutable than ever. But there are a few trends among these young people as they become the consumers of tomorrow.

Generation Y individuals were brought up in a time of rampant individualism, when personality and the freedom of the child were of primary importance. The children began to rebel against this excessive individualism and developed new opinions to counterbalance it. They came to value collective ties, such as faithfulness in relationships and "traditional" concepts of family, to a greater degree than the generations before them.

In their choices, however, they are still extremely individual. There is no question of a return to the well-defined consumer categories of times gone by, which makes this generation even more elusive to marketeers.

The Wisdom of Crowds
Thanks to the breakthroughs of the information and communication age, Generation Y people are, from their earliest age, used to enormous amounts of information. They know there is more information available on any subject than any single individual can comprehend. Data has to

be analyzed on the basis of limited knowledge. Young people are fully aware of this, and it doesn't make them feel insecure.

Young people are self-willed, fully aware of the media, very critical, and used to the best. It is very difficult to place them in neat, recognizable subcultures with similar and largely predictable preferences. What's more, they understand all the tricks of advertising and marketing.

Nevertheless, they are the target of many financial service providers, especially those still in college or university and those who have just graduated. According to Lambert de Kool, in charge of ABN-Amro's Young Professionals, a higher education in most countries predicts future wealth. Besides, the customer acquisition costs for these young adults are far less than the acquisition costs for more affluent customers.

It is important, however, to retain these customers at critical switch moments – for example when buying a first home. If you focus on success with this target-group, you will create the foundation for future success for the entire organization.

An example of this is the HSBC Graduate Mortgage. This target-group is of interest because of their future potential, even though they still have a relatively low income. This is the reason for a flexible, affordable product with lower amortization for the first three years – student loans not included.

For excellent examples of target-group concepts that not only include specific products, but which also specifically tailor services and market movements, we can look to the ABN-Amro Young Professionals program and LKXA, the youth program of the Spanish La Caixa.

The Trend to Authenticity
This trend is about rediscovering old values and traditional concepts, and translating them into modern society and concepts. Authenticity repre-

sents values such as purity and originality. It is the key value in the lives of the young.

The desire for authenticity has consequences for the way young people act as consumers: a product without any brand is better than a "dodgy," inauthentic, artificial brand. Authenticity is not just something that young people aspire to; it is the standard by which they measure all else.

In general, Generation Y believes in the market economy, but the recent economic recession and the attacks of 9/11 in 2001 have made them realize that the world is not as "manufacturable" as once thought or hoped. The world cannot be steered by economic rationality and market thinking; and neo-liberalism does not, apparently, have the solution to every social problem. Young people react to this realization by intensifying their relationships with their peers – those they can count on for help and support. They are calculating as consumers; as people, they want to be there for friends and family.

A Colorful Palette of New Identities

Global Citizens as Cosmopolitans

Only a hundred years ago, most people slept ten hours a day, then eight, and soon it will be six. Only a hundred years ago, most people traveled only 5 miles (8 km) a year; now many people in the affluent world travel 18,600 miles (30,000 km) annually – flying not included. In the old days we got news from our small local regions; now our TV screens, newspapers, and laptops are flooded with daily news from all over the world. In the old days we had friends living nearby; now we can explore virtual friendships around the world.

For some people this lifestyle is wonderful. But if this were everyone's lifestyle, only one culture would be here to stay: a global culture. Cosmopolitan world citizens would be fine with this – but compared with the total world population, they are just one small tribe.

Typical cosmopolitans are self-confident, individualistic, and interested in self-development. They are well educated, earn above-average incomes, have a high pattern of consumption, are pretty materialistic, and

have a fondness for luxury. At the same time, they are tolerant, appreciate their freedom, and are independent, yet socially engaged.

These world citizens have an international orientation, a global view, many interests, and are open to change and innovation. Often they have an urban lifestyle and sometimes an international job. For a cosmopolitan, the globalized world is fun: there are new exotic places to visit, and new interesting things to do. Cosmopolitans associate globalization with prospects of unimagined wealth and well-being worldwide. Among these global citizens are many mass-affluent (almost rich) consumers.

The Attractive Mass Affluent

Many financial service providers are focusing on so-called mass-affluent consumers, the "almost rich," who have large sums of money in their bank accounts. An important part of this target-group appears to be global citizens. This is a good reason for banks to offer a formula that's as worldwide as possible – and it's actually feasible. VODW research shows that cosmopolitan mass-affluent consumers – from Chile to the US, and from western Europe to Russia and the Far East – share similar attitudes towards money and banking.

Robert Hovenier, of Fortis Intertrust Switzerland, identifies a trend of banks and financial service providers opening branches at a rapid pace in regions such as central and eastern Europe and Russia. In these countries, the mass-affluent segment is growing steadily.

Raquel Goshima confirms this for the emerging market in Brazil:

"According to the twelfth Annual World Wealth Report of Merryll Lynch, the number of millionaires increased 19.1% in 2007, behind China and India only. The rise of the Brazilian economy in recent years and expected continuous growth pushed by the upward trend in commodity prices as well as large oil fields discoveries alongside the Brazilian coast, will most definitely create a new mass of affluent consumers."

Tailoring to the Global Citizen

Worldwide service concepts that already target this group include: CitiGold, HSBC Premier, Standard Chartered Priority Banking, ING Personal Banking, ABN-Amro Preferred Banking, and Barclays Premier Banking.

CitiGold is the best example of a formula tailored to the local market conditions in each country. Their offering has a different positioning, different services, different target audience criteria, and different distribution – all under the umbrella of one value proposition.

In the US, CitiGold profiles itself as "personal and privileged," inviting customers to "Enjoy the exclusive benefits of a CitiGold membership: our highest level of personal service, exclusive savings and rewards, trusted advice and guidance."

In Spain, CitiGold isn't aimed so much at clients who like to demonstrate wealth; their Spanish approach is "trustworthy and straightforward," targeting those who are looking for peace of mind and personal service in managing their funds. "When making an important decision you need someone you can trust."

In Russia, however, CitiGold stands for western-style VIP treatment. Targeting clients with a "privileged lifestyle," their service is "offered only to VIP clients" (with over $20,000 capital), who like to demonstrate their wealth. The Russian version focuses strongly on exclusive non-financial services: VIP tickets to theaters such as the Bolshoi, transfer and passes to VIP lounges in the main airports of St Petersburg and Moscow, complimentary accident and travel insurance, and free subscriptions to the leading foreign business magazines. But the question remains if this is enough localization for Russia.

The Troika bank – needless to say, a Russian bank – combines excellent performance and reputation with a pioneering approach to sales. The sales department of Troika first assembles a well-researched database on potential clients, obtaining their information from sources such as luxury car salons. A person who has just purchased a Mercedes, for example, is considered a good target.

Troika's main sales force is composed of good-looking, young female financial professionals. They will contact potential clients, explain to them the interesting options for investing their money, and if necessary meet for dinner or lunch and further explanation and negotiation. It is an interesting fact that in Russia, female sales agents are much more successful at attracting the clients. Young male sales professionals, at this sales stage, would not be as successful. Male advisers normally come in at a later stage of negotiation.

These features not only characterize both the culture and lives of Russia's mass-affluent; they also show that with any global roll-out, you must question if you need or want to localize and to what extent. They also show how strong local players convert their direct consumer knowledge into a competitive edge.

Bob Neuhaus, EVP of Financial Services at TNS North America (one of the biggest market research agencies in the world) and responsible for TNS' Affluent Program, says however: "The current economic turmoil is affecting the affluent. Data from our most recent 2008 research shows that the number of affluent households in the US declined somewhat after years of steady growth. In 2007 there were an estimated 16.4 million US households with $500,000 or more in net worth (not including their primary residence). In 2008 the data project the size of the market at 15.6 million households – a decline of 5%. A shrinking base of affluent investors means that the competition to service this group will further intensify. A thorough understanding of the issues facing affluent people will be the key to being successful."

He continues: "While the US is being affected by the sub-prime crisis and other economic developments, you would think that we would be seeing fundamental changes in affluent asset allocation. However, when asked about their investment approach in the 2008 AMRP, 56% of the affluent indicated their approach has changed very little over the past year; 78% of the affluent consider themselves 'long-term investors' and that long-term pays off. Some affluent see the current economic conditions as opportunities, i.e. 15% said they took advantage of buying opportunities over the past year. Of course, this does not mean they are not concerned; 32% strongly or somewhat agreed with the statement: 'I am concerned the state of the current economy may jeopardize my retirement goals.' However, nearly half (48%) still feel 'confident I will meet my retirement goals.' There is concern that the affluent may no longer take the stability of their financial services providers for granted. With some of the major investment firms and banks taking big losses because of the sub-prime crisis, we may see the affluent questioning their providers' long-term stability and continuity, which can result in more clients spreading their investments across various asset managers. So far this has not happened. Nearly two-thirds (65%) of the affluents' portfolios are managed by their primary providers – unchanged from previous years. Furthermore, switching among asset managers remains steady and low: 17% indicated they moved some assets over the last year, but when asked where the assets went, 38% said they moved assets to rather than from their primary provider. Better performance was the predominant reason for switching (45%), but clearly the implication is that it will take more than a few bumps in the economy to move market share."

Globalization Leading to Nationalism and Protectionism

The process of globalization can also evoke countermovements that threaten its fulfillment. The basic premise of globalization is that competition will sort out the most efficient players. This process, by definition, involves winners and losers. Those who appear to be losing the battle will turn to their familiar political institutions for relief. They won't find any comfort in the valid proposition that the benefits of global growth far outweigh its costs.

In times of economic distress, this phenomenon intensifies. Many people with menial jobs in the industrialized world lose their jobs to colleagues in countries with lower wages. Because of that, they (and their trade unions)

call for protectionist actions by their governments. As for the companies, in general, transnational enterprises advocate free trade and free movement of capital, while companies that are fully dependent on the national economy and political process often push for protectionism.

Globalization Leading to Countermovements

As we described in Megatrend 1, there is growing unrest in the developed world about the threat of being overwhelmed by emerging economies. Especially in times of economic headwind, when growth figures are dropping, as they are now due to the credit crunch, these feelings of uneasiness come to the surface.

If and when such feelings arise, people tend to look for culprits. Even if the cause of the crisis lies mainly in the US, there is still a tendency in the US to point the finger in the direction of emerging economies (mainly China). The Chinese aren't having any problems with growth figures; they are even buying themselves into the American economy using their Sovereign Wealth Funds.

Besides those who oppose globalization for economic reasons, many oppose globalization for cultural or religious reasons. For a large group of people, the world has simply become too large, too fast. They feel threatened by the breakdown of their old world, where they knew what to expect. They're confronted with new games and new rules that they can't or don't want to adjust to.

Instead, they value more traditional lives, and don't want to give them up. Countermovements, such as religious traditionalists and fundamentalists who prefer to shun their societies and modernity, are present all over the world.

Countermovements that Strive for Self-Sufficiency

The common denominator of religious and cultural countermovements to globalization is that they want to stop or even turn back time, to preserve their heritage.

In several regions in Asia, the Middle East, and Africa people want to live as they have lived for centuries – without feminism, without technology, and so on. They are opposed to a single world culture with only

one form of architecture: skyscrapers, which look the same all over the world. They value local architecture, local arts, and local societies with their own codes of conduct, values, and laws. They have their own ways of dealing with each other, and their own definition of humanity. And their resistance is of course perfectly understandable.

Economically, traditionalists would like to go back to a time when their economies were self-sufficient. They despise McDonalds, Pizza Hut, and Coca Cola as examples of a perverted modernism. Traditional forms of saving – purchasing land and real estate, and converting money into gold for dowries – are on the rise in these regions.

In the West, there is also a part of the population, albeit small, that strives to turn back the achievements of globalization. They don't want mangos from Mali or green beans from Kenya; they don't want strawberries or asparagus in the wintertime, coming from the other side of the world.

Some strive for autarchy and self-sufficiency, and less dependence on uncontrollable external powers. The motto here is "out with the big bad world." Others simply don't fancy industrial food. They prefer to eat the pure, healthier, tastier food grown communally in their own regions, and to build with locally available materials.

For example, in the US, a lot of people are actively trying to buy only locally grown food at so-called farmers markets, where small-scale farmers from the region sell their foods. Their reasons for this are to reduce their carbon footprint, to enjoy healthier and tastier food, and to support local small-scale farmers, etc. This trend is especially strong in

The Future of Finance

the West, such as the Seattle area, and San Francisco. An example is the 100-mile diet, where a Canadian couple decided to try to live for one year buying or gathering their food and drink only from within 100 miles (160 km) of their home in Vancouver.

The Reinvention of Local Currencies

A remarkable example of a Western initiative to turn back globalization can be found in the UK. In the Sussex town of Lewes, they are devising a plan to start printing and using their own local money again, inspired by the Devonshire town of Totnes, which launched its own currency in 2007. The town of Lewes once did have its own pound, last in circulation in 1895 – and Lewes locals plan to get it back.

The group behind the schemes in both Totnes and Lewes are part of the "Transition" movement, which is concerned with the impact of rising oil prices and consumption. They argue that the local money will encourage shops and customers to buy local products and reduce their fuel consumption. It's also hoped the scheme will encourage a greater sense of community.

Another example of a new local currency comes from the United States. In 2006 the region of Southern Berkshire in Massachusetts introduced the currency BerkShares (not to be confused with Berkshire, the investment company of super-investor and multibillionaire Warren Buffett). BerkShare Inc., which established and maintains the currency, says: "The purpose of a local currency is to build the local economy by maximizing the circulation of trade within a defined region."

The Rise of New Tribes

Ever since time began, people have belonged to "tribes" – groups that share a language, culture, and in some cases a religion. These tribes spread throughout the world in a kind of Diaspora.

The Jewish Diaspora came about after the decline of Israel in the first century of our calendar. In the same way, the Diaspora of Lebanese, Poles, Irish, Armenians, and Kurds occurred.

Some tribes never had a state. But even when widely dispersed, their numbers are so large that they managed to maintain an international

connection with each other. Romanians, for example, have a worldwide connection with each other.

The same is true for the tribe of homosexuals (5–10% of the world's population), even though its members may not share a language, culture, or religion. Members of the homosexual tribe are based in all countries of the world and maintain a network economy. They help each other worldwide in business. Third-generation Irish-Americans are so proud of their Irish heritage they even celebrate it.

The last few decades have seen a process of "new tribalization." A Diaspora of over 60 million Chinese has occurred throughout the world. Together, this group forms the third-largest economy in the world, with a collective GDP that is about as large as that of their 1.2 billion compatriots back in China. They control the economies of Thailand, Indonesia, Myanmar, Singapore, and Malaysia.

There was also a Diaspora of Indians, who are called the NRI (non-resident Indians), or PIOs (people of Indian origin). This tribe has a total of 35 million people, with a combined wealth of $340 billion. Annually, these people earn the same as the 1 billion people still living in India. Seeing the potential in this group, the Indian government would love to bind these people to India, which it tries to do by offering them fiscal advantages. The government organizes annual Diaspora conferences in Delhi, to which thousands of successful Indians living abroad are invited.

There are 7 million Americans living outside the United States; 1 million Bulgarians outside Bulgaria; an unknown but very large number of Germans or people of German origin living outside Germany (in countries such as Brazil, Argentina, eastern Europe, and the Netherlands); 5 million Hungarians living outside Hungary; more Greeks living outside Greece than in Greece itself; and more Italians living outside Italy than in Italy itself. Tribalization is becoming a trend of major dimensions.

Tribal Networks and Economies

What makes these tribes so attractive in the modern world is the networks they form. Tribe members in all parts of the world are connected to one another, and they put business each other's way – thus forming an economy separate from a nation state.

The Chinese and Indians living outside their homelands create high GDPs. In the past, the Jews and Armenians had already formed economic networks. Now the idea is taking root throughout the world.

There are millions of Westerners working as expats in Asia, South America, Africa, and the Middle East. Diplomats, businessmen, consultants, trainers, bankers, and the like – they, too, value a portable identity and portable nationalism. Very often the British in Asia feel more British than the British living in the UK. Portable nationalism makes it possible for India's Bollywood film industry to export its movies to the Indian Diaspora, who feel even more Indian when they collectively watch their films. This trend toward "portable nationalism" will have consequences for the world in a whole range of areas.

The Hawala System

While tribal economies sometimes use modern techniques, the ancient money-transfer systems also remain operational. Take, for example, the millions of Filipinos and Indians temporarily living and working as housekeepers or construction workers in the Middle East and Gulf States. They often sent their earnings back home to their families by means of an Islamic money-transfer system called "hawala."

Hawala is a means by which a person can send cash from one country to another, without a record of the transaction. When a recipient, even when living in a remote area, needs cash urgently, they can receive it quickly. The sender gives the cash to a hawala broker, who, in exchange for a commission, contacts his counterpart in the region of the receiver. This hawala broker then delivers the cash to the receiver. The clearing of the transaction may be done in various ways; maybe in cash or maybe in livestock or a cancellation of debts.

This money-transfer system is based on the Shariah (Islamic law) and, ultimately, on trust and "honour." It requires an established relationship between the person or business providing the service, and the individual in the target destination who will deliver the cash to the recipient. These relationships are usually built on business or family ties. The contact in the home country may be reimbursed in many forms, including goods sent from the first trader, the cancellation of a debt, or cash from another source.

In this day and age, when more and more poor people work abroad, hawala is growing, simply because it's cheaper than bank transfers and – more importantly – because most of the recipients of these remittances don't have access to bank accounts.

The use of hawala clearly reflects the patchy reach of the banking system in these migrant workers' home countries. Hannah Scobie, Chairwoman of the European Economics and Financial Centre, says: "If you look at the size of transfers and the size of the immigrant population, it is growing everywhere in the world." Estimates for the amount of money transferred through hawala from the UAE are as high as $10 billion a year. Up to 90% of money transfers from the UAE to India use this system – which will persist for now in underdeveloped areas of the world. But as soon as there is a worldwide standard for m-banking, it will disappear.

The hawala system is also under close scrutiny because, as no records are kept and therefore there is no "money trail" to follow, it is also frequently used (or rather abused) for financing terrorism.

From Melting Pot to Salad Bowl

With continuing migration and tribalization, we will find tribes all over the world living together in the same cities and villages. But, whereas in the past it seemed necessary to mix the different cultures into some kind of united "melting pot," in this new environment, people will prefer to stick to the characteristics of their own tribe.

Simply put: people see themselves as both members of a tribe, and members of the new multicultural, multi-religious environment. Imagine, for example, three newly arrived New Yorkers: a Saudi businessman, a homosexual European computer programmer, and an Irish student. While each of the three wants to keep his or her own identity, they all feel like New Yorkers. They are proud of their new temporary home and cherish both their old and new identities – but they want to keep them separate. We see this "salad bowl" approach replacing the old melting pot idea.

In a salad bowl, the different "ingredients" (or tribes) keep their own identities. But the same salad dressing (in this case being a New Yorker) is poured over everyone.

"Glocalization": the Rise of Regionalism

Globalization and the creation of a single world culture are perceived by some as easy and convenient. Others perceive this as increasingly anonymous and alienating. The result is that many people will fall back on some form of regionalism. They will cultivate and invest in their regional identities, improve their knowledge of regional languages, and acquaint themselves with the history and culture of their local areas – even if they weren't born there. The region is back, as if it were the lost time of Proust itself, offering comfort to anyone who feels homeless, uprooted and lonely.

In the context of globalization, this renewed regional focus could be seen as a form of "bicultural thinking," rather than nationalism as we knew it. Pure nationalism interferes with bicultural thinking and acting. It destroys our ability to have several loyalties simultaneously, and it destroys any distance between region and nation-state – both of which are vital to success in the new era.

This new focus on individual regions could be called "glocalization." While embracing globalization, there is a revaluation of local, regional, and personal identity. In practice, these two can go hand in hand perfectly. You act as a global citizen, while at the same time you have a sense of yourself as a national or regional citizen. This is the attitude of the future.

Ultimately, we are all world citizens. Take, for example, a young man in Ireland named Liam who works for an international company in Dublin. As a modern cosmopolitan, Liam enjoys life in an international arena. At the same time, he cultivates his Irish heritage – and can often be found playing the fiddle in an Irish folk band or cooking traditional Irish dishes for friends. By incorporating both global and regional cultures, he is acting globally and locally at the same time.

A Revaluation of Family

Everywhere in the developed world we will see a revaluation of the family. In the past century in Europe, and to a lesser extend in the US, we actually saw a trend that went in the opposite direction: towards individualization and away from the family.

This was made possible by the establishment of the welfare state. The family that had for centuries been the social safety net for the individual was temporarily replaced by the government. In communist countries in eastern Europe and the USSR, it was the government that took care of its citizens – thus making the role of the family more or less redundant. But now that the welfare state is rapidly being reduced in the West and the communist systems have become market economies, the family is again becoming the center of social and economic life.

In Asia, the situation was different. There, the family never ceased playing a central role in society. The most important reason for there never being a welfare state in Asia, not even in communist China, was the fear of its leading to the disintegration of the family.

This is exactly what happened in Europe in the last few decades. Family members generally came to be treated as friends – nothing more, nothing less. Family ties might be maintained for a variety of emotional and economic reasons; but when these no longer existed, as was often the case, there was no real incentive left to maintain family relationships.

However, in the coming era, throughout the world, the family will regain its fundamental role as the cornerstone of society: the base that is always there to turn to.

We are now seeing the first products on the market that target the family. Some of these are driven by a new form of "member-get-member" policy, where the customer base is expanded by using satisfied customers to gain new ones. Standard Chartered Priority Banking uses a "family-member-get-family-member" system that offers a range of family privileges to create loyalty to their bank throughout the family. Privileges such as scholarships for the customer's children are especially effective in gaining the next generation's loyalty to the bank, thus securing the bank its future clientele.

Other players approach this from the perspective of what families are really about. Families are about helping each other – which now, judging from all evidence, is mainly about financing the purchase of a house. With the Virgin Money Family Mortgage, it is now possible to get a mortgage from family and friends. Virgin takes care of the construction only, to assure that your agreements on interest and payments are clear. The Kent Reliance Intergenerational Mortgage is transferable from generation to generation. Only interest is payed on this mortgage; there are no periodic repayments on the principal amount, which can also be passed onto the next generation, which then creates tax advantages when the house is inherited.

The increasing importance of the family is definitively worldwide. Robert Hovenier of Fortis Intertrust Switzerland says: "We have noticed an increase in requests for estate-planning vehicles for wealthy families from not only central and eastern Europe, and Russia, but also from India."

In these examples we are seeing some of the first successful concepts to capitalize on this megatrend. Many more will follow.

The Impact of Demographic Developments

Summarizing, these are exciting times. Not only is the economic world upside down due to globalization, but demographic developments will also be causing shifts in the financial sector for decades to come. Research has identified two important demographic shifts that will take place in coming years.

First: in less-developed parts of the world, the population will increase by billions, because of continuously decreasing mortality rates. All these billions of new people represent not only extra mouths to feed, but also potential producers and consumers for our world economy.

The second most important demographic development will be the aging of the Western world, Russia, Japan, and China – caused mainly by a decreasing birth rate. Some of these ever-increasing numbers of senior citizens will have great purchasing power; others will be poor. The need for health care will increase explosively. And while medical science has made us healthier in old age, this means our retirement period will be longer. The aging population will make it impossible to maintain a welfare state in the West, which again brings up the topic of the original social safety net: the family.

These drastic demographic shifts will cause considerable migration, and result in a world with all kinds of new identities. Parts of mankind will feel at home in this new world culture and embrace it. Many will turn to tribes and happily live in a "salad bowl" situation, meaning they will have no problem uniting several cultures with their own identity; no problem being, for example, 100% Muslim and 100% Londoner at the same time.

To counterbalance the weight of the uniformity of a cosmopolitan culture, many people will also turn their focus on their local regions, giving them a little contrasting color to offset the omnipresent global gray. Yet others will feel threatened by all the new developments and start to resist globalization. They will unite in countermovements in an attempt to turn back the clock – for example by withdrawing into closed communities, or embracing terrorism.

In the coming years, a colorful palette of new identities will develop in the world. Their wishes will be highly diverse, and the financial industry will need to approach each of them differently.

A New Look on Consumer Segments and Value Propositions

New Models for Consumer Segmentation – Again.

Traditionally in financial services, various models are used to distinguish segments of consumers and subsequently serve them with specific products and an equally specific marketing approach.

Criteria used to determine such segments have long been socio-demographic criteria, such as prosperity (e.g. available assets), and life events (e.g. giving birth, relocating). Now, over the past five years, other methods have been added, such as "customer life-time value," and the use of "mentality groupings."

Customer value refers to all future value that a customer represents for the company; in other words, the future cash flow that a customer will generate for the company. By focusing on the most valuable and loyal customers – and not just bringing in as many clients as possible – the value of the clientele is increased.

The use of lifestyle groupings has received an enormous boost from sociologist Paul Ray and psychologist Sherry Anderson. Based on extensive research in the US (for American LIVES), they distinguish three major "subcultures," or lifestyle groups: traditionals, moderns, and "cultural creatives." The uncovering of this latter group has inspired many marketeers.

The cultural creatives (approximately a quarter of the population) care deeply about ecology and saving the planet. They are also committed to relationships, peace, social justice, and self-actualization, spirituality, and self-expression. They, together with their peers all around the globe, are practically the future of the world. Also important is the fact that they are a growing part of the total population, they have average to high incomes, are willing to pay more for added value and quality, and are responsive to innovation. They are, in short, every marketeer's dream.

The increasing importance of tribes, religion, collectives, region, and family is becoming the key to consumer identity – thus forcing us to include these coordinates in any segmentation discussion. They are forming, in fact, the foundation for new target-group concepts – although this doesn't mean we should throw out all the "old" segmentation models.

Growing Importance of Deep Consumer Knowledge

Thinking from this new perspective – of tribes, religions, and so on – it really is a new ball game. What does "care" mean from the point of view of a specific tribe? From what point of view do they approach investments – as a member of a tribe, follower of a religion, inhabitant of a region, member of a family, or strictly as an individual?

Studies like the one by Ray and Anderson are necessary for a better global understanding of the various groups. But we really need to dig a bit deeper to get to the core of the matter.

What we really need to uncover is the consumer's true driving force, the so-called "deep consumer insights." Bill Bernbach, founder of the world-wide advertising agency DDB, already knew this some thirty years ago: "Nothing is as powerful as an insight into human nature, what compulsions drive a man, what instincts dominate his actions, even though his language so often camouflages what really motivates him. For if you know these things about a man, you can touch him at the core of his being." This is not about borrowing, or saving, or investing; it's about what is on someone's mind when he or she needs money or has money to spare.

The disclosure of deep consumer insights requires a method that really reaches beyond traditional market research. It is about being close to consumers, and using our ears and eyes to truly understand what's relevant to them and why. In order to generate real consumer insight you need to immerse yourself in the consumer's world, so you can fill in the blanks in your knowledge and understanding.

"So what else is new? Of course consumers are the most important point of departure. This is what we do for decades!" This is quite a common reaction, but in particular in financial services this is hardly true.

Experience What Consumers Experience

Philips, the consumer electronics multinational, has implemented the consumer-insight perspective into every vein of their organization. Philips CMO Geert van Kuyck says: "Marketeers are generally alienated from the real world. They believe in their own views, in numbers, in quantitative research and focus groups. They think that based on this they can predict something sensible about what drives the consumer. And that's wrong." Van Kuyck continues: "Numbers don't tell you everything and they can send you completely in the wrong direction. Marketeers should throw their traditional approach overboard and go into the world. Only then will they find out what really moves the consumer and what he needs. You only gather insight by experience. By keeping your ears and eyes open. Philips produces products for domestic use. Therefore we need to get into people's homes: look into their living rooms, bathrooms, bedrooms, and kitchens. Forget about those consumer panels and knock on people's doors. And that doesn't only apply to marketeers; everyone who develops products should do this. Researchers, product developers, designers – go and make house calls!"

To say that this way of thinking and working is not yet common practice for banks and insurance companies would be an understatement. The number of managers who have never actually met their own clients is truly staggering. Insight into what is really making the customers tick is sorely lacking.

Target-groups and Distinctive Value Propositions
If we establish that tribes, regions, collectives, and families are important anchor points, then obviously we must use this as a departure point for specially tailored offers. Intentionally, we talk about target-group concepts and not about products. A target-group concept doesn't just apply to products; it also applies to services and how to market them. To touch the right chord, it's necessary to include every aspect of the concept. The service and marketing, in particular, must respond to specific consumer insights into particular tribes, regions, and so on – "or else." For example, some Western banks saw great potential in Europe for ethnic groups with an Islamic background: Moroccans, Turks, Pakistanis, Arabs, Malayans, and so on. Therefore they developed mortgages that solved the interest issue, (according to their religion, Muslims aren't allowed to charge or pay interest) but these products are hardly successful.

"Striking the right chord," as Philips' Van Kuyck has explained, means really studying the target-group, then offering a range of services that shows the group you really understand them.

HSBC Amanah: Classic Islamic Banking

HSBC Amanah show how to do this properly. HSBC Amanah is available for consumers in Malaysia, Indonesia, Saudi Arabia, the United Arab Emirates, and the United Kingdom. Their concept is explained as follows: Islamic banking is an ethical and equitable mode of financial services that derives its principles from the Shariah (Islamic law). The Shariah is based on the Koran and the Sunna of the Prophet Muhammad, and it governs all aspects of personal and collective life.

All HSBC Amanah products and transactions are developed in consultation with independent Shariah scholars and approved by them prior to distribution. HSBC Amanah considers Shariah compliance of its business operations as its most important and strategic priority. This is reflected in its corporate values: "In developing our products and services, we are committed to the highest Shariah standards in the Islamic banking industry." HSBC Amanah has established a broad advisory structure: a Global Shariah Advisory Board with Shariah scholars of international standing, and regional Shariah committees.

This board advises HSBC Amanah on research activities intended for further development of the Islamic finance industry. The presence of renowned scholars from various countries provides an opportunity to achieve further harmonization of Shariah standards and the practices of the Islamic finance industry. Furthermore, HSBC Amanah employs a team of qualified professionals to ensure that the guidance and advice received from the Shariah committees is implemented in letter and spirit. The great depth of HSBC Amanah – the embedded principles of the organization – is something completely different from a mortgage with an intelligent interest solution. And so is their success. HSBC Amanah is an excellent example of how HSBC is truly living its positioning as "the world's local bank."

Similar target-group concepts can be developed for all the groups of this megatrend toward specific identities – from global citizens to tribes, collectives, regions, and families – just as they can be developed for the traditional demographic groups: the mass-affluent consumers, senior citizens, young academics, and working women. These are also fast-growing and financially attractive groups.

Ravi Sankaranarayanan of RBS states: "For banks, developing propositions to specific groups and their specific life stages is crucial. It is evident that financial needs evolve with peoples' changing lifestyles. True family banking is an undervalued proposition – but could well mean a crucial factor in attracting and, even more strongly, retaining them… However, refined segmentation and targeting is not yet as relevant to focus on in emerging markets, where focus on basic service delivery, doing what you promise to do, and simple things like 'more feet on the street' can often drive your sustainable competitive position. There is a large bankable population out there that you can get to by keeping it simple."

Just to inspire you, here are some more specific ideas for tailoring service concepts.

Input for Target-Group Concepts for Senior Citizens, 'the Flipside of 55'

We shouldn't generalize senior citizens. We can distinguish five different segments within 55+ baby-boomers, each with a different mentality and lifestyle:

- Whoopies: wealthy, healthy, older people
- Cheery price-hunters: fun, independent, digital savvy
- Early adapters: outgoing, individual, innovative
- Careful types: social, conservative, traditional
- Inactive socializer: average, social, slow spender

Whichever segment you choose, there are some generic dos and don'ts for targeting your aged 55+ consumers. Do focus on real insights and highlight the positive aspects of aging. Don't mock older people and never use granny clichés.

VODW research outlines seven things to keep in mind while targeting 55+ consumers:

1. Convenience is a key reason to buy for 55+ consumers. Integrate convenience in your concepts by offering additional services.
2. An aging mind can only hold so much information. Focus on ease of use and safety in product development.

3. Boomers are information seekers. So offer extensive and realistic information in your market communication.
4. 55+ consumers love to feel young, energetic, and good-looking. Tap into their need to age in a healthy way.
5. Baby-boomers value their social network. Make sure your products and services promote their social lifestyle.
6. Price quality is more important than just price (transparency is the key word).
7. All channels can be used, even the Internet, but boomers still love the postman. ☐

Input for Target-Group Concepts with a Regional Perspective
The region where you live is your "home." You feel connected there, you feel safe there. And you strongly identify with the region, which is where you have your roots.

- Every region has its own regional bank. Insurance companies will return to their roots: to the regional collective, a new version of the mutual insurance company, or cooperatives. Of course, regional banks and insurance companies can be facilitated by large players. Their brands are regionally rooted and have a high degree of authenticity. You will see this in the look and feel – but mainly in the staff. They live and carry the brand.
- Regional investment funds. These are forms of savings and investments that can be directly linked to the region. Invest in your own region – in local real estate, regional companies, or estates. "Buy" streets in your region, just like Monopoly.
- New alternatives to traditional savings and investments. Much like investments in Italian wines and Guest Invest, a concept that allows people to buy a hotel room and earn money from the rental income.
- Investments in local communities. Customers make their money (savings) available to the bank, and the local bank invests this in projects that support the local community.
- Attractive mortgages for local high-potential housing clients. To prevent customers from leaving the region, they receive attractive conditions, comparable to the tax breaks used to attract companies. ☐

The Future of Finance

Input for Target-Group Concepts for Families

As families become more and more important in the future, they will not only include parents and children, but also the grandparents. Cousins, nephews, and nieces will have closer ties and begin sharing more with each other with the return of the old safety net: the family.

- Pension funds and insurance companies will offer all-in packages for families. The working family members pay for it, and the entire family is assured specific retirement benefits. Cell phone companies already offer this kind of family deal.
- At the moment parents and grandparents start saving when their (grand)children are born, having in mind: "So you can start studying when you're 18." This becomes: "So you can start taking good care of your parents when you're 50."
- Cheaper (medical) care insurance will be available if you arrange for volunteer helpers (children, cousins, nephews, or nieces) yourself. As there will be fewer available caregivers, making your own arrangements will lower your premiums.
- The "Family" bank: the Smith family, for example, might set up the Smith Bank, and build a mutual capital as a family. This capital will form the foundation of their financial services. All the insurances and financing are based on this family capital, as well as the mutual risk profile. By creating your own bank, you do what Blogger is already doing: creating an online direct interpersonal banking platform. With a few simple clicks, you create your bank and build your family community. This is not as remote a possibility as it might seem. (For more about this, just look at Megatrend 3.)

The Need for Backward/Forward Integration

The effect of aging on the Western world will be dramatic. Ever more seniors will start paying less in taxes, while making more and more claims on social benefits. As the working population shrinks, there will be fewer people available to fix dented cars and broken windows, to change the locks after a burglary, or to take care of the sick and the elderly. This problem will be only partly solved through new migration flows and the use of technology. We expect that financial service providers will anticipate this development through backward and forward integration.

Backward Integration as Prevention

In this case, "backward integration" refers not so much to upstream links to the production and marketing chain, but rather to the prevention of certain undesired situations.

Damages (fires, car accidents, disease) cost society much more than prevention. People are getting their PhD on the subject of prevention, because society simply can't carry the costs of healing and repair. Consumers will more consciously influence, if not determine, their own future, in an effort to do their socially responsible best. And the core business of insurance companies will shift to prevention.

Prevention will be partly technology driven. Insurance companies may demand more home security, which will result in fewer burglaries and fires – or a more rapid response from the fire department.

We will see similar technology in cars. Already, indemnity insurers seek to prevent damage instead of covering it – for example, with the requirement of indoor parking. Such policies attract risk-averse people and improve the loss ratio.

International databases, like those of Audatex and Dekra, register all car damages and repairs claimed with member insurance companies. These contain a wealth of information that has, until now, barely been used to pro-actively prevent damages. For example, there would be considerably less parking damage if parking assistance systems or navigation systems were used more often. Also, the color of your car has an influence on the likelihood of getting into an accident. In the future, your onboard computer will probably protect you from fender benders, as it will help you stay out of trouble. Because of these advances, the various non-life insurance policies may well show a spectacular decrease in price.

The future is near: Norwich Union is planning to use GPS satellite-based navigation technology to track cars as part of a new, pay-as-you-drive insurance scheme, which will lower premiums for many drivers. The in-car device is the size of a DVD case and is fitted with an emergency button that allows drivers to alert someone in the event of a breakdown or accident. The insurance company said the new pay-as-you-drive policy will cut premiums by up to 30% per year for some drivers, such as those who don't use their cars in the morning rush hour.

Statistics from the Norwich Union and the British Department for Transport show serious accidents are more likely to occur at night, that motorway driving is up to ten times safer than driving on local roads, and driving during the weekday morning rush hour is 50% more likely to result in an accident than driving on weekends or evenings.

An in-car GPS device will in the future store information on every car journey, and each customer will get a monthly itemized insurance bill based on how much and when they used their car, what kind of road they used, and how many miles they drove.

Health Insurances with Intel Inside

Technology will enable health insurance companies to become virtual health advisors, sometimes working together with a healthcare institution. An insurance advisor – acting not as a teacher, but as a "coach" – will be able to help consumers achieve a healthy lifestyle at the right time, in the right place, in the right way. They will receive tips for this healthier life style through a personal home device.

We foresee many home aids to help with a healthier life. From remote health checks that diagnose malfunctions earlier, to help with self-medication and recovery – these technological advances with be an

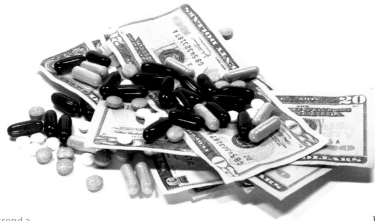

absolute necessity, with an increasing number of senior citizens and decreasing number of people to care for them. Databases and models to curb damages and to guide the flow of claims (similar to those of Audatex and Dekra) will benefit the effectivity and efficiency, and with it, lower the total costs of medical care. The use of this kind of technology will be part of the services health insurers have on offer.

Moreover, databases and new models for controlling damage claims and claims flow, like Audatex and Dekra, will improve the effectiveness and efficiency of health insurance – and thus its total cost. In the health insurance of the future, the use of technology will be part of the service.

Preventive Medical Care

We will also be seeing health insurance companies that organize health trips and health centers for their customers. Based on a monthly health check (already possible remotely), they will determine when the customer needs to go to a health care centre. Ten years from now, you could be going on a health trip several times a year, to Thailand for example, sponsored by your health insurance. Within a week, you could have minor surgery, follow a diet, get nutritional supplements, kick the habit, or receive psychotherapy. This kind of "maintenance service" could keep you going for another year. Insurers may make it mandatory for the over-50s.

Because many medical complaints are stress-related, there will be de-stressing courses developed where clients will be taught how to meditate, practice yoga, or exercise. Health insurance companies will become important promoters of sports. With the advance of technology, it won't be long before they can check on how much relaxation you get, so your health insurance premiums can be adjusted accordingly.

Educating Money Management

Taking care of ourselves will become increasingly important. Banks and insurance companies will actively help us with various courses that answer questions such as: how do I protect my family and my assets? How can I become and remain financially independent? How can I do more with less money? How do I minimize my medical expenses?

Banks will begin teaching schoolchildren how to manage money responsibly. The first examples already exist.

- Toyota is teaching children how to finance the purchase of a car. Whyville is a popular virtual world for kids aged between eight and fifteen, with its own newspaper, government, museums, and beaches. It also has its own economy, with "clams" as currency. The site has over 2 million registered users.

    To introduce the new automobile brand Scion, Toyota introduced this game to teach children at an early age about the brand, and how they can borrow money to buy a Scion in the virtual world. A virtual advisor helps them through the loan process, teaching them all they need to know about borrowing. It also links to online resources on financing, leasing, and interest. During the ten days of its campaign, the name Scion was mentioned more than 78,000 times in chat sessions and many cars had been virtually sold. The kids could "pimp the car up" to their own liking and take it for a spin to their friends place.

- ING's Postbank also wants children to learn how to handle money responsibly. So, with games-developer IJsfontein, they created the concept of Blue World, a digital game environment where children learn about money. When they open an Easy Blue childrens account, the kids receive the Blue Box, a digital piggy bank. And when they connect the Blue Box to their computer with a USB cable, the Blue World opens up in a special way. This digital play-and-learn environment is safe and protected. Savings that are physically deposited in the Blue Box appear as virtual money (points) in the Blue World. With these points, you can buy all kinds of goodies and create your own unique Blue World – and learn to recognize coins, compare prices, and count, exchange, and manage money.

Forward Integration as Problem Solving

The current expectation is that when you retire, you'll receive a monthly amount from your pension fund or social security. The problem is that in twenty years' time, money alone will not be enough. By that time, an aging population will see more senior citizens than people who can actually care for them. Then, instead of being paying institutions, the financial service providers will become problem solvers. Instead of transferring money, they will need to provide people, organize care – and, again, pay more attention to prevention. Then a mortgage will become a "home plan," combining mortgage, renovation, and maintenance in one product – after all, labor will be more scarce than money. They might also provide for a second home in Sweden, say, including domestic care, of course, due to global warming southern Spain will no longer be attractive, and besides, the aging population there will have become such a problem that it's no longer possible to find a nurse.

"Is forward chaining in its most literal meaning really a global trend?" Zurichs Theo Bouts wonders, "Providing customer-centric services is very localized. It can be funded by a global provider but at the end of the day it needs local delivery. How can a global life or pension provider orchestrate a business network like that? Solving that will give a competitive advantage."

Tilman Hengevoss, CMO and Head of Corporate Development at Zurich Switzerland, has a concrete example: "We have been applying this problem solution concept successfully over the last decade and have thus achieved a clear market differentiation in the Swiss insurance industry. We moved away from 'the check-handling business', i.e. paying for claims but leaving the repair process to the customer, to a fully integrated services provider in case of an incident. This approach is a win-win concept as the customer is released from the burden of restoring his life to order – it is simply done by Zurichs partner network. But also Zurich has the advantage of managing the claims process at significantly lower costs, which again pays out for the customer in more attractive premiums."

New Business Models
Obviously, financial service providers will engage in partnerships with companies that provide complementary competencies. The future of banking and insuring will not be business as usual with the usual parties. From this perspective, we expect to see a variety of new entrants.

For the next twenty years we need to think of temporary employment agencies like Manpower, Randstad and Adecco or parties that are used to adopting different business models fast, such as General Electric.

These are parties that add something crucial to the service. Think too of large pension funds. Why just pay out, if you could mean something to your customers? Really being there in moments of truth is what it's all about.

The First Success Factor: Simplicity

Increasing local and cultural diversity does not really relate to "one size fits all." It again introduces a balancing act – one that is even more critical in view of the desire to roll out concepts worldwide overnight. To keep these new value propositions well organized, simplicity is essential. The solution here is mass customization: like an assortment of Lego blocks that with relatively little effort will appeal to a range of target-groups. Those are important arguments for simplicity, but seen only from the provider's point of view.

Earlier, regarding real consumer insights, we established that many managers hardly ever meet with clients, and therefore have no idea what makes them tick. This, we suspect, is also the problem underlying the products they offer. One wonders if many financial service providers ever actually buy their own products and experience, for themselves, their customer service. Regarding which, here's how one customer replied in a recent survey: "Something you might ponder when shopping online for insurance, pushing around a basket full of potential purchases, after having completed an array of questions, is that you have to search in vain for the a virtual check-out. It makes you wonder: Do these people really want to make money?"

Within the industry, the word "simplicity" is often used to mean stripping away service. In the guise of convenience and cheaper prices for the customer, the actual goal is none other than saving costs – which is not what we mean by simplicity.

What we do mean is making it as easy as possible for the customer to do business with you – which includes products, pricing, service, marketing, distribution, and organization.

In the financial industry ING Direct is, obviously, exemplary for simplicity as a guiding principle. Dick Harryvan, a member of the board of ING Group and CEO of ING Direct, says: "Making up new products is easy. Banks and insurance companies do it all the time. Actually there's no stopping them. The average bank has 200 to 300 products. But usually less than ten of those products account for 80% of the total turnover. The rest is dead weight. In a sea of products like that, everyone loses oversight. A customer with a specific question never gets an instant answer. So what do you do when you devise a concept for a new bank? You get a piece of paper and you say: we will take one, simple, transparent product and with that, we break open the market. After that, we may add a handful of products, maybe ten or twenty, and that's it. We keep it simple, because simplicity affects everything, internally and externally. Both customers and employees know exactly what to expect. That's how we did it at ING Direct."

The Second Success Factor: Authenticity

On the one hand we are all becoming world citizens. But in such an enormous world without borders, people search for an identity. They want products with a known history. There is increasing sympathy for "authentic" brands, that people know from the past. This is reflected not only in purchasing behavior, but also in their friendships, the music they favor, and the role models they choose.

This is why sports heroes have become so popular. Sports is the last frontier of evident authenticity. A team that's up to bat is not acting or playing a role; they're just giving everything they have to win the game. The talent, personalities, the passion, joy, and the pain are all pure. The game is unpredictable, raw, unedited, and unscripted. It's authentic.

Authenticity means "to be real," with real roots and a real history. It also means "to be original," in this case with a genuine mind and personality, and knowing what to expect of someone. The increasing importance of authenticity with the choice of brands and products is completely in line with the countermovements of globalization, as described in this megatrend. Tribes, regions, religions, and family all characterize themselves with a high degree of authenticity. When servicing these cultures – whether target-groups or subcultures – authenticity is a must.

Get Real and Get Customers

Few industries have become as commoditized as financial services over the past three decades. Banks in particular have pushed customers out of branches – the one place where they could create an experience – to make them use automatic teller machines, then voice-response systems, and finally the Internet. Today, the only way to differentiate is to go beyond financial services to stage experiences so engaging that potential customers can't help but pay attention – and pay up as a result by buying the company's offerings.

Moreover, in today's Experience Economy people no longer want the fake from the phony; they want the real from the genuine. For any offering to be successful, therefore, it must be perceived by customers as real. Customers increasingly expect all types of businesses – including financial institutions – to represent themselves, their places, and their offerings authentically.

In order to be perceived as real, every financial institution must state its own identity: what it is. What is the self to which you and your offerings must be true? Secondly, you must carefully identify how you represent each offering, to ensure that it is what it says it is. What exactly does your bank say about its offerings, its branches, and itself? If you do not know the answers to these questions, you cannot possibly hope to be viewed as authentic by your customers. In particular, to help you understand how to represent your identity in the marketplace, there are five key elements that provide the necessary guidance in setting the standards for authenticity.

Firstly, think of who you call yourself via naming. Designate any dimension of your enterprise to render that thing more authentic. The Walt Disney Company, for example, refers to the founder and thereby to the company's origin, associating it with a real, live, breathing person who brought this entity into being.

Secondly, consider what you say you are through your expressed statements. Think of your choice of media and the statements you make about your bank, your offerings, your customers, and your employees. The easiest way to be perceived as phony is to advertise things you are not. For the way to advertise in a way that comes off as incredibly authentic, think of Unilever's "Campaign for Real Beauty" for Dove.

The third element is where and when you are encountered in your established places. ING Direct created European-style coffee houses in the US where financial professionals, in the role of baristas, engage customers in real conversations about their financial needs, creating a place-making experience that does a terrific job of generating demand for its offerings. And Umpqua Bank in Portland has put the "retail" in "retail banking" by creating branches in which people actually want to spend their time.

Next, think about why you say you are in business, your declared motivations. Learn from the Ritz-Carlton, where hotel managers take employees through its three-sentence credo every single day. Which public ideals for which you claim to exist do you hold to, and what are the incentives to encourage those ideals?

Finally, consider how you show what you are. All displayed appearances beyond text, including your logo, symbols, colors, and so forth need to induce a specific set of perceptions from others about you. Heinz Co. added "1869" to the logo – the date of the company's founding – and changed its packaging to impart perceptions of natural vegetables as a means of rendering authenticity. How do current and potential customers perceive the total sum of your representations?

Authenticity, like the Experience Economy that brought it to the fore, is not something that matters for only a year or two. Although it may take a while – some companies take decades to learn how to do it well – there is no reason not to start here and now to embrace this new management discipline. If you desire to be perceived as authentic, do everything in your power for your institution, its places, and its offerings to be true to what you say you are. ☐

Professor Joseph Pine II is co-founder of Strategic Horizons and co-author of best-sellers "Authenticity: What Consumers Really Want," and "The Experience Economy: Work Is Theater & Every Business a Stage."

Nurturing Authenticity With Inspiring Stories

More and more companies understand the power of storytelling. Regardless of B2C or B2B marketing, people do not want more information. They're flooded with it. At the end of the day, they want trust.

Facts do not create trust, only more questions. To create trust we need a story: a story that strengthens the belief in our dreams and ideas to really fulfill their promise. Storytelling is one of the most powerful tools we can use to present the truths of our products, services, or company.

Stories have sticking power. Stories create buzz and brand advo-

cates. They help customers and other stakeholders share opinions and experiences (as we will see in the next megatrend) – and customers value each other's opinions far more than the industry's. Word of mouth is the strongest way to advertise our qualities. This buzz is fueled by a good story. A meaningful and inspiring story can turn satisfied customers into true fans of our products and services, and "propagandists" for our ideas. However, the story must be authentic and real. As customers become more and more marketing savvy, they easily see through made-up tales. An inspiring story also builds a company's image and nurtures company pride among employees. "Living the brand" is about fueling and reinforcing its authenticity in a genuine fashion.

"Progressive is a US insurance company that shows, through its approach, great authenticity. It also realizes simplicity for its customers, and, on top of that, creates stories that their customers love to pass along," states Joseph Pine II, highly acclaimed expert in the fields of experience and authenticity.

Conventional industry wisdom says that insurance can count on a very low degree of involvement from customers. This makes it all the more difficult to seriously grow – but not for Progressive.

In the 1990s, Progressive discovered a consumer insight that was at odds with conventional industry wisdom. There are certain moments when customer involvement simply can't be higher for insurance: namely a moment of serious damage. This, according to Progressive, is the moment of truth. This is why this company made excellent service at the moment of damage, or truth, a core value of its strategy.

Currently there are thousands of SUVs driving around the US, insured by Progressive. When a customer is involved in a collision, Progressive immediately acts – often arriving at the scene before the police. They immediately take care of everything, leaving the customer to quietly recover from the shock. He or she will be completely pampered (with a tasty cappuccino if possible). The drivers of these SUVs don't just fill out a claims form. Thanks to mobile technology, damage can be estimated on the spot. Therefore, in two-thirds of cases, a Progressive client can have the claim amount transferred to their bank account within hours. The time for reimbursement has been reduced from months to a few hours – and counterparties just stand by and watch.

Fortunately for the counterparty, a Progressive driver has no problem in helping them too (also with a cup of coffee). You can guess the results. The counterparty would have loved such service from their own insurance company. On the spot, they ask the driver how to get a policy from Progressive. The drivers often respond to this by taking out their laptops and immediately enrolling them. This has become the most important sales method for Progressive. You can guess how often such a positive experience gets repeated to family, friends, colleagues, and acquaintances. It is indeed a nice story to tell.

Thanks to this strategy, Progressive is without a doubt the most successful indemnity insurance company in the US. In 1998 Progressive was number twenty on the list; seven years later they were number four – and more importantly, number one for profitability.

Megatrend 3

A Connected Society, New Marketplace Dynamics,
and Compelling Customer Experiences

September 24, 2035

Lillian is happy. She just woke up after a twenty minute powernap in her new sleeping capsule. This capsule connects your current mental and physical state with your desired state. After calculating the deficits, it automatically fills the air in the cabin with all the energy and vitamins you need. The capsule will also communicate with your doctor if necessary. New medications or vitamins are delivered within twelve hours after napping.

In the bathroom, the interactive mirror shows Lillian her agenda for the day, news updates, and the weather forecast. It also shows the changes in her bank account and digital bills. She pays them instantly by clicking on the mirror. She's saving money for a weekend trip to Tokyo next month. The saving meter shows that she has reached 80% of the required budget. She decides to deposit an extra 10% from her running account. A simple click on the mirror does the trick. This way she definitely has enough to spend on the weekend.

The minute she turns off the shower, her espresso machine automatically serves her favorite macchiato. All appliances in the house are interconnected and communicate with each other. No need to spend too much time on things that technology can do for you. Food is ordered and delivered automatically. Home insurance is updated automatically every day, so any new furniture, home appliances, and electronics are instantly insured.

On her way to work, Lillian decides she needs a new house in São Paolo. She has been commuting between Amsterdam and São Paolo for two years and is tired of staying in boutique hotels. Wondering what kind of global mortgage she can get, she checks the Internet in the car for information. Mortgage-specific consumer sites show that PinkOrange is well matched with her needs. PinkOrange offers mortgages specifically designed for Amsterdam – São Paolo commuters. On the PinkOrange site, she speaks with an advisor who gives her more information on specific questions. He tells her how she can choose a peer-to-peer mortgage, or even build her own mortgage at PinkOrange. He sends her a customized offer that she can instantly sign with her E-dentity. She sends a message out on the PinkOrange network to ask if anyone has spotted a nice house in São Paolo. Two options pop up within seconds. It is good to live in a connected world. ☐

A Fast-Spreading Revolution

Technology has brought drastic changes into our lives. The introduction of electricity, the light bulb, radio, television, faxmachines, computers, aircraft, cars, photography and film – all have changed our lifestyles and the way we spend our days. Technology is so integrated in our daily lives, we're no longer aware of it: technology and mankind have become one. Now you can't leave home without your cell phone or even imagine life without the Internet – and the revolution is still in full swing.

We are going to discuss those inventions that will have the most direct effect on the financial industry, radically changing the way our banks and insurance companies work.

When describing this megatrend, we won't go into all sorts of new technologies that we can expect. They will be obsolete by tomorrow. Instead, we are looking at the effect technology has on the way people live their lives and make use of these services.

The Impact of The Internet

The Internet really has caused the most revolutionary changes, in all aspects of our existence. The financial branch has been deeply influenced by this technology in the past decade, and more changes are on the way. Some see this as a menace, but for most of us it offers new possibilities and opportunities.

Within ten years, the Internet has caused rigorous changes in the rules of the game for the markets and financial service providers. The way financial products were sold ten years ago has become completely obsolete. The following points roughly describe the impact of the Internet on financial services:

- *The connected society.* Thanks to the Internet, consumers have become empowered. It has given them the tools to deal as equals with the providers of financial products and services. Empowered by the Internet, consumers can provide each other with product and purchase advice – and even offer each other products or services (peer to peer). Now the challenge for the providers is not to find as many consumers as possible, but to become a part of this new marketplace.

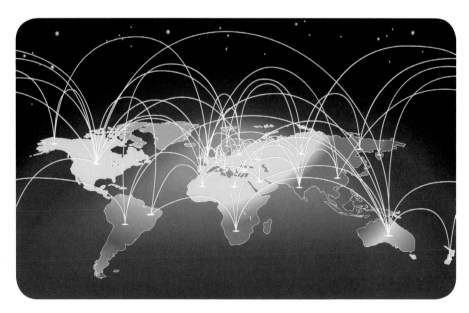

- *New marketplace dynamics.* The Internet initiates completely new dynamics in the industry. New links appear, and old links disappear or take on new functions.
- *New paths of purchase.* Thanks to the Internet, consumers are orienting themselves differently, as they choose and buy products and services in a drastically new way. Suppliers of financial products and services must reconsider any business model based on the old paths of purchase.

Online Banking and Insuring

The growth of online banking and insuring depends on country-specific Internet penetration, the banking and insurance culture, and the perceived product complexity, and its use is different for each step on the paths of purchase.

Both online banking and insurance have taken off in recent years. This growth is expected to continue in the future, with Scandinavia leading the ranks in Europe.

Internationally, we see big differences in the various countries. Those differences are mainly determined by the speed with which they embraced the Internet. Countries that were using the Internet in the 1990s – the US, UK, Scandinavia, the Netherlands, and Germany – are also ahead as far as online banking and insuring are concerned.

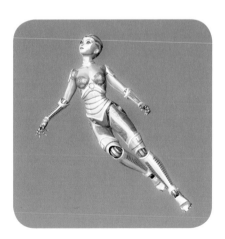

The penetration of the Internet depends mainly on computer possession (meaning prosperity) and the availability of broadband service. In a country like Indonesia, broadband service is many times more expensive than in a Western country, and the population is less prosperous. In Russia, approximately 25% of the population uses the Internet compared with 67% in Germany.

Two other country-specific factors determine the penetration of online banking and insuring: the speed with which they do or do not embrace technological innovations in general, and the specific banking and insurance culture.

Countries that are accustomed to negotiating product prices will prefer going through channels that allow them to do so – and that's not the Internet. Italy is an example of such a country. The British, the Dutch and the Germans, on the other hand, with a greater degree of "self-direction," prefer to manage their banking via online channels (and are topping the list in online banking and insurance in Europe).

Besides these national differences, there are product differences. For simple products such as car, home, and travel insurance, the perceived risk is low. People are more inclined to buy such products from "A-to-Z" online. In the UK, for example, half of all car insurance is now bought online, and this is expected to increase to 80% in the next decade. For products with a higher perceived risk, like mortgages and retirements, it's a different story.

Finally, the use of the Internet for banking and insurance is different for each step in the purchasing process. Despite modest Internet use for actually purchasing mortgages, it is widely used during the orientation phase. For other products that are easy to compare, such as non-life insurance, savings accounts, and investment funds, the Internet is the most used information medium in mature markets. In the past year Google saw a 42% increase in the search of the terms "mortgage," "car insurance," and "loans" – although this doesn't necessarily lead to actual sales. ☐

A One-Time Technology Leap or Permanent Technical Revolution?

Technology is currently developing so fast and having such a big impact on the financial industry that not even supervisors can always keep up. And they're not the only ones: government regulators and even the risk managers of banks themselves are frequently lagging behind. Many innovative financial products have been marketed without comparable expansion of bank risk-management – which means without the necessary checks and balances in place.

In Nout Wellink's words, "What I actually wonder is if this technological development is a 'leap', a temporary phenomenon that we'll catch up with in the near future, or is it something that will just keep going, so we can never catch up? And the main question then is whether regulators and supervisors should want to stop it – because imagine if you had kept the Wright brothers from flying, just because they didn't first get their pilot's license."

The Connected Society

New technology is not only changing the way in which governments, NGOs, industries, and businesses work; it also influences the way people think and behave. Technological developments cause top-down models to make way for more horizontal social models. This is characterized by Harlan Cleveland, the American political scientist, educator, and diplomat, as the "nobody-in-charge society."

Both the Internet and the international monetary market are examples of this horizontal model. With the introduction of each new generation of information technology (every two to three years), our society becomes less centrally managed, and the products people buy and exchange become increasingly "virtual."

When a physical product is purchased, there is an exchange of ownership. But when an idea, a vision, or an opinion is sold, both the old and new owner possess it. Cleveland explains, "If it's a thing, it's exchanged; if it's information, it's shared." The transformation we are currently experiencing is due to the fact that the Internet is "shared" by billions of people.

The Internet democratizes. It keeps people from blindly trusting authority and makes them seek advice from other citizens or consumers. The web functions as a kind of collective brain, from which conclusions or decisions are distilled in time. One-way messages from political leaders to citizens or from financial service providers to customers have really become out-dated. Citizens and consumers have been empowered and will need to be treated as equals. The best way to approach them is through dialogue.

The Rise of Soft Power
Thanks to the enormous influence of the Internet we see the rise of "soft power." Soft power is the power gained by "winning the hearts and minds" of the consumer for your propositions, so that voluntary participation replaces force.

The term "soft power" is attributed to the American political analyst Joseph Nye, who defined it as "the ability of a country to persuade other nations to participate in its aims without applying any force." But soft power is not only used by nation states; non-governmental organizations use it extensively, and companies can learn from them and apply it as well.

The Internet stimulates the rise of soft power because it works as an enormous (political) platform, where opinions can be shared. Many of the networks that arise have a common cultural identity or social value, or similar religious, political, or corporate ethics. Many are small and will remain so; others grow into large organizations with a great deal of economic and political power. In the future, these virtual networks will become more important than geographical networks.

Social Networking and Consumer Decisions

Citizens are taking back power from governments and companies, and they do this through online networks and communities on the Internet.

An online community is a group of people with common interests, who meet each other in a shared online environment and exchange content or cooperate in other ways on a regular basis. Think for example of MySpace, Facebook, MSN Spaces, and LinkedIn.

VODW E-commerce specialist Hong-May Cheng says: "Internet communities are spaces in which we can network without borders, and where we can enter or exit at any time of day. Internet communities are surprising, personal, sometimes recognizable, and sometimes shocking – but always authentic and from the perspective of real people. More and more Internet users are members of one or more online community. In the future, no one will apply for a job with a company without first checking LinkedIn, to see if there's anyone they know who's already working there." Twitter is an example of an emerging new community form. Twitter is, in fact, an intermediate step towards a completely integrated on- and off-line world.

Social networks like these are not only popular in Europe or the US. Approximately 40% of all 50 million Koreans are active on Cyworld. In Brazil, Orkut is really big. Patrick Degenhardt, a founding partner of Kiron Integrated Marketing in São Paolo, Brazil: "Orkut isn't just another social network. It is in fact the most visited website in Brazil. Orkut really has become part of the Portuguese dictionary in Brazil. It's amazing to hear people talking about 'their' Orkut, as if it was a part of themselves.

When there was an outage of the service for a week, millions of kids were literally disconnected from society, as many of their friends are only known to them through this online service – friends with no name, only 'nicks' [online nicknames]. Orkut is now a measure of someone's popularity: the more friends they have, the better."

Twitter combines blogs with instant messaging, which is therefore called "microblogging." With Twitter, users send emails or Twittersite text messages called "tweets," of up to 140 characters via SMS. These then show up on the Internet page. The pages are continuously viewed by other users who, for example, might want to form an opinion before buying something.

Wesabe is another example of "a community of real people dealing with real money issues." It is a community for financial overviews and decisions. The basis of Wesabe is a kind of account booklet that you manage on the Internet, to get an overview of your financial situation. Additionally, other site users can view your personal situation anonymously and give you tips from their day-to-day experience for managing your finances or achieving specific goals.

As Cheng says, "The importance of social networks on the Internet will only increase in the coming years. Nowadays our identity is often determined by the products that we use and the brands that we buy; but in the future this will shift to the communities in which we participate."

However, Susan Greenfield, Professor of Pharmacology at Oxford University, Director of the Royal Institution and a Member of the House of Lords, states that we lose our identity in cyberspace. Screen life and screen culture are fundamentally different from real life. She wonders what a "friend" in a social network such as MySpace really means. It is something completely different from in the real world, she assumes. "A strong identity is not a necessity there. If the scale tips over to more and more online experiences instead of participation in real life, your identity also becomes blurred."

The Power of Bloggers

Hong-May Cheng says that "the power of the bloggers is interesting in this respect: That the consumer has more confidence in the opinion of unknown fellow bloggers than in the well-intended advice and commer-

cials from corporations – not only for light issues such as music and travel, but also for sensitive issues like financial services and health care."

Public opinion as well as leadership opinions will be influenced more often by the bloggers who provide content and commentary on weblogs. With no media presence behind them and often no journalistic experience, they operate freely and independently. Their opinions are accessible to all – and they count. They are the proverbial flea on the hide of the established opinionating media.

Interesting here is the research done by Forrester Research on the extent of people's involvement with Internet communities, and their level of activity. For this research Forrester divided society into four types:

1. *The Creator* – the 10% of the European population that maintains their own sites and blogs.
2. *The Critic* – the 19% that participate in forum discussions and writes reviews.
3. *The Collector* – the 9% that join a social networking site.
4. *The Couch Potato* – the 63% that reads blogs and reviews.

Each group has its own dynamic and specific need for interactivity. The creators look for a platform for their activities; the critics look for dialogue and reactions; while the collectors and couch potatoes only want to get content. In terms of "soft power," the creators are the ones with the most influence. They influence not only the people in their own target-group ("our kind of people"), but also people in all other segments of the population.

The Wisdom of Crowds

Confidence in the offered information is crucial. For this reason, people prefer the unbiased opinions of their fellow consumers, no matter how rough and rugged, to the beautifully wrapped messages from stakeholders. Consumers are smart enough to estimate how much truth a story contains. When two negative judgments face off with 35 positive ones, the two critics are not going to carry much weight. This is the "wisdom of crowds." If a company tries to rip off a customer, before long you will find a site where this company is being crucified. There are countless readers of these angry, sarcastic, or hilarious messages, in which companies or products are ridiculed and their services skinned alive. The opposite is also true. When a company is very service-driven and customer-friendly, customers don't hesitate to offer praise in a blog or a forum. And research shows that people would prefer to judge positively rather than negatively. For companies, these online communities are places where reputations can be made or broken. Reputation management will become an important new competency for companies.

The younger people are, the quicker they are to see through a commercial message. Consumers inform each other on the Internet about how to interpret marketing messages from companies. Sometimes they make a game of it: what emotions are they targeting here? What tricks are they applying here? How are they trying to persuade me? The "they," in each case, is the provider of a product or service in some commercial.

How to Become Part of Online Networks

For companies, these networks will become important as places where their reputations are made or broken. That is why one of the most important questions that financial service providers should ask themselves is:

how do I get them to discuss my product with integrity, without me or the company losing our integrity ourselves in the process? The issue now is how to become part of the (uncontrollable) public opinion. How do we stay informed? How do we participate in the discussion? In companies, reputation management will be an important new competence.

Cheng speaks of "distributed content": it is no longer a matter of attracting the consumer to your site or content, but getting your content to the consumer in those places where he or she goes to find information and orientation. Examples of distributed content are the so-called RSS feeds, used for newscasts.

Then there are "widgets," the handy computer tools that provide information about traffic or icy road conditions, offered by car insurers. The SmartyPig widget can be used by a consumer to indicate personal savings targets to all the visitors to his or her site – if visitors wish, they can contribute. And, as already mentioned, the Wesabe widget can track the balance of all your bank accounts worldwide.

The Egg Money Manager from Egg, while not a widget, is still based on the principle of really engaging in consumers' lives and offering additional value. This online space allows consumers to easily see all their online accounts in one place, whether the accounts are with Egg or not. With just one password, you can enter your personal space and visit the Internet sites of your other banks with one click.

The Money Manager is an easy way to access and oversee the status of all your accounts. This reinforces the image Egg has an Internet bank and existing customers will visit the Egg site more often. The results for Egg are an increased level of trust by consumers, a more durable relationship, and an increase of 20% of the total customer value.

Going With the Flow

Some "old school" companies try their best to come up with ways to lure consumers to their sites in order to influence their opinions – and sometimes it works.

Amazon successfully applies "social networking" – for example, by offering buyers the opportunity to leave reviews on the site. This only works if those reviews are believed to be uncensored. Consumers don't expect Amazon to take an interest in whether product A or B gets a good or bad review. But reviews show that the platform is objective, and so the site is perceived as reliable.

Besides Internet retailers, some corporate sites offer the consumer large amounts of information. Nowadays you can find (uncensored) customer forums, with chatrooms for customers to discuss among themselves and with company experts. The providers can then draw lessons from the remarks and questions that customers come up with.

A nice example of a forum is on Hewlett-Packard's corporate site. Customers ask their questions, and answers come from other customers. On average it takes about a minute to get an answer to a question. The person providing the answer is given a score by the questioner. Those scores provide a kind of status on the forum, which stimulates people to provide even better answers. Hewlett-Packard moderates the forum and interferes when there are actual errors in the discussion. Input from the discussions is also used for knowledge management in their customer contact center and product development department. By providing the forum, HP got fewer customer contacts, but increased customer involvement in the company.

An example from the financial sector is the SunTrust Mortgage site, where you can ask questions, share ideas, or give advice. Accessible to everyone, their forum is for consumers, by consumers – as well as the experts of SunTrust, who gain more insight into "what's happening" and can more quickly react to problems and opportunities. But according to Cheng, this is still a bit of "old school" thinking: "Compare it with judo: going along with the flow is much more effective and efficient. What you should really do is use your existing powers to think creatively about what additional value you can offer in the discussions consumers will have outside of your own sphere of influence anyway – like it or not."

The KEB Dotori Bank: A New Internet Service

Cyworld is the leading online social network in South Korea. Cyworld is quite similar to the US-based Facebook and MySpace. Obviously, "Cy" stand for "cyber", but it also refers to the Korean word for friendship.

The beauty of the service is that people are able create a horizontal network in the online world by establishing a circle of friends with other users. Members use Cyworld to nurture friendships, online as well as offline, through a so-called "minihompy", a mini-homepage that includes a message board, photo gallery, and friends list.

Seven years after the launch in September 2001, Cyworld has around 20 million users from a population of 49 million. Needless to say, Cyworld plays a key role in Korean Internet culture. Cyworld is extremely popular among young people (teens to thirties). When young people meet for the first time, they exchange "cyaddresses" rather than phone numbers.

Cyworld has its own virtual currency, so-called "dotori", that allows members to purchase specific services, e.g. 5 dotori for a wallpaper. This is why the Korea Exchange Bank (KEB) decided to create Dotori Bank.

Dotori Bank targets potential customers in their teens and twenties who do not have the opportunity to enjoy regular banking services compared to other age groups. Dotori Bank offers them easy and fun access to banking services with the cyber money used in Cyworld.

Dotori Bank handles deposits and loans, in a new definition that seamlessly fits the Cyworld concept. For deposits, a customer puts dotori in the bank, and receives the principal and interest on completing missions designated by the bank, e.g. participating in a viral marketing activity for the bank. In the case of a loan, the customer repays Dotori by performing similar bank-designated missions.

The impressive growth of the Internet as well as the retirement of elder generations will accelerate the shift of customer contact channels from offline (branch counter, ATM) to online (Internet-based service) in the next decade. Most bank transactions will be done over the web without customers having to go to branches.

Competitive advantage of the financial industry will lie in convenient and diverse functions of the Internet banking system, rather than the number of branches. Consequently, banks are likely to prioritize marketing through online networks with customers.

KEB is actively engaged in a range of online activities aimed at attracting new customers in their teens and twenties who are likely to grow into a major customer base in the future.

Part of this strategy is to utilize the online network among existing customers (with the aid of member-get-member and viral marketing techniques) to form a network with these potential new customers, increasing their familiarity with the bank, thus inducing them to choose KEB as a main bank. The KEB Dotori Bank is the perfect example.

We expect that with this strategy, KEB will play a major role in the online arena of the future, another step closer to becoming a world-class bank in North-East Asia. ☐

Richard Wacker is CEO of Korea Exchange Bank (KEB).

E-dentity: Privacy and Liability

E-dentity is one of the most important issues for the future of the financial branch. The customer now has various pass numbers, pin codes, passwords, and so on – the logistics of which are too complicated. In the future, it should become possible for each citizen to have an electronic identity, or "e-dentity." This would be individually determined and used for every financial transaction, regardless of which financial institution you happen to approach. It would all be managed through a central portal. So when citizen X gets pin code Y, it could be used for every bank, pension fund, and insuranc company.

In the US and trade blocs like the EU, such e-dentities could be possible within five years. At that point, the digitalization of the rest of the financial services will probably happen very quickly. It will then be much easier to switch banks or insurance companies, which is nowadays still a cumbersome process. Transnational traffic will also be much easier, as network solutions shorten the distance to the consumer and provide maximum flexibility.

The End of Privacy?

As our lives become increasingly digital, we leave more and more digital traces: with all the online sites we visit, with the physical items we use for digital payment and loyalty programs, and of course with the parties involved in our financial affairs. As digital payments continue to replace physical payments, we will only leave more.

Like it or not, privacy is becoming a thing of the past. More security cameras are appearing in the streets and other public places. The very equipment that was considered an intrusion into our privacy is now becoming our friend. To safeguard our security, we are increasingly prepared to give up privacy. We are willing to have our bags and bodies searched at public events, and in museums, airports, and shopping centers – especially those who live in countries where terrorism is commonplace.

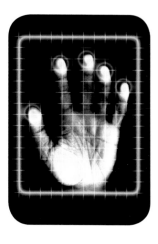

New Marketplace Dynamics

The Rise of Peer-to-Peer Networks

One way people can now thwart the power of big corporations and governments is in the use of peer-to-peer computer networks: networks in which all connected computers are equivalent and all participants roughly have the same possibilities at their disposal.

Peer-to-peer (P2P) processes occur in "distributed networks." In distributed networks, autonomous agents freely determine their own behavior and linkages, without the intermediary of obligatory hubs. With social networking technology, people started sharing information, but with peer-to-peer networks they can start to share and exchange "stuff."

P2P is often described as a "barter economy," as P2P processes contribute to forms of "distributed capitalism." The massive use of open-source software in business (such as Linux) is enthusiastically supported by venture capital and large IT companies (such as IBM). This is creating a distributed software platform that will drastically undercut the monopolistic rents enjoyed by companies such as Microsoft and Oracle – much like Skype and VoIP are radically redistributing the telecom infrastructure.

Peer-to-Peer Loans and Mortgages

Well-known examples of peer-to-peer networks are the music-sharing sites Kazaa and LimeWire. The music industry lost much of its power and influence because of these networks, where music is shared among users. In banking we see the emergence of a specific kind of P2P: peer-to-peer Internet lending networks. The *Wall Street Journal* predicted $100 million in P2P loans for 2007, with an increase to $1 billion in new loans by 2010. One of the first P2P lending sites was Zopa (Zone of Possible Agreement), developed by James Alexander in the United Kingdom in 2005. Now, in addition to Zopa UK, you can find Zopa Italy, Zopa Japan, and Zopa USA.

One year after Zopa, the American equivalent, Prosper, was launched. Besides being a place for P2P lending, Prosper is also a kind of social network. People who want to borrow money can leave extensive profiles on Prosper for potential lenders. They can also join one of the Prosper Communities. There are communities for Microsoft employees, Christian investors, women entrepreneurs, and for people who are in the business of horses. There is a community for Geek Power (nerds lending to other nerds to develop, for example, the ultimate computer game), and a community for families with autistic children – to name just a few. This taps precisely into the tribalization we introduced in megatrend 2. Most P2P lending sites are national, because financial laws and regulations are different in every country. In France, for example, it is impossible to lend or borrow from Zopa or Prosper; but since spring 2007 there is a local site for P2P lending called PrêtP2P. Likewise, the Dutch now have their Boober; the Chinese have their PPDai; and the Germans their eLolly.

In the mortgage market, a network called Home Equity Share operates on a similar P2P principle. Focused on the US market, it is a remarkable initiative in these times of the sub-prime lending crisis. Home Equity Share matches private investors with those who are looking for a house but lack the capital. Potential investors and buyers prepare their profiles on the website. These are then matched and together they buy the house and become "shared owners."

How Do P2P Lending Sites Work?

Individuals looking for low-cost loans create listings that detail how much they want to borrow, what they're planning to use the money for, and how much they're willing to pay in interest. People with money to lend can go through the listings, which include details of potential borrowers' credit histories and their pictures, which makes the transaction more personal. They then bid on the loans they want to fund. Lenders can choose their risk level, and both lenders and borrowers can specify the rate of return or interest rate they're demanding or willing to pay.

Some sites, like Zopa and Lending Club, work with pooled lending: the lender lends money to a pool of borrowers with similar credit ratings. Other sites, like Prosper and Kiva, work with direct lending: the lender lends money to a specific borrower, based on their credit rating. In this model, evidently the risk is greater.

The fact that the P2P lender knows where his or her money is going, and what it is being used for, makes this kind of lending attractive to many people. But they don't just choose P2P lending because it's more personal. They also do it because they want to oppose the big mainstream banks (anti-corporatism); because of the comparative financial fairness of social lending; because of its ethical and social premises; because of its supposed transparency; and because of the accompanying sense of community and feeling of connectedness.

A study by the Social Futures Observatory from October 2006 states: "The combination of financial attractiveness and a series of value systems based on ethicality, philanthropy, community, and individualism is likely to mean that Zopa's future will be very favorable."

Should Traditional Banks Fear P2P Lending Sites?

Newly emerging types of financial relationships like P2P lending may rival more traditional mainstream financial services and prompt a need to re-examine their proven model of traditional banking.

But not everybody agrees on the future success of these initiatives. One expert says: "Actually Zopa is a regular bank. It is still small scale, but when it grows, it will have more staff and we will need to carefully calculate the risks. That's the core task of any bank. Now it still has a sympathetic flair. The borrower knows the lender. And people might give $100 each to a starting entrepreneur. Why? Because they like the guy's picture. But in fact it's just a modern kind of gambling. I don't think it will really take off – and if it does, it will be just like any other bank."

From Outsourcing to Crowd-Sourcing

Companies have been outsourcing to cheap Asian countries for years. Now they're taking it to another level, using social networks such as MySpace, Second Life, and a multitude of other virtual communities for their business solutions. This phenomenon was labeled "crowd-sourcing" by Wired journalist Jeff Howe.

Crowd-sourcing is all about user-generated content. Wikipedia describes it as "the act of taking a task traditionally performed by an employee or contractor, and outsourcing it to an undefined, generally large group of people, in the form of an open call. For example, the public may be invited to develop a new technology, carry out a design task, refine an algorithm, or help capture and systematize or analyze large amounts of data."

Examples of companies that crowd-source are Getty Images, which recently paid $50 million for iStockphoto, a website where more than 23,000 amateur photographers upload and distribute their stock photographs.

Besides corporate sites that use crowd-sourcing, there are open innovation marketplaces such as InnoCentive.com, NineSigma.com, Openinnovators. net, and YourEncore.com. Here, companies and entrepreneurs pose their questions concerning innovation to an anonymous crowd. Sometimes suggestions are given for free, but increasingly the best ideas get paid. For specialists, giving advice and proposing ideas can also be a way to get attention and assignments for their own business.

Companies have to beware that crowd-sourcing can also irritate consumers. When people are confronted too often with questionnaires from companies that "want to improve their services for the benefit of you and your fellow consumers," they get annoyed and cynical. The same is true when they notice that the companies posing the questions don't take their comments seriously.

Take computer company Dell: on their website they asked "the crowd" what they most wanted Dell to improve or supply. From day one, the reply was new software: Ubuntu Linux instead of Windows. Dell listened, but only to a certain degree. It now supplies Ubuntu Linux, but only scantily, because Dell doesn't want to offend Microsoft. For "the crowd" that asked for Linux, this is an incentive not to buy Dell hardware anymore.

Open-Source
The tables have turned in the past decade. In the past, companies ruled the game; now the customers rule. Companies know this and are preparing for it. One consequence of this awareness is that companies are starting to apply the "open source" method.

Open source means that you disclose certain corporate information and provide people with free access to the source material of your end products. You then invite people to further develop the product or invent new applications or alterations.

The open-source philosophy was developed in the software arena and made popular by Linux, who actually disclosed all the source material for its software. Usually only a limited amount of corporate information is disclosed to third parties; these selective open doors are called APIs (application protocol interfaces).

With APIs in hand, suppliers and consumers can use each other's services. The results are "mash-ups": new solutions and enterprises that are established out of already existing companies. For example, Google Earth allows others, through an API, to disclose specific geographical information, such as the location of ATMs, bank offices, insurance advisors, affiliated physical therapists or shops.

eBay is in fact an open-source platform. Consumers can set up their own businesses there. As a company, too, you can try to be a creative part of this open-sourcing.

The German company Sparschwein (German for "piggy bank") offer an alternative way to save money. The proposition is simple: "Empty your garage and fill your piggy bank!" Sparschwein calculated that Germans have "stuff" worth more than €20 billion stored and unused in their garages and cellars. Now they can give their stuff (if it's worth over €50) to a Sparschwein agent, who will sell it for them on eBay. Sparschwein will deposit the return (minus a handling fee) directly into the customer's savings account with the "Deutsche Kreditbank." In one year, Sparschwein provided customers with €56 million and earned €3 million for themselves.

The essence of the open-source philosophy is that companies need to open up. By offering access to their techniques and concepts, the companies themselves gain access to an enormous, worldwide reservoir of creativity and entrepreneurship. Third parties can then use parts of their ideas or company to develop new ideas and companies – which in turn makes the company stronger. Open-sourcing is a new kind of partnering: worldwide collaboration without barriers.

New Paths of Purchase

Offline – Online, Offline – Online...

New communication technology has totally changed the way consumers orient themselves before purchasing a product. Ten years ago, if you wanted to buy a CD player, you would go to the nearest store and ask for whatever you'd heard about – for instance – in the commercials. The salesperson would express some wisdom about the various brands, and you would happily leave the store with your new CD player.

Nowadays when consumers want to buy a product, they switch effortlessly from offline to online environments. The purchase of an iPod, for example, might go like this: First, you call a friend who has one to see what his or her experience has been. Then you look on the Apple website to see if the iPod is compatible with your laptop. For more neutral advice, you check out CNET. Subsequently, you may surf to Amazon, where you've made some purchases in the past. The consumer reviews on Amazon are all positive, but the price is disappointing. So you go to the nearest Apple store, where you can actually hold it in your hands – and you fall in love. On the price comparison site pricescan.com, you discover that Amazon is only a few dollars more expensive than the cheapest retailer. You don't know the retailer, and you've had good experiences with Amazon. So you surf back to their site and buy your iPod.

Patrick Degenhardt says "Even in Brazil, a country of noted social disparities, it is now common to see people with a page showing the TV they want to buy printed from the Internet, entering a shop and asking the sales person if they can match that offer. In panic, they usually agree."

The entire orientation and purchase cycle looks completely different because of the Internet: before you shop in a store, you gather your information online and often end up making your purchase there.

For financial products, such as car insurance, savings accounts, and mortgages, the orientation and purchase cycle looks entirely different from the way it did ten years ago. In markets where Internet use has matured, most product orientation is happening online in a variety of places, such as supplier sites, consumer and comparison sites – with the integration

of the Internet and cell phone creating an additional channel. From time to time, the consumer might switch to a call center or visit a bank. When it comes to the best channel for the actual purchase or closing of a deal the consumer will make the most suitable choice.

The Call for Transparency

In the past fifty years we have seen the consumer market grow exponentially. Where we used to see about five "classic" products in the dairy section of the supermarket, we now see dozens of new variations on those products. You can hardly see the forest for the trees.

The same is true of financial services. The number of suppliers grows every day, with each supplier regularly expanding the range of its products. Consumers are calling for more transparency.

Because of the increased influence of soft power and social networking, the call for transparency is becoming louder. Consumers are more empowered, and they want to know exactly what a product is about and what the producer is up to. They want to know, for example, if their insurance company is doing anything to protect the environment, or if their bank is investing in the weapons industry or in industries that use child labor.

Technology has made it possible to view products side by side and compare them at home, and is a major cause for the demand for transparency. Whereas you previously had to leave things up to the "independent" insurance broker or sales person, future consumers will be more in the driver's seat.

Transparency and Comparison Sites

Comparison sites play a big role in providing transparency, and thus a very big role in the new paths of purchase. For those who want to insure their cars for instance, many good comparison sites can be found. How these sites are set up and how they make money will vary.

Some comparison sites are just information sites, offering no option to directly buy your insurance. These purely informative sites earn their money through advertising: they offer only their logo, or logo with telephone number, or the option to forward an information request to the insurance company. Some sites not only rank insurance based on price, as most sites do but also use qualitative criteria. On some sites, customers can leave reviews and ask or answer questions in a forum. Other comparison sites enable you to also immediately buy insurance. The revenues from these sites come mostly from commissions and in part from advertising revenues.

Banks and insurance companies are already buying stakes in comparison sites, as they become an ever more important link in the decision-making process of consumers. By participating in these sites, the companies gain an enormous insight in the choosing behavior of the consumer vis-à-vis the products of the competition. Of course they are tempted to redirect traffic on the comparison site straight to their own channel. But tampering with the objectivity of the comparison site will automatically lead to the loss of authority and, with it, popularity. So these new shareholders aren't very likely to sink to that level. Not the smart ones, anyway.

Comparison Sites as Drivers of Choice
All products and services will become much more transparent over the next ten years. Soon comparison sites will compare not only the price, but also the quality of service. As soon as this happens, pricing competition will shift to a competition for quality of service. Thus, the logical evolution of comparison sites will make service much more important. The travel site TripAdvisor, which offers quality assessment of practically every hotel in the world, is "bookmarked" by every frequent traveler. So they are not making their choices based only on price.

In recent research by VODW, respondents could choose from three fictitious weekends in Paris. The first one for €175 was ranked 5.5 (from an average of 100 responses); the second one for €200 was ranked 8.0 (based on one response), and the third for €225 was also ranked 8.0 (based on 100 responses). A staggering 77% chose the third option. The high ranking combined with a large number of assessments allowed them to ask a price that was approximately 25% higher. The empowered customer loves lists that allow products or services to be compared for quality. Here's a non-digital example.

The German magazine *Focus* annually publishes the *Große Ärzte* ("Great Doctors") research, which compares the reputation and performance of medical doctors. For every specialization in the medical field, there is a list of the best-known doctors: for example cardiologists, surgeons, and doctors specializing in knee or hip operations. They can all be checked with regard to reputation (among colleagues), their quality assurance and improvements, and recommendations by patients.

There are also Internet sites that put the medical profession into comparison lists. Vimo.com is an American search engine annex and comparison site covering just about the entire US medical sector. Here you can not only compare medical insurance quotes and buy medical insurance, which is the core of the site; you can also compare doctors and dentists by price and service, based on customer reviews, and compare medical procedures by experience, hospital, and price, as well as all kinds of information about medication.

NOTICE

1. CHECK OUT TIME 24 HOURS.
2. AFTER 24 HOURS A PART OF THE DAY WILL BE TREATED AS FULLDAY CHARGE.
3. SPITTING AND DRAWING ON THE WALLS ARE STRICTLY PROHIBITED AND THOSE ARE SEVERELY CHARGED.
4. MAINTAIN SILENCE AND CLEANLINESS IN THE ROOM.

Bricks and Clicks

What makes a consumer go directly to the store to make a purchase one time, and go the Internet to make their purchase the next time?

Research shows that it doesn't really matter much to the consumer if they do business physically or virtually. The channel itself doesn't matter. What matters is satisfactory service and experience. Did the contact feel personal? Did you feel listened to? Was the service friendly, proactive, and empathetic? And beyond that, if your questions are answered adequately, how much effort does it take to get things done?

It was thought that demographic factors – mainly age and social class

– determined consumers' preferences for specific paths of purchase. But research shows that other factors play a role: the season, weather, time of day, and the people and locations involved in the transaction. If a customer wants to contact his financial service provider on a Saturday morning, for example, he might have to go about this differently than he would on a Monday morning.

As a customer, you want the orientation and purchase channels to align seamlessly, no matter what path you choose. This is a big challenge for many financial service providers, but it's nevertheless possible.

For example, at First Direct all channels are fully integrated. If a client is having a conversation with an agent on the phone, while paying a bill or requesting a product online, each channel knows what's happening on the other channel in real time. The same goes for online teasers. Let's

say a consumer has logged on, and a banner pops up offering a loan at a certain amount. It would instantly be stopped if the customer had already spoken to the call center and obtained information – and vice versa.

This is a more holistic approach: one customer and one set of information. Here's an example of this customer-centric focus. If a customer calls the call center with a complaint, the agent who takes the call will "own" that complaint throughout the entire organizational process – which may even mean going to the CEO for a signed response. This may seem overblown, but it demonstrates the customer-centric culture – and the perfect multi-channel response.

Jeremy Alwyn, Head of Bank Distribution Europe at Zurich Financial Services, adds an extra dimension: "Not many years ago, insurance was typically sold by a trusted advisor, normally a tied agent or a broker. Today the role of the trusted advisor is also increasingly being played by banks, motor manufacturers and retailers. These new distributors are now developing a multi-channel insurance distribution approach of their own within their branches, dealers, or shops through to their customer contact centers. Their distribution confidence is growing to a point where they are comfortable with comparison engines on their websites. These new providers have moved faster than many insurers in changing their distribution model. Underpinning all of this is the trust the consumer has in their brand."

Professional "Chatters"

The role of customer contact will change in the future. In a market where products and services are looking more and more alike, and where products can be purchased at many distribution points, the supplier who makes every customer contact a personal and special experience will be the winner.

Conscientious use of each channel will be crucial. But while each channel focuses on its own additional value, there will be seamless alignment with other channels. In the past, when online customers had questions, they were forwarded to email addresses and phone numbers. Now – thanks to a new generation that grew up with chatrooms – suppliers will also turn to chats to field questions and remarks. Moreover, on the Internet it's faster to link to a chat session, than to a phone – and besides, chatting is quicker. Then you have your answer in no time. With no more waiting hours or days for an email response, the use of chat sessions actually results in more conversions.

Chat sessions run in part on companies' own chat bots (programmes that converse with people). Researchers expect that in ten years time about 15% of companies will use chat bots for customer contact – but as well as an automated "chatter," they will use more flesh-and-blood chat experts.

In 2006 Bank of America realized 800% more mortgage sales. What's their secret? They proactively approach people who spend a lot of time on their site. Bank of America now employs 100 chat experts.

Image: The Missing Link

Another growing trend is the use of visual communication. When talking about the use of imagery, most people think of video conferencing or Skype – but that's not what is meant here.

The Eye Catcher from Ex'ovision is an excellent example of this next generation of video communication. Three things make all the difference: an almost life-size picture, eye contact, and superb quality of sound and vision of broadcasting quality. The overall effect is that, in seconds, the person you're talking to seems to be sitting right in front of you. You can look this person in the eye and see their body language, as if they were sitting on the other side of the table. Increasingly, the Eye Catcher is being used by multinationals for better personal communication, without the travel. This dramatically reduces the number and costs of flights – and more importantly, lost travel time. Most recently the Eye Catcher is being used in the front and back offices of financial service providers, to facilitate direct customer contact – and thus make the transition to physically unmanned advice shops. This development enables financial experts to be available in many locations, without their having to travel or physically be present. Moreover, they can be reached outside regular business hours, at home, or, for that matter, on the other side of the world.

New Roles for Physical Distribution Channels
In the channel mix, the Internet has become the general point of departure and overall reference. With the exception of day-to-day shopping, very few consumers buy products without first doing some research on the Internet. And the Internet is often the first contact point between the consumer and supplier – which drastically changes the role of the physical path.

Traditional suppliers are already questioning what to do with those expensive "bricks" in these times of Internet competition. With few exceptions, they are drastically reducing their branch offices. In their remaining offices, they are experimenting with new concepts for paths of purchases.

Rabobank has started a shop concept that guides people in the use of direct channels. If this shop becomes successful, it will automatically eliminate itself in several years' time. Other suppliers are experimenting with video kiosks. Using equipment similar to Eye Catcher, experts can speak live with a client, without actually being present.

Child of Our Times

Technological advances have changed the behavior and needs of customers everywhere in the world, and especially in the financial sector. Nowadays customers want their bank to be transparent, easy to deal with, and inexpensive. They set the rules and know what they want. Their bank has to be accessible 24 hours a day, seven days a week; increasingly through the Internet, but also through the familiar bank branches that are visited when important decisions have to be made, for example when buying a house. Looking ahead, personal contact will continue to be an important added value.

When I was young, my father used to take me with him to the bank every Friday night. He had his own company and every week he would deposit the money he earned, hand in his fund transfer slips and withdraw some money. I always thought this a wonderful weekly ritual.

Technological developments have turned the financial sector upside down. These days, a Dutch person visits his bank three times a week on average, primarily via the Internet. A number of years ago, people thought that the Internet was just hype, but it has become an essential part of life. And people want to make use of the practical advantages of modern technology. Against forty or fifty people who visit an ING bank branch in the Netherlands every day, 1.5 million people log onto our banking website. Customer contact has increased enormously compared with the past and the nature of these contacts has changed. The transactions my father used to settle at his bank branch are now taking place via direct channels, without the intervention of counter staff. Yet, customers want a bank branch in their neighborhood, to have access to professional advice on, for instance, mortgages or pension products.

What is true for the Internet is also true for the bank branches: excellent service and accessibility are vital. This means extended opening hours, equal to those of shops, and during the evening as well. This also means that it should be possible for clients to get service in every branch in the country.

In the future, too, banks will have to adjust to the changing needs of customers. The strong increase in direct distribution channels will continue, such as the Internet, direct mail and call centers with specialized units for certain products and services. At the same time, there will be a growing need for professional advice on the more complex products, also because the world around us is becoming more and more complicated. This requires a good match between the customers' needs and the expertise of the employees.

Financial institutions will have to take the extra step to acquire and retain customers. In the future, when it becomes more difficult to distinguish through products and services, personal and perfect service will be a decisive factor.

Nick Jue is CEO of ING Retail Netherlands.

Reinventing the Branch

The Umpqua Bank in Portland, USA, was established as a lifestyle concept. A super-trendy bank, it has a contemporary vision and hip offices. They are committed to creating a new customer experience, because "Umpqua = not a bank! It's a Lifestyle." As they say: "Enjoy the small moments, bank wisely, and live well." Their redefinition of the banking concept is inspiring, engaging, relaxing – and even a little bit quirky. And it has been implemented at all levels.

The Portland office has a stage for community events, and they also host yoga, movie nights, and an Umpqua book club. Regarding products they developed four personal "blends" (product and service packages). A test on their site will reveal the best blend for you. Crucial to their success, according to Ray Davis, the CEO of Umpqua, is the staff and the culture that they've established.

Customer service is key. Every manager receives training at Ritz-

Carlton. Employees get a broad-based training that enables them to assist the customer with just about anything. Instead of "return on equity," they aim for "return on quality." Here's a bit of trivia: Umpqua's personnel turnover is only half that of most banks, and this small bank scores high in the Fortune 100 "Best Companies to Work For."

The Deutsche Bank also asked itself what the bank of the future should look like. Their starting point was to create a bank where people are pivotal; the result is the Q110 in Berlin. In this completely furnished bank of the future, there is a Trend shop with exclusive products developed by top designers; a comfortable lounge where customers can enjoy coffee and a salad or sandwich, listen to some music after completing their bank business, or simply relax; there is a Kids Corner, and a Forum where clients can get video information on the advantages of various products. They also have a "gallery of wishes," where people can talk about their dreams for the future (based on a research project, Deutschland Wunschland). The office is a complete experience for all senses.

The Italian Mediobanca, originally an investment bank, introduced CheBanca! – a concept aimed at the younger population. Where other banks' concepts for the young are almost fully carried by the Internet, the physical bank office plays an important role with CheBanca!. The hundred planned office branches, look nothing like the traditional bank office, however. They look modern, have no barriers or counters, and have lots of technology. Also, you will find space there to chill out and somewhere to "park" the kids.

The Future of Finance

Common to all these concepts is that the role of the shop and staff has changed. Instead of focusing on sales transactions, they are focusing on personal experience and advice. The physical experience is much more important and the senses are pivotal, particularly taste and smell – which you can't enjoy on the Internet.

The Importance of Personal Experience
In 1999 Joseph Pine II and James Gilmore published a book called *The Experience Economy*. They suggested that after the agricultural economy, the industrial economy, and the service economy, we have now landed in the "experience economy." In this economy, the suppliers of products and services must provide the customer with a memorable experience. That experience becomes, in fact, the final product.

The customer experience is a factor that's especially ignored in the financial sector. Many customers experience banks and insurance companies as unwieldy, closed, bureaucratic institutions, which pay no attention to service or the feelings of their customers. Since companies in other sectors are paying more and more attention to the customer experience, people come to expect a similar focus on customer service from financial service providers.

Ravi Sankaranarayanan of RBS confirms this: "It is indeed the case that not enough focus has been given to the customer experience. The financial sector, relative to other industries, has only recently had to deal with increased competition and more sophisticated customers who demand better service. We were previously in the luxurious position where increasing our customer base and revenues were a given. But times have changed. Especially in emerging markets, where we as an international bank compete against established local banks, differentiating ourselves on the customer experience is key to growing our market share. Ensuring that we understand what drives customer loyalty and client engagement and deliver on that at every touch point is now becoming a crucial part of the way we do business."

As briefly mentioned above, financial service providers don't pride themselves on emotions. Their focus is still mainly on product advantages, and any focus on customer service is mainly to keep costs to a minimum.

These are very important issues. Nevertheless, it doesn't mean that financial service providers can't have a close relationship with their customers. Often there is frequent contact with customers, and banks get free insight into their consumer behaviors. This frequent contact and insight could be seen as assets – and used to give completely new meaning to customer relations.

The Future of Finance: Real Branded Experiences?

From a consumer standpoint, finance is plagued today with a major image problem: as far as banks are concerned, the feeling is that there is little difference between banks. Certainly their advertising differs, as do their identity codes and claims. Low-cost bank services do of course also differ from the high-end services, revealing two major segments. But within these segments, one is struck by the resemblance of conditions, rates, services, relationships, and CRM processes. All banks claim that they have a great consultant who will make a proper diagnosis of the client's portfolio and deliver great counseling, etc.

From the banks' own standpoint, this may be a good thing. All studies show that the determinant of loyalty is high satisfaction, or even delight. But they also show that people rarely quit a bank even if they are not very satisfied; in fact they tend to downgrade their expectations and believe that it probably won't be better elsewhere, as the whole sector is being plagued by problems caused by the proliferation of services. This opens an avenue for a "blue ocean" type of innovation.

Finance is in fact a relationship business. As with medicine, what creates a lot of buzz about a doctor is certainly that he or she recommended the right treatment. But it's a known fact that the patient's psychology plays a great role in its own salvation. We like to be listened to, really, deeply, as whole people, not only as portfolio holders. We like to have a personal consultant, the banker himself, almost exclusively to ourselves. This is not possible, of course, but we want to consume this myth.

Now is it really impossible? Web 3.0 is coming and that, feeling of an exclusive relationship will be soon available. We also want to have a sense that we are living a highly branded experience. All airline first classes are not the same: Singapore Airlines stands above all others.

Banks should benchmark the best airline companies. They would understand how much differentiation is possible in the experience itself, which should highly reflect the deep values and culture of that bank, not simply the wishes of targeted clients. Simply being consumer led leads to a marketing of resemblance. Banks should also be brand-experience led. ☐

Jean-Noël Kapferer is Professor of Marketing at the HEC School of Management in Paris.

Cell Phones Combined with The Internet: the Promise of Anytime, Anywhere

Along with the Internet, mobile communication offers the promise of anytime, anywhere. The effects of technology cannot always be predicted by their inventors or developers. Cell phones are a good example of that. Originally designed as a "phone," the cell phone is now used to take photographes, play video games, and check email. Many things we now do on our PCs – researching products or finding shops – will be done on the cell phone.

Generation Y people already use their cell phones to buy music and videos, post photos to social networking sites, access location-based services, send peer-to-peer payments, and access e-commerce offerings. With the increasing availability of high-bandwidth, mobile web access, and a new generation of mobile devices such as the iPhone, the fast-following baby-boomers may soon use their cell phones for buying gifts for the grandchildren, and not just for talking to them.

The financial branch is tremendously influenced by the cell phone – Internet integration. Cell-phone banking has been possible for some years in the industrialized world, but is still restricted to viewing ones account balance and making transfers. Now we're simply waiting for a low-threshold way to introduce a mobile version of the digital wallet. The GSM Association started an international trial last year with Master-Card and Visa, and telecommunication providers are conducting trials with banks.

Some of these trials are very simple. The Japanese Internet bank eBank introduced MailMoney. With this email money-transfer service (the first in Japan), money can be transferred by simply specifying the recipient's name and email address, even if his or her bank or account number is unknown. Transactions can be made around the clock, using email addresses from a cell phone or PC. An account can be applied for 24/7, simply by filling in a form from a PC or cell phone. The application is completed by sending a fax to eBank or a copy of some personal ID, which can be a driver's license or even a photo sent by a mobile – it's that easy.

Graham Tocher, responsible for TNS Finance Asia Pacific, Latin America, Middle East and Africa, and for TNS' global Mobile Payment capabilities, tells us from Singapore: "We've seen a lot of countries embarking on pilots and trials with mobile payments during the last couple of years, ranging from the US, and the UK, to the Middle East, Africa, and several APAC

The Future of Finance

countries. Although the number of countries involved in some level of mobile-payment development is considerable, our annual TNS Global Technology Index survey shows that there is still limited take-up and usage of mobile payments, apart from countries like Japan and Korea (16% and 8% of cell phone users respectively). This is considerably higher than the global average of 3%, with Western developed markets like the US and most European markets sitting at low levels of scoring (0% to 2%).

"Overall, we see that awareness of mobile payments remains very low in most developed markets: ranging from 39% in Italy, 41% in the US to 52% in the UK, whereas in frontrunner markets like Japan and Korea, awareness is at the high 80% level."

When asked about the future of mobile payments, Graham Tocher says: "In our global research we do see that while current awareness and usage levels are underdeveloped, consumers still show a considerable level of interest in the idea of using their cell phone to make payments. On a global level, 25% of current non-users are very or quite interested in using their cell phone to make payments, with Developed Asia being the frontrunner at 40%, regions like Africa, the Middle East, and China at the 30% interest level, and European countries and the US at a lower level ranging from 10% to just under 20%. So consumer interest for mobile payments is definitely there, and we believe is destined to be the next breakthrough in retail banking channels. What we see as a key barrier to take-up, apart from sufficient merchants accepting mobile payments and universal standards, is security: consumers still have to be convinced that their financial data will remain safe. Once these reassurances are in place, along with a suitably prevalent distribution network, the challenge then will be to stimulate behavioral change – but we don't see this as being too huge a task – and the necessary patience to allow this to build towards mass adoption."

Ravi Sankaranarayanan adds: "People underestimate the pace in which emerging markets in central and eastern Europe and the Middle East embrace new technology and adapt new ways of banking in a matter of years, leapfrogging so-called developed markets in, for instance, western Europe, where there is a legacy in both the behavior from clients and the banks that service them, which make changes more difficult."

M-banking for The Underbanked and Unbanked

To introduce Megatrend 3 and its technological developments, we talked about what drives the penetration of online financial services – and why penetration is highest in the rich Western world. Now we will look at the enormously equalizing effect of mobile banking.

Cell phone banking has been in common use in developed countries for some years now. However, the real potential of "m-banking" may be to make basic financial services more accessible to the world's millions of "underbanked" people.

These are consumers who have no more than one transaction account in a traditional financial institution (a bank or credit union). Many of these consumers rely on alternative providers, such as check-cashers and payday lenders, for some or all of their financial transactions. Underbanked consumers are not only found in developing countries, but also in industrialized countries. Though estimates vary, they clearly represent a significant portion of the population in the US – as many as 40 million households.

At least half of the underbanked have some kind of transaction account; but they lack deeper asset-building and credit relations with financial institutions. Despite their weak links to banks, they constitute a substantial market for financial services, spending at least $13 billion a year on more than 340 million non-bank transactions alone.

Research suggests that the underbanked in the USA tend to be younger and less educated, with lower incomes than the general population. Non-white families are four times more likely to lack a bank account than white families.

Notably, the fastest growing demographic segment in the United States is also profoundly underserved: 35% of all Latin American and 53% of Mexican immigrants do not have bank accounts. But despite their limited use of traditional financial institutions, underbanked people exhibit a strong desire to save and invest their money. New technologies, such as mobile financial services, may help financial institutions serve the underbanked in ways that are profitable for both companies and customers.

Developing Countries in the Lead

In 2007 the cell phone became the first communications technology to have more users in developing countries than in the industrialized world. According to the GSM Association, more than 800 million cell phones were sold in developing countries between January 2003 and December 2006.

On the other hand, traditional banking is very poorly developed in these countries. Compared with the industrialized world, the majority of this population is not just underbanked, it's unbanked. On a continent like Africa, there are great barriers to banking services. These include the high cost of opening an account, the very limited number of bank branches and services, and the remarkably bureaucratic need to verify identity on a continent where identity documents aren't always available.

With m-banking, there are not only advantages for the people in developing countries, but the banks also win. Since m-banking transactions cost far less to process than transactions at a cash dispenser or automated teller machine (ATM), or at an office, banks can make a profit handling even small money transfers and payments.

In Kenya, with a population of about 37 million, there are only 3 million bank accounts. But their local mobile banking system, called M-Pesa, is already used by 1 million Kenyans.

In South Africa, approximately 35% of the country's 16 million residents without bank accounts are estimated to own cell phones. Mobile financial services technology has proven a particularly promising way to reach residents of rural townships with few traditional financial institutions, and an unmet demand for financial services. The South African company Wizzit allows users to conduct phone-to-phone payments, pay bills, and buy airtime (phone- or text-message credits) using SMS technology. A method regularly used south of the Sahara in Africa, is to pay someone in airtime for his or her cell phone, by sending the code from scratch cards by textmessage (SMS).

SMART Communications, a company providing wireless services to 15.4 million subscribers, created a nationwide network of retailers in the Philippines, through which customers can load airtime directly onto their phones, without using scratch cards. With this infrastructure in place, customers can more easily load and withdraw cash from their mobile wallet accounts. SMART has since leveraged its market share to convince merchants and utility companies to accept m-payments from its phones. SMART's bank partner, Banco de Oro (BDO), holds all the cash that passes through the network and takes full responsibility for compliance and account protection.

So players from outside the financial industry are seeing possibilities. Approximately 175 million people in South America don't have a bank account. Nevertheless, 70% have a cell phone. In the very near future, Telefónica, the Spanish telecoms multinational, will launch a mobile banking concept in cooperation with Inter-American Development Bank (IADB). IADB is the largest of the regional development banks, and was founded to stimulate economical and social development. Speaking of possibilities, nearly half of the adult population in eastern Europe doesn't have a bank account either.

New Forms of Cashless Payment

Cashless payments can be made in many ways. The most common is to load credit onto a smartcard. There are two basic types of smartcard: those with or without contact. Contact cards require physical contact with a card reader; they are often sucked into a reader and then ejected when the read or write operation is complete. Contactless cards have hidden chips and aerials, which can be read when placed close to a reader. They, too, offer very efficient processes, and their readers suffer fewer mechanical failures. But contactless cards are more expensive and have problems of their own. Often cardholders don't hold the card close enough to the reader long enough for the transaction to complete.

As we've already seen, cashless payments are also possible via cell phone, as seen in Africa. As well as cashless payments via cards, in the future there will be biometric methods for paying your bills. Already, experiments are being carried out with payment by fingerprint, although many experts think this method of paying is unsafe. Other biometric identification methods, such as the iris scan, are safer as far as cashless payment is concerned.

> identity matched
> access granted

PayPal and Google Checkout

Payment systems such as PayPal and Google Checkout are somewhat special cases. Officially they are not banks, which means they don't have to comply with strict banking requirements. You could call them "non-bank banks." With PayPal you can make a payment using the email address of the receiver. However, you do need an external credit card or banking account. Generally, PayPal is also free for international payments. The person who receives the money, however, does pay a fee when he or she transfers the money to their own bank account.

Companies like PayPal and Google actually created a financial "loop." With the proximity of a banking portal, they developed a portable payment module that the customer can use anywhere with access to the

Internet. PayPal actually uses the "borrowed authority" from banks. PayPal bought eBay when they noticed that half of all payments were made with their system. In mid-2008 the company had more than 500 million users, and that number will grow quickly in the near future.

Although PayPal is officially not a bank, the company has applied for and received a banking license in Luxembourg. Anticipating future developments, Google has also applied for a banking license for their Google Checkout. Although Google claims in the public media that they have no intention of becoming a bank, it may well be that later on – maybe through iGoogle – they will offer all kinds of tailor-made financial products. They may also start offering other kinds of services. PayPal, for example, offers its customers "WordPress," a web application that lets you create your own blog. When WordPress becomes integrated with PayPal, you will be able to offer products and services on your blog, which can then be paid for through PayPal.

In the future, PayPal will probably offer many other plug-ins that you can then use to offer more financial services to your own community – beyond mere payments for a T-shirt or some advice. Imagine the creation of a piggy bank, mutual insurances, collective investments in sustainable enterprises, and examples such as SmartyPig (for collective savings). Technology makes all kinds of creative opportunities possible.

Goodbye Cash Money, Hello Contact-Free Payments

Whoever thinks he or she still needs cash money in the future is mistaken. A credit card, a cell phone, or any other object that can hold a chip with an antenna will do. Over the last decades, the credit card has become widely accepted as a means of payment. The advantages are obvious: credit cards are fast, easy, and reliable, whether at home, abroad, or on the Internet. Moreover, purchases are usually insured if payed by credit card. A basic need of a consumer is control: consumers want to determine and control the purchases they make. Where a means of payment is concerned, the perception of security and reliability is also essential. And of course, it has to be cheap, fast, and accepted anywhere. The latest developments in the field of payments are, evidently,

taking this into account. Thanks to innovation, payments and cash withdrawals will become ever faster and more secure in the future.

One of these innovations is EMV: a platform for contact-free payments devised by europay, MasterCard and Visa, which increases the speed, and – more important – the security of payments. With the latest EMV card it is possible to make a payment by merely holding it in front of a terminal. In the London Underground, this new method of payment (Oystercards) has proven itself very successful in a matter of only months. Another innovation in payments is via the cell phone. This form of payment is enabled by NFC (Near Field Communication) technology. You simply move your phone across a scanner, the NFC chip inside is recognized and the payment made. Contact-free paying will become much more accessible through new standards and technologies.

Because the technological and financial hurdles of mobile Internet are becoming lower all the time, the number of people using mobile Internet will increase, also causing the number of mobile shoppers and mobile payments to increase substantially. The introduction of the Single European Payment Area (SEPA) also helps. SEPA is working on standardization of payment systems and products, in order to ceate a single European payment area. As numbers of mobile Internet users – of whom over 30% are interested in mobile shopping and improved accessibility of mobile payments – rise, webstores may well consider the implications of the mobile channel for their industry. Without a doubt it it is only a matter of time before a large proportion of consumers is won over by contact-free payment. At the moment, 63% of Europeans still pay with cash money and only 37% with their bank cards. These percentages are expected to be precisely the other way round by the year 2020. Contact-free payment is the future.

Michiel Wielhouwer is Country Manager for Visa Europe and Arie van Dusseldorp is Marketing Director of LaSer Nederland.

Realizing Engaging Customer Experiences through a Creative Industry

A Shift of Power

Technological development can't be stopped – even if we would like to try. Moreover, the pace at which the rules are changing is picking up. Power to the people? "You ain't seen nothing yet!" New financial concepts invented by playerswho are not traditionally part of the industry? Prepare to see a whole lot more of that. New paths of purchase? We will have to chase our consumers even faster, and then we will still have a tough time keeping up with them.

Every prediction we make on this subject will be caught up by reality, probably even before this book even goes into its next print. This is simply a fact of the Internet age. What we are able to envisage is how the powers will shift even further. And that will already be dramatic enough.

Everything Remote, No More Middlemen (Disintermediation)

Technology will be so integrated into daily life in the future that the perceived difference in quality between physical and digital functions will disappear. Digital arenas will even become more trusted and easier to use; they will seem "closer" and more immediate. In the future, banks may only exist online. And the term "online" falls away as an abstraction, because online and "real life" become one.

All services of banks, insurers, and pension funds will be available remotely through the successor of what is currently known as the Internet. Bank offices and insurance agents as we now know them will have all but disappeared. Which is fine, as they are no longer needed. The person (or hologram) I see on my screen will be virtually sitting at my table.

With the virtualization of financial experts, customers will demand personal contact only if and when they don't trust the service, or need help getting through the bureaucratic jungle. If that jungle doesn't exist, there's no need for personal contact. If a consumer would still like someone come to his aid, however, he will have to pay for it, as that visit apparently has "real value."

Our mindset is still to think hard about how to add value to physical branches, to the bricks. This will change in when we begin to ask what issues are we really not be able to solve remotely, and where does our physical presence still add value?

Distribution will be completely driven by technology, and the entire distribution chain will be reorganized. What we've seen with the Internet in recent years will repeat itself, only in an even more dramatic way. And if insurers try to maintain the current imperfections for too long, they may well find themselves confronted with a re-insurer who will try to skip links in the chain.

In this section we have explored new paths of purchase. Who could foresee five years ago that consumers would orient themselves and purchase products the way they do now – and who would dare to predict what things will look like five years from now?

One thing we do know is that the paths of purchase will continue to change, due to many new functions and enterprises that for now only exist in the imagination of Internet entrepreneurs. We also know that an ever greater portion of that path will shift online.

Robert Hovenier of Fortis Intertrust Switzerland puts this in perspective for private wealth services: "Depending on the type of financial services, for the high-end level of these services, clients still would like to look their banker in the eyes when starting a professional relationship. Only after that is the client prepared to benefit from their virtual services. Again, various compliance-driven regulations require that you have met the client in person before entering into a professional relationship."

The Chinese insurer New China Life (NCL) demonstrates that remote sales are also possible for products that are complex or require advice. Their Bejing branch is fully equipped for selling even the most advice-sensitive life insurance by telephone. At NCL, telesales has a higher status than personal sales; employees must have at least a year's experience as a sales rep, before they are allowed on the telesales team. Also, the salary is considerably higher. A conversation with a client lasting an hour and a half is not unusual.

From Bank Branch to Experience Shop

Some physical presence will remain, but your future bank branch will look more like a Starbucks, where you can also take care of some financial business, than today's bank branch. It will offer more of a "lifestyle experience" than personal service. Like the high-end shops on Fifth Avenue in New York or Via Montenapoleone in Milan, the main purpose of each "store" will be to tell the story of the company, to emanate the brand. Their focus will be on the company and not so much on concrete customer service. This applies not only to banks, but also to insurance companies and pension funds.

To remain relevant and recognizable, financial service providers must visualize their business. (Think about the Umpqua Bank and Q110 of the Deutsche Bank, which we talked about earlier.) With the brick buildings going out the virtual door, so will some costs. But experience tells us that we shouldn't overestimate this.

On our way to this future, we envisage bank branches and insurance agents maintaining their roles for those people without access to technology and those who don't fancy such frills. This also goes for those with questions that have proved impossible to answer remotely, and, of course, for those in countries where progress isn't so fast-paced.

The Future is Now

The future is no mystery. It will bring the same dramatic changes we've seen in recent years, only faster. It's here already in the use of technology, increased competition, new consumer behaviors and needs. For many, these aren't opportunities to embrace and rise to, but unknown challenges to be feared and ignored.

The question now and in the future remains a simple one. How will you and your company stay relevant? Why will people choose your financial institution over another – or instead of their favorite retailer-now-banker? These questions are urgent now and will remain so. As technology advances, how will your company use it not just to improve speed but to enhance your company's essential relevance and purpose? As consumer behaviors change, how will your company's delivery systems respond to

The Future of Finance

surprise and delight your customers? Every institution will have different answers, of course. But each must address a few specific areas if they are to be successful in the long-term.

The first is your company's culture. It is your organization's distinct purpose and personality and, if successful, it is the reason your employees get up and come in to give their best not once a week but every day. It can differentiate your company from the competition in profound and practical ways: improving morale, productivity, customer service and product innovation. But you must care for it constantly, and charge your team with considering every day how to strengthen it, protect it, evaluate it and perpetuate it.

The second is the experience your customers have whenever they interact with your company, whether in your branch, through an ad, or on the Internet. Does the experience exceed your customers' expectations? Or does it reinforce the negative perception many consumers already have of our industry? This is critical for all companies but particularly for banks. As competition increases outside the industry, including from retailers adept at connecting with consumers, financial organizations must view the delivery of products and services not as transactions but as opportunities to connect with and engage their customers. To transform going to the bank from an errand into a lifestyle choice.

Delivery systems are the third critical piece to the future of financial institutions. Our industry must embrace innovation and technology as successful retail and entertainment organizations do – not as something to be feared and ignored but as a new channel to connect with, engage and delight their customers. Will mobile banking replace branches and online banking? That's not likely to happen any time soon. Is it a powerful

opportunity to provide customers with convenience? Absolutely. And it's more than that – if you've made your company culture and customer experience top priorities, you can use this new delivery channel to connect with and know your customers more intimately, making your company indispensable in the process.

Address these three areas and your company will be well-positioned now – and well into the future. It's time to stop relying on how things have always been done and start imagining how they can be done.

Ray Davis is CEO of Umpqua Bank.

Re-Intermediation

The opposite of disintermediation is "re-intermediation": the return of the middleman – but in a completely different form. The previously mentioned "comparison sites" are an example of this role. Gradually

they became essential in selecting the best offers and best transparency. From there, it's not very difficult to take the next step to paid advice. The successors of comparison sites will enable us to compare all products, without doing these comparisons ourselves. We can leave that to a robot. The robot will search the web for the best offers from trusted parties – and not only that, it will immediately act if it sees ways for our money to do better. When there is no more fear of technology, this is possible.

By the way, this is not science fiction. Similar robot technology is being used all over the Internet by comparison sites to fill out their price tables. With PriseWize you can subscribe to a so-called contract manager that keeps track of the expiry dates of your energy contract, home-owners insurance, and so on. It will then show you better offers and even cancel your old contracts if necessary.

Many peer-2-peer networks, online social networks, and entities like Google and Morningstar have strong ties with their members. We can expect consumer organizations and knowledgeable bloggers, for example, to become new intermediaries, or links in the chain – each with its own angle. The insurance agents of today hardly seem to realize that they have all the necessary weapons at their disposal to claim a new role. Like no other, they have insight into the service performance of the insurers. If the thousands of insurance agents that all countries have aggregate this knowledge and could make it available to consumers in a comparison site, they would have, at one stroke, reclaimed the front door to the purchasing process from the comparison sites which, almost without exception, only compare price and product features.

A countermovement is returning to us an improved version of the familiar advisor. Because of the enormous amount of available information, it will be crucial for most people to have a neutral, reliable information broker. If they're not comfortable in the digital arena, then advisor reliability will be even more important, especially in the financial world.

People who work hard or spend a lot of time abroad have other things to do than arrange their financial affairs. That is why private bank Insinger de Beaufort developed "Shoe Box." Shoe Box provides you with a private "office" and financial experts at your disposal. The principle is simple: you collect all your receipts, invoices, and so on, in the shoe box. Once a month, they're collected and Insinger de Beaufort then arranges all your financial affairs, working closely with your financial advisor and your civil-law notary. So all the manual work – the administration and management of accounts at various banks – is left to Insinger de Beaufort. The Shoe Box service is not cheap. Including financial planning, it costs €815 a month for three years, and is available for existing Insinger de Beaufort clients as well as people who bank elsewhere. The proposition is clear: no more hassle with financial affairs, thanks to complete outsourcing.

The benefits to Insinger de Beaufort are better insight into a wealthy consumer segment, better insight into the overall financial position of customers, and new leads for private banking when non-clients apply for the Shoe Box service.

Bob Neuhaus, EVP of TNS North America, says "In these uncertain times, affluent investors may be seeking more advice. Advisor usage in the US, which took a big hit after the Internet bust and 9/11, has been climbing steadily over the past five years. This year, 71% of the affluent use a professional as their primary investment advisor, up from a low of 57% in 2004. Should these percentages hold over the next year or two, financial institutions will be in an excellent position to further strengthen their relationships with their affluent clients. In fact, of the

71% of affluent that use a professional as their primary advisor, more than half (58%) indicate they turn to the same company for advice and asset management. And the strength of this relationship seems to be holding steady: 79% of the affluent who use a professional advisor as their primary advisor indicated that they will continue to use them at least at the same level as up to now, with only 5% indicating they will drop or replace an advisor over the next year."

Neuhaus continues: "The biggest opportunity may be to target those affluent not currently using an advisor. But providers wishing to tap into this group may have some rather large obstacles to overcome. Self-confidence and trust are chief among the reasons, affluent investors cite for not seeking professional advice; 40% say they feel they 'do better managing their own investments than using a professional' and 29% say they 'do not trust advisors to act in their best interests'. One quarter say the 'wealth of information available makes a professional advisor unnecessary.'"

Transparency, Authenticity, and Simplicity

In the financial world, transparency, authenticity, and simplicity will form a trinity. With the demand for transparency, financial service providers will have to formulate their answers simply. Transparency and simplicity are a must if the branch is going to become truly authentic or "real" – in the sense of being truly and recognizably relevant.

I want to know exactly how the bank calculates the interest it charges me. I want to understand each factor that determines my car insurance premium. I want to know what ends up where – and who exactly is managing my funds. What is the vision and track record of this service provider?

The Egg Money Manager we saw earlier and the Japanese eBank are good examples of the importance of simplicity. Another example is the Virgin One Account, which combines mortgages and savings. All savings are automatically used to reduce the mortgage – reducing the duration of the mortgage and the amount of interest paid. A simple tool enables the consumer to see how much the mortgage can go down.

The Paperless Mortgage from First Houston Mortgages is another example of simplicity. All administrative matters, such as the signing and review of documents, are handled electronically. This reduces costs, accelerates the service, and makes the entire process easier for the consumer.

Christof Göldi, CEO of Delta Lloyd Germany, tells us: "As a consequence of a new law in Germany, insurers are obliged to ask their clients about their health in great detail if they, for example want to buy insurance against disability. Often, it's difficult to get the right information. We are the first insurer in Germany to have an underwriter with a medical background call the customer directly and personally go through the questionnaire with the client. That saves both the client and us a substantial amount of time, so it simplifies the process for everyone."

These are some forerunners of service simplicity. Why, you might ask, wouldn't every financial service provider want the same level of simplicity? When getting car insurance, do you really need more than a license plate number and personal identification? Behind these two means of identification there is a world of data already known: the specifications of the car, damages from the past, whether the car is well maintained, even the most driven routes, their proneness to damage, and if the driver in question has been a good boy or girl in the past could be distilled from those two data. This is more than enough to provide a fully customized insurance policy – and no need for any more forms. We can't wait for the new e-dentity! But to be honest, we are doubtful if financial service providers will actually use this tool to make our lives easier, and not just as yet another additional security check for themselves.

Simplicity is becoming the guiding light for customers: not only simplicity of product design, but also pricing, touch points, marketing, the entire delivery process. This means an end to products we don't immediately understand; an end to the insane range of products that are impossible to choose from. It spells the end of so-called "clever" contracts that don't reveal their consequences – so that before you know it, you may have to sell your house. It is the end of complicated pricing tables, the end of useless forms, the end of websites that sends you on a one-way trip into outer cyberspace, the end of FAQs lists, which, again, don't include your particular question – and the end of the bureaucratic jungle that none of us likes!

This doesn't mean that the challenge of financial service providers will also become simple. Piet Verbrugge, Chairman of the Board of Delta Lloyd Bank Belgium, says: "Simplicity is the core of our strategy. Our goal is: simplicity in products, simplicity in advice and simplicity in company structure. I was educated a mathematician, that's what made me realize the importance of simplicity. Explaining mathematics to non-mathematicians is only possible if you are able to do that in a simple manner. Simple is not the same as uncomplicated. To be able to explain anything in a simple manner, you really need to know your stuff."

The Future Is EaZy

Convenience and simplicity are key consumer trends – and the call for transparency is loud and clear. This made us at Zurich Financial Services decide that we should focus on making life as easy as possible for our consumers as well as our partners.

In 2006 we decided to introduce EaZy in Zurich Global Life. Not as another project, but as a way of life. We have formalized EaZy in our organization by promoting the concept of "easiness" to a leading principle for products, sales, services, communication, etc. "EaZy" best practices have been collected worldwide and serve as inspiration for the organization. To make EaZy a way of life, in each country "EaZy Challengers" have been appointed: employees assigned to continuously explore opportunities to introduce and implement the concept into all aspects of the business, and consequently measure and monitor the predefined results.

By making things EaZy, we improved our customer and distributor satisfaction and decreased our time to market and cost levels. The result: a steep increase in sales and profitability. Some examples are:

- We replaced technical product brochures by "sales stories": clients telling their real-life experiences and explaining in a very down-to-earth manner why they needed life insurance. With success the stories stick. The result is a 7% sales increase.
- Reducing the number of application forms from eighteen to four and application questions by 50% significantly decreased the number of "drop-outs" during the application process.
- We installed a save desk that called canceling customers. One third of them could be saved just making an effort to communicate with them.

- Replacing a technical confirmation letter about their upcoming maturity to an easy-to-read letter that included a fitting reinvestment offer tripled the reinvestment rate to 38%.

Simplified, easy products do not diminish the added value of the agent and the broker. If products and processes are easier, the agent has more time to add value: to address and assess the real needs of a client. This is an essential step to building a relationship rather than doing a transaction. Our clear and tangible results speak for themselves – and the numbers in terms of additional sales and profit even more. Proven success boosts this way of thinking. It is, however, not easy to be EaZy. It requires time, has technological implications and must become a way of life. That is not simple to achieve.

Everybody in our organization needs to ask him or herself on a continuous basis: "Can I make this easier?" – from call agent to administrative staff, from manager to receptionist.

The EaZy way of thinking is what makes Zurich Global Life unique. EaZy is embedded in our make-up and is therefore difficult to replicate. EaZy is not "for sale." For Zurich Global Life, it will be one of the most important and sustainable growth drivers of our future. ☐

Paul van de Geijn is a Member of the Group Executive Committee of Zurich Financial Services.

Competing on Service Level

When all products and services are completely transparent, you will know exactly what you're getting, and you will be able to compare the competition before you buy. Simplicity and convenience will become the hallmarks not only of financial products, but also of the purchasing process. Service is increasingly the most important distinguishing factor for any bank or insurance company. In the same way Tripadvisor compares hotels, comparison sites will soon be looking not just at prices, but also service. As soon as consumers have more insight into the quality of service, prices will become less important.

Imagine that the current comparison sites for car insurance expanded their range of hard facts: the percentage of claims paid in full; the number of phone calls needed on average to get a claim paid; the time it takes for a decision to be made, and to receive the money in your account; the number of satisfied customers; and the number of legal disputes. When this kind of data is included on comparison sites, the set of purchase criteria will change. The future of finance is service!

This trend will be enhanced by the declining impact of the "weapons of mass marketing." The power of advertising will decline, media will become more fragmented, and consumers will watch less TV. The marketing messages delivered through these media are bound to lose much of their punch.

Walter Capellmann, founding partner of Capellmann Consulting in Düsseldorf, and an advisor of multinational financial service providers both inside and outside of Germany, stresses that it is important to use the right definition of service: "Reducing service to pure customer service means to miss some essential moments of truth. To make a difference in the market, the integration of services in every step of the contact chain will be increasingly important."

"The distinguishing factor of any service won't just be the technical excellence (such as availability, speed, or competence) – it will be the relevancy of the services. In times of literally ubiquitous information relevancy very often means 'simplicity'."

"Creating this kind of simplicity for the customer will very likely be a challenging and ambitious task in an environment that is highly dependent on complex administration systems and IT-driven processes on the product side. But those companies who understand 'service' as a way to make their offers and products easily understandable and relevant in the eyes of the customer will set new standards for success – especially in complex world of financial services."

Moments of Truth

Service moments are moments of truth. This will be even more the case in a future of increased transparency. The case of Progressive insurrance (pages 173-174) shows how you might score as an entrepreneur. In moments of truth a financial service provider – generally seen as a low-involvement category – can engage a customer, make a lasting impression, and create a real ambassador to pass along your story. This is customer advocacy in the most literal sense of the word. The financial services sector used to revolve around administrative organization. Now it is developing into a creative industry.

Scott Osman, Managing Director of Brand Experience at Hachette Filipacchi in New York, foresees the superlative of experience: "There is a shift in the way consumers perceive their participation with the brands they buy. In the coming years, they are looking for something deeper, for shared values. Slowly, but accelerating rapidly, purchase decisions are being made by the quality and ethics of a company, not just by the products and services they provide. We can observe this in the amount of cause-related marketing and the application of cause on packaging in order to influence purchase intent. But this is just the beginning of a sea of change." More on this with megatrend 4!

Businesses and Banks: Working Closer Together than Ever Before

The future for both the business and the banking world will be dominated by digitalization. Paying via your cell phone in the store is already a reality. Tests on eye and fingerprint scans as a method of payment are currently being carried out. Between 2010 and 2015 we will be considering these methods as normal.

The impact of digitalization goes much further. Businesses will determine for themselves when and how they contact the bank – via the Internet, email, chatting, Skype, phone or dropping by. And that includes all products and services: increasing credit limits, taking out insurance, authorizing fingerprints in order to use the online accounting program, or a letter of credit for an import from China or India. For each client, products and services must be accessible, understandable, and able to be arranged via all channels. Company computer systems will communicate on a one-to-one basis with the banks, which is both easier and cheaper.

The customer will occupy center stage at last – and rightly so. Websites that sell books give us a taste of what's in store. They inform us of the status of the order: whether it's in stock, with customs, being shipped, or at the post office. Soon, this is not just how it will happen with an order for a bank card, but also with your company's credit. Is the account manager ready with his report? Is the application included on the agenda of the credit evaluation committee? Who does what and when will be immediately visible. Websites with price comparison services will force banks to define even more clearly their price-quality-service ratio. The quality of service is under constant vigilance through reviews and comments on virtual communities, and businesses help each other to keep banks alert. The banks will have to try even harder to please their clients.

Digitalization has made frontiers irrelevant. This is reinforced by further internationalization. Trade barriers are declining and foreign markets are becoming more accessible. These trends are continuing. Within a few years, throughout the whole of the EU, there will no longer be any difference between domestic and foreign payment transactions and bank account numbers and bank cards will function in all European Union countries. Business conducted by companies and banks will become more international.

It appears, however, that people themselves do not change through internationalization. They still retain their naturally strong attachment to their immediate surroundings. This also applies to entrepreneurs and businesses; they have a more international orientation and yet keep a local office. You can remain at the same location in the Netherlands and still conduct business in all corners of the world. The same applies to banks – operating internationally from a local branch.

There are more things that will remain the same. Even though at the start of the millennium some forecasters thought otherwise, economical cycles will always remain. The fact that taking more risks will ultimately result in more profit remains the same. And however communication capabilities develop in the future and however differently we will experience the world, the core of the banking business will remain. In the present lies the past, and in the present what will come. About one hundred years ago, the Raiffeisen-Boerenleenbank in the Netherlands was in a position to finance businesses in the agricultural sector and in SMEs far more competitively than the regular commercial banks. This was not just because of the nature of these cooperative banks, which were striving not to maximize profit but to maintain continuity. The main reasons were that they had much better information available to them to be able to advise their clients and calculate the risks they were taking with them. Through their local involvement, they were familiar with the business and the markets, and they knew exactly where the risks were. The basis for this was trust. They had the courage to back their customers when some of the commercial banks were afraid to.

A hundred years ago, now, and in a hundred years' time, banking is about commitment, knowing and understanding each other, and thereby trusting each other. In a future where there is an abundance of information, it will not automatically become easier. Of course, there will be systems to help assess creditworthiness. Customer support is really not a question of "positive standard credit-scoring by the computer." Being able to recognize and acknowledge entrepreneurship remains vital. For this you need to build up a relationship and look each other in the eye from time to time. The bank that knows how to combine these fantastic new communication capabilities with this intrinsic value has the future in its hands – and also its client. In the future, banks and businesses will work closer together than ever before.

Joop Wijn, is Director SME, Rabobank in the Netherlands. He was formerly Minister of Economic Affairs in the Netherlands.

Megatrend 4

A Revival of Ethics, an Emphasis on Health and Happiness, and New Missions for Financial Services

April 2, 2028

It's early Monday morning. Jim and Clark log in for a virtual meeting with the other members of their team, who are up and about in locations around the world. Everybody logs in through the virtual meeting system.

While just sitting at home at their dinner table, suddenly through three-dimensional projection, 3D images of their colleagues appear around the table. Some are still sleepy due to the time difference, but they're there at their computer, dressed up in a suit and tie anyway. They can look each other in the eye, as if they were physically sitting together, even though they are all in their own homes. No one really has to travel to meet for work anymore. Virtual meetings arose as a way to use less energy, decrease pollution, and prevent global warming – a trend that emerged at the beginning of the century.

So Jim and Clark exchange views and ideas for about an hour. Decisions are made for the company for the coming week. Then everybody says goodbye, logs off, and tackles their part of the job. Jim remembers a time when you had to actually physically meet all your colleagues. Unimaginable now, but people voluntarily traveled for hours, enduring traffic jams, delayed airplanes, full trains, and other inconveniences, just to go to work. Now all that has changed. The low-energy economy of the 2020s stimulates people to travel less. If they do travel, they use cars that are no longer fueled by oil or gas. And although occasionally they miss the sound and powerful feeling of the good old gas guzzlers their parents used to drive, they enjoy their new cars. Jim's dad even had an SUV, imagine that! Solar energy in particular enables people and companies in their areas of Europe to live a more secure and peaceful life than ever before. They are not really putting a stop to global warming, but nevertheless their new lifestyle makes them feel good. Thank goodness they are no longer so dependent on all sorts of volatile governments for supplying them with energy, maybe even financing terrorism in the process.

Then Jim's VirtualMe pops up with a message: they have an invitation for this year's Oil Baron's ball in the Emirates! Although its name is now a complete anachronism, it is still the ultimate place to be seen for the successful young professional. And why shouldn't they go? They might even win this year's Ewing Award for the Happiest Person category. But then Jim's VirtualMe calculates that theirs will be a virtual presence this year, as they don't have enough CO_2 rights in the bank. Well, maybe that's for the best: no physical traveling gives Jim a chance to spend time with his daughter as well as being the soul of the party.

Globalization and technological progress lead to increased prosperity and well-being. They also create new challenges and moral choices for the world – and for demographic developments like the aging population. In this chapter we focus on the developments that touch on ethics, food shortages, challenges like global warming, and the consequences of medical advances, as well as the revival of religion and spirituality.

A Call to Ethics

In this new era, when there are not only global possibilities but also threats coming from every corner – German sociologist Ulrich Beck talks about the "risk society" – we hear a worldwide call for more ethics.

With increasing globalization, there is a danger that people with evil intentions can divert to places on this earth where laws or their enforcement are lacking. Think, for example, of the dumping of toxic waste, the expired medications in Africa, and child labor in South Asia. The development of new technologies brings new and different ethical issues, for example with stem-cell research. If we don't solve these problems, we will wind up with an immoral kind of Wild West – hurting everyone in the end. But which authority can or wants to take on such a heavy moral task?

The Economic Impact of Climate Change

Climate change will change the face of the twenty-first century world. Worldwide, there is a growing awareness of the serious impact human behavior has had on the climate. And there is not only the problem of a changing climate, but also the problem of an eventual depletion of important raw materials and sources of energy, especially oil and gas.

While public opinion in the industrialized world is convinced of the necessity of taking painful measures, in developing economies the initial emphasis is on economical growth. But even there, people will be confronted by serious environmental pollution and natural disasters, and will soon realize that we can't continue on this same path.

Not only will consumers gain more environmental awareness, and adjust their buying behavior accordingly, but governments will also take action. Internationally as well as nationally, environmental goals will be established and regulations will be adjusted. Environmental tax will be a recurring issue in the coming years. For some industries, this means difficult times ahead. Automobile and aviation industries will need to invest heavily in clean technology, if they want to survive.

At the same time, this changed perception of the environment and energy use will offer many opportunities. Products will need to be adapted to these new conditions, and new durable forms of energy will need to be developed. In the coming decades, many investors will be attracted to sectors such as durable energy, clean technology, waste management, and water supply. The environment and climate are important issues, and being active in this area as a company is also commercially attractive and sexy.

With so many companies advertising their environmental awareness, we are seeing the inflation of the "green" phenomenon. Companies proudly claim that they work in a "climate neutral" way. Their CO_2 emissions are compensated for by the purchase of green energy or by planting trees.

Others see new market opportunities in the areas of environmental sustainability and energy. Cars are becoming hybrid and may, in the not-too-distant future, run on hydrogen. Conscientious celebrities drive hybrids, which has helped to win over many car owners. The trade in carbon emission rights is booming.

The Growing Focus on Water

Due to climate change, some regions in the world will be confronted with a surplus of water. The warming of the earth leads to a rise in the level of sea and river waters. It seems not unlikely, therefore, that certain coastal areas will have to be evacuated in the future. It is essential to take measures – for example in the form of new embankments to hold back the sea.

In other areas, there will be shortages of fresh water. In the worst case scenario, some areas will turn into desert. Many things can be done about this. Fresh-water streams can be distilled from sea water, as already done in Israel and Dubai. It is also possible to recycle water, as is already done on modern cruise ships. On shore, too, used water from toilets, washbasins, and bathrooms can be purified and reused.

If the price of fresh water rises high enough, there will also be a large market for recycling water in the home. What's more, "fresh-water pockets" have been discovered in the seas of the world, for instance along the coast of Saudi Arabia. These are reserves of fresh water in the sea – often hundreds of meters below the surface and separate from the salt water. At the moment it is too expensive to exploit these pockets, but if fresh water becomes expensive enough, exploitation will become profitable. The Saudis are already looking into this – much to the dismay of Uruguay. With some of the largest fresh-water reserves in the world, Uruguay thought this "new gold" would bring them golden times in the twenty-first century.

The French bank Société Générale is one of the financial services companies that turned this notion into new products. It offers an alternative way to invest in water, in the form of warrants based on the World Water Index, which started to quote in February 2006.

In coming years, we will see more investment products based on the dangers and opportunities connected with water and other global challenges.

A Temporary Commodities Bubble

Right now the world is dealing with spiking oil and food prices. These price increases can partly be explained by a growing demand while supply remains the same. But the main cause is not insufficient production; it is speculation on the markets that deal in futures for food and commodities, the so-called commodities markets. The same goes for the current shortage in the food market, which is not structural. Capacity for commodity production could even be increased.

In past years – and particularly after the onset of the financial market crisis in 2007 – more institutional investors appeared on the commodities market. These include the so-called index investors, such as pension funds, university endowments, and Sovereign Wealth Funds. In the past decade, the share of "long positions" (positions that benefit when prices rise) held by financial investors has grown from one-quarter to two-thirds of the US commodity market. In only five years, from 2003 to 2008, investment in index funds tied to commodities has grown twenty-fold, from $13 billion to $260 billion. This, along with regular investors, draws in speculators: opportunistic, short-term investors looking for a fast profit.

The steep rise in the price of commodities looks like the next bubble we will have to face. The shape of the bubble is this: financial analysts repeatedly raised their price forecasts as oil prices soared, drawing in new investor flows and speculators who have pushed prices to still-higher levels, leading to still-higher price forecasts. These are the classic ingredients of an asset bubble, with financial investors driven by a herd instinct while chasing past performance.

From an ethical point of view, there has been a lot of potential criticism of speculation on commodity markets, and this will only increase. The rising prices of fuel and gas will cause many people who are already living on the poverty line to get into deep trouble. In developing countries, these rising prices will threaten the poorest populations with hunger and starvation.

Legislation to control similar commodity market speculation will be tightened in many countries. And the man in the street, with his small retirement invested in a large fund, will increasingly hold that fund accountable.

All Money is Green

From eco-ugly to eco-iconic

Until the twenty-first century, most ecologically justified products were ugly, expensive and tasted bad. Those who bought them did so because they valued the "good cause" more than the aesthetics or price advantage. But in recent decades, the green product has developed considerably.

Many green products went from eco-ugly to eco-chic – meaning ecologically justified, but with premium quality comparable to less-sustainable products. For the producer of eco-chic products and services, the sustainable characteristics were not the goal. They were just a means of putting a better-quality product on the market – because, at the end of the day, consumers are primarily interested in quality. With the new sustainability trend spreading across the world, a huge new phenomenon is developing: products and services that are "eco-iconic." Eco-iconic products and services are environmentally friendly. They express this through their design or accompanying story. Thus, the environmentally conscious consumer of such items can justify this purchase to his friends. A "new style" eco-label will elevate the status of these products, and people will happily display their environmentally conscious choices.

Trendwatching.com describes eco-iconic like this: "Eco-iconic works both in the world of traditional status symbols (build a green brand or product, advertise the hell out of it, and make it recognizable to the masses, which in turn makes it easy for buyers to gain respect from strangers), and as part of the status-stories phenomenon. This involves providing buyers of little-known eco-brands with conversation starters and story details, to get a status fix from their peers." This eco-iconic trend coincides with the increasing importance of the storytelling trend that we described in Megatrend 2.

A recent worldwide survey by TNS called Global Shades of Green, for which more than 13,000 consumers across seventeen countries were interviewed online, found that concern for the environment continues to grow worldwide, particularly in Latin America. Kimberly Bastoni, SVP of TNS Custom Marketing and Development, and in charge of the TNS Global Shades of Green survey in the US, says: "It is not just concern for the environment that is growing: worldwide, people are beginning to actually change their behavior to benefit the environment. For example, 26% of the US respondents actively seek environmental products. Active behavior still lags behind favorable disposition, though: 53% of Americans are willing to pay more for eco-friendly products, but only 26% are really taking action."

From the TNS Global Shades of Green survey, eight unique segments emerged, which were grouped into four categories:
-   Green is the right thing to do
-   Green is practical
-   Green is cool
-   Green isn't a priority

Bastoni explains: "The 'green is the right thing to do' category is the most enviromentally active group. It includes segments like Eco-Centrics: high education and high income urbanites, actively doing their part to protect and improve the environment. A segment in the 'green is cool' category is the Eco-Chic group: young adults who see being green as something hip and chic, it fits their lifestyle. For example, the 'green is cool' segment says about the Toyota Prius on various blogs, monitored by TNS Cymfony: 'The Prius has become more than just a way to save money. It is *the* cool car because it's small and understated and high-tech'."

Realizing Corporate Responsibility

The term "corporate social responsibility" (CSR) is so often used, it's almost a management fad. But even we can't get around it. Every company plays a role in society. Companies that are aware of this and – more importantly – act accordingly can be seen as socially responsible organizations. They take account of the environment, strive for better working conditions, are active in the community, and make more sustainable products.

In the past, a company simply had to be big and get its brands well known. That was proof enough of reliable products. Modern-day consumers look beyond that. They are more critical, and they are truly choosing products on the basis of what they know about companies. Whereas reliable used to translate into "large and well known," it is now synonymous with credibility, reputation, and social responsibility.

"Good examples of combining business and social objectives are the Spanish *cajas* [saving banks]," says Reggy de Feniks. "The 46 *cajas* are regionally orientated and manage more than half of the assets of Spanish families and companies. Being regionally orientated, the *cajas* invest an important part of their profits in social activities – sometimes even as much as half of their profits. These activities range from cultural initiatives to the maintenance of cultural artistic heritage and conservation of the environment. The amounts run into the billions of euros. On the list of the 50 largest philantropical institutions in Europe, La Caixa holds 3rd place, while Caja Madrid and Caixa Catalunya repectively claim 27th and 30th place.

Ethics and Employer Branding

Among other things (such as aging), Western countries will face a tight labor market in the coming years. Companies will need to put their best foot forward to attract good personnel. The workforce will need to be not only convinced by the money, but will be paying more and more attention to the company's image.

VODW research shows that it's extremely important for top talent to know that the company they work for is connected to global trends. Active policies and tangible results in the field of sustainability are of growing importance to job candidates and current employees alike. They want to work for a company that makes them proud. They want to see their own moral standards reflected in the company's policies. Then the company will appear more attractive to work for. When employees feel a sense of company pride, they tend to be more loyal and stay longer. Companies that maintain ethical standards will have less trouble finding personnel. Meanwhile, sectors that pollute (oil companies, for example) will be dealing with a serious shortage of quality personnel.

Due to the credit crunch, financial service providers don't score very high in the labor market. Also, employer brand has suffered. Still, there are exceptions. In Spain, the Banco Santander, for example, was declared the best company to work for by the magazine *Actualidad Económica*. According to José Luis Gómez Alciturri, Director of Human Resources at Banco Santander, this is predominantly due to the culture, with principles such as dynamism, innovation and ethics. In his experience younger people have changed their preferences compared with what they used to be: "Nowadays they are concerned that the company cares about the environment. That is a change in values. It would be stupid to think that they [new generations] only ask for salary and holidays. Nowadays they look for responsible companies that help them with their career and give them security."

Stimulating Ethical Investment by Legislation

Corporate responsibility will become an integral part of doing business. And those who don't do business sustainably will ultimately be forced to do so by external pressures: the media, politics – and the law.

The fact that ethical investment has grown since the beginning of the new century is due, in part, to a growing awareness of sustainability. But it is also due to the considerable influence of legislation.

In the UK, sustainable investment received a boost in 2000 when a law was passed obliging pension funds, from that moment on, to indicate which social, ethical, or environmental factors influenced their choice of investments. Thus, the UK set a new standard, which many other Western countries followed. After that, similar legislation was passed in countries such as Australia, Sweden, and Germany.

Other government measures, such as taxes on CO_2 emissions, indicate investment choices for green investors, and show that sustainability and profitability can go hand in hand.

Financial Service Providers are "Going Green"

When choosing financial service products, many clients nowadays don't just ask which party's offering is cheaper or where they get the highest return on their investment. They also ask in which assets their money will be invested.

Environmental issues are coming to the fore in the industrialized world. Financially strong baby-boomers – concerned that they're leaving their children with an uninhabitable world – will increasingly demonstrate social awareness in their banking decisions. The notion of being a guardian of the earth will become an important aspect of Western banks, pension funds, and insurance companies.

Jeremy Alwyn, of Zurich Financial Services, sees clear opportunities for general insurers in this respect: "In the future, insurers will have to consider how they repair damaged property. Policies will need to allow for best practice in terms of using local materials, recycling damaged goods, and meeting local environmental standards. This is a passive move by both commercial and retail customers to improve the environment. For insurers, however, this clear demonstration of CSR shows how non-manufacturing companies can have positive impact on the environment."

Most banks have already started green funds. Allready they can see that investors want their money to create more sustainability, not more CO_2 emissions. Some banks have completely specialized in socially responsible investments. The Triodos Bank, for example, active in the Benelux, Great Britain, and Spain, plays a significant role as an opinion leader in this arena.

Today's consumer can get much information about the environmental impact of his or her bank. In the Netherlands, the Friends of the Earth organization released a report in 2007 comparing the national banks on a "green scale." In this report you can read, for example: "The largest Dutch banks have an estimated €118 billion outstanding in investments in producers of fossil fuels. Thus they have a shared responsibility for a yearly production of 594 million tons of CO_2, more than three times as much as the total yearly emission of the Netherlands. By comparison, investments in sustainable energy are dwarfed."

Edward Monchen, a partner with ForGood and a specialist in sustainable business solutions for financial services, says: "Although banks, insurance companies, and pension funds have a much smaller carbon footprint themselves, they do have a large influence on the corporate social responsibility (CSR) policies of the companies they invest in. Their clients will ask more and more for green or sustainable products. The Dow Jones Sustainability index and other SRI indices are already a good start."

There is clearly still much room for improvement. Therefore, future comparison sites will include the environmental (un)friendliness of financial products, so consumers can make choices based on sustainability.

Edward Monchen points at Banco Real from Brazil as an example of a large bank that has taken this a level further, by elevating sustainability to their core strategy: "As a result, Banco Real won the 'Financial Times

Sustainability Award' in 2008. The bank won the prize not only because of its desire to built a better future for our planet and the people living on it, but also because it achieved a higher financial performance. A true Triple P performance. The following quote from Banco Real after they won the prize sums it all up: 'When we initiated the process of inserting sustainability into our businesses, our aim was to build a new bank for a new society, and reinforce the role of banks generally as agents for economic and social development. We began by substantially reducing the environmental impact of our activities and looking at our products and services as a means of transforming society positively. We have innovated our product portfolio with solutions such as carbon credits, and fostered local development through our microcredit lines. We now offer customized financial solutions, combining financing with advice on how to adopt environmental and social practices. We have also started to share our knowledge with clients and suppliers in a structured manner to shorten the path to be taken by companies towards sustainable goals. Even though it is difficult to objectively prove the relationship between sustainability and financial results, our results have improved year after year, and our performance has strengthened the bond with our clients and other stakeholders."

Green Financial Products

Besides the obvious investment funds, we are seeing more and more "green" financial products. Here are three good examples.

Several automobile insurers offer rebates to owners of hybrids and other energy-efficient cars. Farmers was the first US insurer to offer a hybrid vehicle discount, beginning in California in 2005. The thinking behind this was that hybrid drivers were more responsible, and they would therefore be more careful and claim less damage. This appears to be the case. The driving records of hybrid users are top-notch. In Canada, Kanetix insurance company has their hybrid motorists showing clean (or fairly clean) driving records: 88% never have any tickets; only 2% have two or more tickets; 90% have no at-fault accidents; and only 1% have two or more at-fault accidents. Simply put, hybrid motorists are very attractive and responsible customers.

British Cooperative Insurance offers eco-insurance for cars. This insurance is eco-friendly at no extra cost. Cooperative Insurance promises to offset 20% of your car's CO_2 emissions by investing in projects such as reforestation, renewable energy sources, and third-world education. Furthermore, cars in Tax Band A (those that emit less than 100g of CO_2 per kilometer) receive a 10% discount. And appointed mechanics are paid more by the provider than by any other in the UK, to ensure they recycle materials such as used oil and old bumpers.

Rabobank launched the so-called KlimaatHypotheek ("Climate Mortgage") for people wanting to save energy and contribute to a better environment. With this type of mortgage, the client receives a reduction on interest for that part of the mortgage used for energy-saving amenities – for example double-pane glass, roof insulation, the replacement of old heaters, or installation of solar panels. The effect of this is that clients can afford to make eco-friendly investments in their homes.

Environmentally Friendly Investments

As more and more investors take into account the environmental effects of their investments, more large institutional investors will start watching for sustainability as well. Decisions will be guided by long-term ethical and short-term prudential arguments. A higher purpose and higher profits will no longer seem so incompatible.

The rising price of oil and gas may be seen not only to cause trouble, but also provide opportunities. All eyes are now focused on the development of alternative energy sources. Some of these energy sources, such as wind and solar energy, have been around for some time. Some will need to be developed into new types of energy, such as oil from algae.

Several banks in recent years began specifically investing in renewable energy. Dexia Group, together with Rabobank, financed a large windmill park off the coast of IJmuiden in the Netherlands. In southern Spain, Banco Santander in cooperation with BP Solar is developing the largest solar thermal power plant in Europe. A characteristic of this form of energy is that it involves an inexhaustible source. There will always be wind, the sun will always wind and the sun will always shine. Both these projects are being developed by the sustainable energy company Econcern – according to KPMG, it is one of the fastest-growing companies on the planet, and is often dubbed "the Shell of the twenty-first century."

A remarkable new type of energy of great interest to the financial world renews our interest in the space program. In the 1960s, the United States and Russia had political reasons to engage in space travel. Now, the participants include the US, Russia, China, India, Japan, and Europe (ESA). They have all announced plans to journeys to the moon – this time not for the expansion of territory, but for the extraction of minerals. The great amount of Helium-3 on the moon is an ideal fuel for nuclear fusion. Nuclear fusion with Helium-3 is very appropriate in this context. It releases very little radioactivity, and its fusion process is easy to control. While this element barely exists on earth, there are millions of tons of Helium-3 in the soil of the moon, deposited by solar winds. It could be fairly easily extracted and transported back to earth under pressure as a liquid gas. A load of 25 tons of Helium-3 would be sufficient to fuel the total energy consumption on earth for ten weeks. Investment in the space program could increase explosively in the near future.

Edward Monchen of ForGood puts this in perspective: "As long as the remuneration of traders in dealing rooms is solely based on a single P (Profit) they will not be incentivized to invest in Triple P (People, Planet, Profit) stocks."

The Carbon Disclosure Project

For large investors, information concerning a company's "greenness" will increasingly become key in investment decisions.

A recognized international platform that provides such information is the Carbon Disclosure Project (CDP). This collaboration of institutional investors efficiently accesses information on corporate greenhouse gas emissions, on a global scale. When investors collectively sign a single request for data, it is sent to the companies for completion. The aims of this project are to inform investors of the risks and opportunities of climate change, and to inform the management of these companies of shareholders' serious concerns regarding the impact of green issues on company value.

So far, four CDPs have been completed. The first questionnaire, sent out in May 2002 to the Fortune 500 largest companies, was backed by 35 investors. In February 2007, a request for data on a fifth CDP was backed by 280 institutional investors – with assets under management of $41 trillion. This questionnaire was sent to over 2,400 companies. The results are freely available at www.cdproject. net/responses.

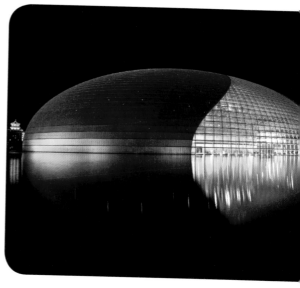

The CDP demonstrates investors' interest in accounting for carbon. Having grown from a core of dedicated SRI investors, this initiative has expanded to cover a large group of institutional investors.

In the future, carbon reporting will be the norm. But it's unlikely in the short-term, due to a lack of resources and reporting mechanisms. Investor initiative will most likely push this through more quickly than government regulatory or accountability changes.

Where Carbon Footprints Lead

The financial industry frequently uses carbon footprint analysis to translate the emotional advantages of going green into financial terms. The calculation of a company's carbon footprint, from a financial perspective, involves evaluating the percentage of carbon intensive companies in a client's portfolio.

Excessive carbon emissions translate into significant costs for companies. Advocates of a green approach in finance espouse the need for firms to analyze the cost of controlling carbon emissions, as well as the need for advisors to play their part in identifying, managing, and reporting carbon costs found in investment portfolios.

In Europe, since 2005 we have been working with a system of trading CO_2 emission rights to combat global warming. Every company is allowed

to emit a certain amount of greenhouse gas. But their actual amount of emissions determines if the company needs to buy additional emission rights (carbon credits), or wether they have surplus rights that they can sell. Every year more companies are forced to reduce their CO_2 emissions. Such reductions are often realized with the implementation of new technologies.

Some companies can invest fairly easily and cheaply in clean, energy-efficient technology. Doing so takes them below the emissions standard. For other companies, such investments are simply too expensive. So these companies may choose to buy carbon credits from the more compliant companies. In this way, all companies are paying for the reduction measures of some companies. The market automatically selects the cheapest ways to achieve their country's environmental goals.

What we foresee is increased investment in those companies that have drastically cleaned up their act or reorganized their production process, so that they can sell carbon credits as an additional source of revenue.

JPMorgan subsidizes the sale of efficient wood-burning stoves in poor countries at $6 apiece. These ovens are so efficient that they actually yield carbon credits. These can then be sold to companies so they can compensate their emissions. Each stove generates approximately $10 to $15 worth of carbon credits annually. If you can sell, say, about 10 million of these stoves in a short time, it doesn't take an economics professor to calculate the potential turnover – and more importantly profit – of this business.

Values Revalued

Religion and Spirituality Revived

According to the most recent statistics, people are becoming more religious worldwide. The number of adherents to the major religions is increasing relatively faster than the world population. Meanwhile, the non-religious and atheist population is stagnating: the annual growth of the non-religious (0.8% a year) and atheists (0.2%) are far lower than the growth of the world population (1.2%).

Of the major religions, Islam is growing fastest (at a rate of 2.1%). The growth in the number of Christians (1.3%) is only just higher than the growth of the world population. And while the emptying of western European churches continues, this doesn't necessarily mean that people in these regions are becoming less religious.

Faith is now being experienced much less within the orthodoxy of a particular denomination or church. Frederic Lenoir, editor of *Le Monde des Religions*, a supplement to the French newspaper *Le Monde*, writes that "ultramodern individuals distrust religious institutions... and they no longer believe in the shiny future that science and politics are painting. Nevertheless, they are still confronted with the great questions of origin, suffering, and death."

This is why people believe again. It all seemed so wonderful: man taking hold of the rudder in a responsible humanistic manner, thanks to science and technology. But alas, in the second half of the twentieth century, it proved less likely that we could shape the world through science and technology than we thought.

A similar realization can be seen in Asia, where a religious revival is also making itself felt. In China, Falung Gong is on the rise. There is a renewed use of the centuries-old tradition of feng shui, or energy teachings, even in ultramodern Asian skyscrapers. Thai high-flyers increasingly send their children for a short stay in a monastery, where Buddhist monks currently play an important social role as community builders.

In South America, the Catholic Church is losing ground, but evangelical and charismatic movements are booming. Their religious services, which attract millions of people, are often held in the open air or in concert-halls and stadiums. In addition, in a country such as Brazil, there are large numbers of followers of Afro-American religious groups, such as Candomblé and Umbanda. Spiritualism is also widespread and growing there, as are Pentecostal communities. Africa is also seeing the growth of Pentecostal communities – along with a strong growth in Islam.

In countries such as Russia and China, the demise of communism made way for a resurgence of traditional religions: in Russia, Eastern Orthodoxy; in China, mainly Buddhism. Christian missionaries have also set their sights on the millions of Chinese – following on from their earlier successes in South Korea and South Vietnam, where a large part of the population converted to Christianity in the past few decades.

The revival of religion makes sense, especially in Western society, given the ever louder call for values and standards. With greater globalization, people sense greater threats and have a greater need for values and standards that protect their everyday lives. With rapid and widespread change, a sense of insecurity has seen people increasingly turning to religion and spirituality to provide them with a sense of security, safety, and a moral handle on the world.

The increasing importance of recognizing such values is also demonstrated by the way somebody like Nelson Mandela is worshipped – to almost mythical proportions. Also, Barack Obama's popularity can largely be explained by the values he radiates.

New World Values

Values and standards will not only become more important in the future. Nout Wellink asks us to also consider the changing values and standards in these times of economic and political power shifts. He points out: "In China, the government has a much more prominent position than it does here. The government reaches into the private life of the average Chinese – something we would not accept in the West. On the contrary – we want to reduce the role of government even more. China also has a completely different idea about democracy and the notion of human rights."

Wellink is right and this is confirmed by a quote from the *China Daily*, defending against criticism of their human rights and the Olympics: "We [the Chinese] have implemented the biggest human right there is: we are able to feed 1.3 billion citizens."

To some extent we must agree. The World Bank estimates that between 1990 and 2004, at least 400 million Chinese have been lifted from poverty. Since Deng Xiaoping's economic reforms began thirty years ago, extreme poverty has disappeared, and the average Chinese person has reached an acceptable living standard. With that comes a certain level of security and peace – no small thing!

In the past century, the Western world has indulged in the arrogance of thinking that we are ahead of the rest of the world. This would lead us down the path of rationality, freedom, equality, and secular democracy. But with the increasing power of countries like China, we may need to compromise somewhat on our seemingly obvious values and standards. China is a giant – one that in the foreseeable future will most likely own one third of the world economy. And this giant is not prepared to just trade in its values and standards for ours. We Westerners will need to ask ourselves to what extent we're willing to adapt to the values and standards of this new giant.

What goes for China also goes for countries such as Russia, and the oil countries in the Middle East. A major acceleration in the transfer of wealth has, in the past five years, shifted trillions of petrodollars from oil consumers to producers. This has altered the world balance of power. And Western ideas about civil society, the environment, and women's rights may well be replaced by new sets of values.

We also see this in the business world of today. In the sale of luxury car maker Aston Martin by Ford, Shariah-compliant structures were followed. Kuwaiti investors had demanded this.

A Revaluation of Democracy

Democracy is the political system at the heart of Western culture. But fewer and fewer people in the West are prepared to fight for the values of democracy. And in countries that are new to democracy, there are doubts about the blessings of this political system.

In Russia, many people value stability more than democracy. With today's global competitiveness, many companies are all too willing to submit to authoritarian regimes to gain new business. Paying lip service to values such as human rights is considered bothersome and counterproductive. The Indian Minister of Commerce and Industry – who is normally proud to be living in "the world's biggest democracy" – recently groaned that he sometimes wished for the kind of fast, uncomplicated decision-making processes the Chinese have.

In a democracy like the Philippines, rising food prices (dictated by global markets), incompetent governments, and rampant corruption have made a farce of the institutions that allegedly work for the people. On the other hand, great progress has been made using the Chinese model. Its increasingly open economic system and closed political system seem attractive to many third-world countries. Personal happiness is not defined in terms of free elections, a free press, or freedom of assembly; it is defined in terms of opportunities for economic advancement and stability.

According to recent polls taken by social scientists at the World Values Survey, people in Moldova, a poor but formally democratic country, are among the least happy in the world, while the inhabitants of the People's Republic of China, a one-party state, are among the most optimistic. Maybe we in the West should get used to the idea that not everybody in the world thinks democracy is the best political system.

The question for the West in coming years will not be which countries will open up to or adopt our Western model of parliamentary government. There is no question that many things can be done more easily in an authoritarian system. "Who wouldn't prefer to do business in a country that doesn't have free labor unions? Who would pass up the chance to reconstruct entire cities, without the public getting to have its say?" asks prominent author Ian Buruma, who advises against preaching purism in matters of democracy.

Aid Through Microcredit

A consequence of the revival of ethics is an increased attention to good causes, like aid to people in developing countries. The sense of social responsibility is growing in the Western world, in part because people know that governments are leaving it more and more up to them.

For some years now, people have preferred to provide development aid in the form of a financial innovation called microcredit, instead of donations, because with microcredit their money is used more productively.

Muhammed Yunus, the inspiration and inventor of microcredit, has very convincingly stated that "a dollar given to charity can be used only once. The beauty of a social business is that it extends the life of the dollar." You can, for example, give $25 in food aid; but the same amount of money will buy a fishing rod, with which the beneficiary can catch his own fish – and possibly sell or trade this fish for vegetables. This is the principal behind microcredit.

According to McKinsey in his report *CEO's on Strategy and Social Issues*, social responsibility is not only being seen in the private sector, but also in companies: "Making globalization's benefits accessible to the poor, through micro-finance among other things, is one of the four most important issues that companies need to tackle in the near future, if they want to remain successful."

Muhammad Yunus and His Grameen Bank

In 1976 Muhammad Yunus got the idea to found a bank especially for the poor. Banks normally don't want to finance the poor because they are not considered to be credit-worthy; moreover, small loans don't interest banks. Yunus, however, did start to provide small credit loans to the poor, naming his bank the Grameen Bank.

The loans have to be repaid with interest, and anyone who borrows money from the Grameen Bank must promise to comply with sixteen rules, including promises to educate their children, repay the loan, renounce the dowry system, and become members of a small group of borrowers. Those small groups eventually take care of social control and discipline, ensuring better repayment than with the classical banks.

Yunus' initiative turned out to be very successful. In 1979 he convinced the Central Bank of Bangladesh of his idea. This immediately led to expansion of the project. Yunus' bank is now the largest in Bangladesh – with some 2 million customers, more than 90% women – and has spread to over 35,000 villages. Partner institutions are active in 35 countries, and certainly not only in the third world.

In 2006 Yunus received the Nobel Prize for Peace for his initiative. "Sustainable peace can only be achieved if large groups in a population have the capacity to free themselves from poverty," said the Nobel committee.

Microcredit is on the rise. Especially after Yunus received the Nobel Prize, celebrities and dignitaries, such as the Dutch Crown Princess Máxima, started to work for this good cause. Between 2001 and 2006, the total volume of microcredits grew 525%, from $4 billion to $25 billion. Not surprisingly, micro-financing institutions (MFIs) started to pop up everywhere in the world, even in Western countries. A branch of the Grameen Bank started in 2008 in the US is providing microcredits to poor Americans. Since January 2006, there are 3,000 microcredit institutions, and 113 million people have received a microcredit, of which 82 million are among the poorest.

Still, according to the World Bank, more than 1 billion people are living in extreme poverty (1.3 billion according to the UN in 2006), which means having to live on less than $1 per day. So, only 10% of this target-group has been reached. Estimates say that half of those billion people

(500 million) have a microcredit enterprise. But fewer than 10 million of them (only 2.5%) are able to obtain a loan from a traditional bank or credit institution. The MFIs that aim to provide loans to this enormous underprivileged group need a lot of capital. Not only to lend, but also to develop their own organization. This makes it a coveted investment for "social investment funds," the social variant of the "green funds."

Micro-finance

As a member of the Advisors group to the UN International Year of Microcredit 2005, I had the privilege of meeting many micro-entrepreneurs on my travels. It is striking how women are empowered by micro-finance, and not only economically. When you invest in a woman, you invest in her whole family. Her children go to school, the whole family gets better healthcare, and she is given a voice in her community.

The biggest challenge is not how to do micro-finance, but how to do it on a big enough scale to make a real macro-economic difference. I am convinced that to move to the next level, profitability will be crucial. Good financial services come at a cost, no matter what the social objective. To reach the very large number of poor people who need financial services, micro-finance must become commercially viable. Micro-finance should no longer base itself on charity. It should be a self-sustaining system. If we want to reach hundreds of millions of unbanked people, a viable, efficient and profitable micro-finance system is essential.

Institutions I visited, such as Equity Bank and KREP in Kenya, among many others, are good examples of why pursuing profits should be welcomed, not feared. Both are now profitable, while banking the previously "unbanked", through providing them with a whole range of financial products. When I spoke to them, what really encouraged me was the fact that even as they grew and became more profitable, they increasingly thought primarily about their clients and how to serve them better.

Being profitable has enabled these institutions to provide credit and financial services to many, many more people, with greater efficiency and lower cost. Other micro-finance providers should follow their example. But to do so, they will need a government and regulations that help them to achieve this, rather than getting in their way.

They will also need professionals, such as competent loan officers, internal auditors, treasurers, and so on. Currently, these professionals are in short supply in many developing countries. This is something where donors can help, and I encourage them – which means many of you – to invest in training the people who can make micro-finance work.

There is also a need for mainstream financial service firms to get more involved in nurturing the growth of micro-finance. At the start of the year, many of the bankers I

spoke to were reluctant. The encouraging thing is that, after speaking with them some more, they started to get excited about the potential of this new market. Some of them realized that in their specific areas of expertise, there was something tangible that they could do. I applaud them, and urge others to join them. We need the experience of mainstream bankers to help this sector grow. ☐

Her Royal Highness Princess Máxima of the Netherlands is a member of the United Nations Advisors Group on Inclusive Financial Sectors.

This column was compiled from a speech given by HRH Princess Máxima of the Netherlands before the UN International Forum to Build Inclusive Financial sectors, November 7, 2005, in New York.

Empowering Women

Banks that provide microcredit are a success. Since the inception of micro-finance in 1974, more than 100 million poor have received micro-credits (with an amazing repayment rate averaging 97%!). The majority of them are women.

The empowerment that results from this capital payment is enormous. Empowerment isn't just convenient for these women and their families; it also provides an important economic impulse. Erlijn Sie, co-founder of the Micro-credits for Mothers Foundation, and Director of micro-credit organization HandsOn, adds: "By giving a woman the possibility to borrow money, her social status within the family and society grows. In our experience, women become more assertive and gain more self-confidence, which in its turn has an enormous impact on her children. UN research also showed that a loan to a woman benefits the children and community sooner and more effectively than when the loan is issued to a man. In any case, the poorest families depend mostly on the income of women. And don't forget: most poor people are women."

How Does Micro-credit Actually Work?

Renuka is an entrepreneurial but poor woman in Sri Lanka. She folds and sells envelopes made of recycled paper. She buys this paper from a local supplier, and she sells the envelopes to people in the neighborhood. Micro-credit for Mothers provided Renuka with a microcredit of €80, through a local partner, charging interest in the form of community work. What this means is that when the school building needs to be fixed, the women who received loans will take care of it.

Renuka used her loan to open an account with her supplier. A deposit of €80 was the condition for opening an account. Thanks to this account she can buy recycled paper at a much reduced rate, and she can buy more paper at once. Meanwhile, eight of her neighbors are working for Renuka, folding envelopes. She herself sells the bundles of envelopes in the city. Repayment of the €80 was no problem for Renuka.

This real example shows why microcredit is considered a powerful tool. The cost of loans is low, but the benefits are enormous. The community, neighbors, and children all reap direct benefits from the credit – and it's an inspiration for all. ☐

P2P Variants of Microcredit

Personal stories like Renuka's are inspiring. The success of microcredit will increase when lenders get to see the concrete results in the lives of the borrowers. Peer-to-peer variants that facilitate microcredit would certainly also be successful. The paid interest could pass onto the broker, while the borrower repays the loan provider. Several variants already exist. There is the provision of microcredit where the "giver" bears part of the costs – think for example of Kiva.org. There are also peer-to-peer variants, where the loan is auctioned off to the one with the best conditions (i.e. lowest interest). An example here is MyC4.com. Yet another emerging concept is the financing of MFIs themselves through Internet marketplaces. MicroPlace, founded in 2007, is a wholly owned subsidiary of eBay, Inc., providing consumers the possibility to invest in MFIs, against a moderate return on investment, thus giving the working poor a chance to escape poverty.

Microcredit: To a Broader Perspective

Marilou van Golstein-Brouwers, managing director of Triodos Investment Management and former member of the Group of Advisors for the United Nations Year of Microcredit prefers to talk about micro finance rather than micro credit: "For example access to saving facilities can be crucial to help poor people build their assets or help them bridge periods with unexpected expenditures that otherwise could be disastrous.

Our vision is to develop micro finance institutions into a fully-fledged and integral part of the financial sector in developing countries. The creation of an inclusive financial sector, a sector where the majority of people have access to financial services, will provide a sustainable basis for a balanced social-economic development."

Happy Healthcare

Growing Wellness Industry

In a time when no one has enough time, when we must deal with new technologies, worldwide competition, and aging, we are placing ever-greater value on good health and wellness. People the world over want more control over their bodies and are becoming more vocal.

Healthcare and wellness will therefore become increasingly bespoke. New medical developments and holistic relaxation centers will offer this possibility. Medical innovations financed by banks and new financial stakeholders (such as electronics companies) will influence the worldwide healthcare industry.

At the same time, we will see new moral issues arise, if and when the medical industry enables all of us to live to one hundred or more – at a time when the world population is exploding. The rich will naturally be able to afford longer lives, which will lead to heated public debates. The medical use of animals and stem-cell technology – used in part to 3D-print new human organs – is also expected to intensify. Large investments will be made in these areas. Susan Greenfield, the already quoted Director of the Royal Institution, says that boundaries are becoming increasingly blurred. Where does medical care as a therapy stops, and where does medical care as a means of "finetuning lifestyles" begins?

Meanwhile, the wellness industry is expected to soar, especially in the US, Europe, Japan, and southern China. This booming business will also attract large investments. Senior citizens in particular – with their spare time, money, and desire for pleasant lives with minimum stress and maximum relaxation – will put great value on wellness. Spas, thermal baths, and other public wellness facilities have a good future in this market.

High-Tech, High-Touch Healthcare

Every three years, the memory capacity of chips quadruples, and the performance of microprocessors increases by a factor of four to five. Not only is memory capacity is increasing exponentially, but also the processing speed of computers and the resolution of digital cameras. This phenomenon is called "Moore's law," after the man who first described it: Gordon Moore, one of the founders of the chip producer Intel. Moore's law will also affect healthcare: the healthcare of the future could be characterized as "high tech, high touch." We will also see medical technology getting smaller and smaller, becoming nanotechnology. Thanks to miniaturization, pumps, valves, and chromatographs can all now fit on a single chip that can be used to analyze DNA, air, or food.

What consequences will these developments have for the medical sector? Much of this new technology will enable people to monitor their own health. With their own PDA, or "personal digital assistant," they will be able to analyze information about their physical condition at home. A lab chip will perform home blood tests. If necessary, medical histories can be updated interactively every day, creating remarkable possibilities for early diagnosis.

Introducing The Gene Passport

In 2008 consumers were given the possibility to have a gene passport (gene map) created. Until now, only the well-to-do could afford this passport: for the lovely sum of $350,000 you could order one from a company such as Knome in Cambridge, or the Beijing Genomics Institute. But in coming years, the price for a gene passport will go down – and when commercial partners (such as insurance companies) begin to see their benefits, everybody will get one.

With the arrival of the gene passport, we will soon know which diseases we might get at what age. If your passport indicates that there are no serious diseases to be expected, then maybe you don't actually need health insurance. Of course, you might still get the flu, fall from a kitchen ladder, or get into a car accident; but for such things you could take out another kind of policy, or draw on your savings.

In the future we will not only be able to detect a cancer gene, but also be able to remove it. And in the next phase (somewhere around 2050), you will be able to get self-restoring cells implanted in your body, meaning you would never get sick anymore. At which point, health insurance will be a thing of the past. In the future, we will not only be able to remove disease-causing genes, we will be able to influence them by nutrition, according to Michael Müller, a Professor of Nutrition, Metabolism and Genomics at the Wageningen University. Conceivably, product wrappers in the stores will

interact with the chip in your gene passport and indicate whether the product is suitable for you, or maybe even beneficial. Of course these data are stored, much like the old fashioned customer loyalty programs, and then used to intelligently source products that fit your genetic profile.

New Missions for Financial Services Companies

The Most Important Value

For consumers, the ethical behavior of companies will become an increasingly important driver of choice. Therefore, it will be seen as normal and necessary for financial service providers to develop in this direction.

Ethics par excellence "walk the talk." Consumers in a more transparent everyday world look critically at how financial service providers behave and in which companies they invest. Under pressure of these same consumers, companies pay more attention to corporate social responsibility, thus making the circle complete. Ethics will be an important driver of the industry in the years to come – no matter what happens. The credit crisis has caused this process to accelerate even further.

Giving New Meaning to Solidarity

Together with aging, migration, and basic ethics, medical progress will lead to new ethical questions and renewed consumer pressure. Not only financial service providers, but also governments will be expected to have opinions on these questions.

Aging issues are rapidly approaching. With each passing day they are causing, within and among countries, a larger gap between rich and poor – even within an economic bloc like the European Union.

Who plays a role in finding solutions to these differences, and what does solidarity mean under these circumstances? Pension insurers will take the initiative. As the big retirement problem is a large millstone around their necks, then it becomes the problem they need to solve – together with the government. And they need to do so from an international perspective, because differences between countries can be even greater than those within the countries themselves. No one in Europe wants an Italy, for example, where 50% of the population has insufficient income. Moreover, the predictable value of DNA places a time bomb under the conventional solidarity principle on which most types of insurances are based. Which party is going to insure someone who has been shown to have a high probability of one day dying of disease Y?

Why should I pay a high premium (due to my unhealthy neighbor), when my own future looks to be, literally and figuratively, without worries?

Perhaps people will be willing to contribute for those within their family or "tribe," but not for hordes of strangers. Large collective contracts are coming under pressure, which may create opportunities for smaller collective agreements to be made, with strict and specific affinities. Ethical issues linked to these and other developments such as gene passports will undoubtedly become an important topic for heated debate.

We, meanwhile, need to redefine exactly what solidarity means. And because this affects the core of the financial community, it's imperative that financial services companies take the initiative in this discussion.

An Active Role in Solving Global Problems, The Twelfth Pillar

Consumers' changing mentality, ecological and demographic pressures, and medical and technological developments are all external pressures to which, come rain or shine, financial service providers will have to react. In addition, there will be new challenges that the financial community initiates itself. As a result of far-reaching internationalization and consolidation within the branch, the financial industry has developed into the twelfth pillar of power.

"New style" financial services companies, purified by the credit crunch and with proper oversight, are well positioned – through their worldwide presence and interconnectedness, their financial weight, and investment policies – to wield an instrument that actually influences what will and will not develop, anywhere on the globe.

One aspiration that befits this position is to develop and use it to play an active role in solving important social issues and global problems.

Guiding Global Warming

From this perspective, financial service providers will start to participate actively in world issues like global warming. Obviously, sustainable energy projects are good investments: wind and sun are, after all, continuously available and free, providing a practical and predictable cash flow. Their investment power will enable them to quickly play an active role – unlike large energy companies which must finance various new developments from their own profits, and are severely handicapped by vested interests (oil refineries and coal plants that have not yet been amortized). Financial service providers will not only invest in sustainable energy, they will also develop investment products in sustainable energy, to reduce the effects of global warming and the depletion of natural resources. They will invest exclusively in cradle-to-cradle concepts in sustainable companies – and the financing of projects that harm the earth would be denied.

With regards to worldwide poverty problems, they will invest in innovations in food production, in areas where hunger is imminent, and drive systems such as microcredit programs to tackle poverty in the third world. Futhermore, they will only collaborate with other financial service providers, specialists (e.g. the Grameen Bank), and NGOs that bring specific knowledge to the table, or have affinities strongly rooted in community engagement (e.g. the World Wildlife Fund or Greenpeace).

In order to create greater credibility, it is crucial for providers to have stricter global supervision, as mentioned in Megatrend 1.

Promoting Well-being

An "active role" is not limited to the big global issues such as climate, water, energy, food, and waste. Think, too, of an active role in the chal-

lenging areas of care-giving and health: enabling people to stay healthy for longer, improving the quality of hospitals, and so on. Think of financial institutions financing universities – after all, what is a "knowledge economy" without knowledge? And think of the many ways to stimulate the integration and economic position of migrants.

When governments encounter difficulties in mutual cooperation, making solutions difficult to realize, the large banks, insurance companies, and pension funds can play an active role. This kind of scenario also fits the Kondratieff wave model and the previously mentioned trend cycles of approximately sixty years. Up until the 1990s, consumers were concerned with prosperity. Their concerns are now more about well-being, concerns that in twenty years will be pivotal. Of course, the financial service providers of that time will have taken this into account, as making a contribution to well being is pivotal in their strategy, their products, and their services. It will evolve into an underlying way of doing business.

Paradigm Shift

Research by the American sociologist Paul Ray into "cultural creatives" shows that these people feel responsible for what is happening to the earth and bear personal responsibility for their way of life. According to Ray, this is a group – about 15% to 20% of the European population – who initiate change and are open to a paradigm shift. And it is precisely this group who are reaching out to organizations like Triodos Bank, to translate their concerns into practical action.

The cultural creative's enthusiasm for positive change is heartening, because change is precisely what's needed. With the backing of growing numbers of people, the financial system could be very different. Triodos Bank, a sustainable bank founded in 1980, illustrates what's possible. It taps into this body of interest by consciously choosing to stay close to the real economy. As a result the bank, which now has offices in the Netherlands, the UK, Belgium and Spain, is not involved in the sub-prime mortgage crisis and is continuing to grow at similar levels despite the credit crunch. We invest savers' deposits directly in sustainable companies and stay in direct contact with the entrepreneurs who run them. We choose not to invest in loan packages when the individual loans have been granted by another bank.

We aim to maximize sustainability, embracing the need to be profitable as a means to an end. Profit shows an organization is working efficiently, but says nothing about the content of what it's doing. We, on the other hand, start with the content of an activity and ask: "How can this contribute to sustainability?" Then, as bankers, we ask ourselves, "Is it viable?". If our professional judgement is correct, profit should follow almost automatically.

This approach represents a radical departure for conventional financial institutions. It means reappraising the role of our money and its place in the economy. And reappraising the way a bank is organized. Our oversubscribed depository receipt issue in 2007 made it clear that people appreciate a structure which protects against hostile takeover bids. For a long time it was criticized as old-fashioned, unsuitable for a modern, transparent bank. But views have changed. The slogan "not for sale" used in promotion – a clear statement that the bank and its identity are not some tradable entity – resonated with large numbers of people.

Our starting point is a long-term relationship with borrowers – and that's not for sale either. As a bank, we are responsible for the money we lend. If there is a problem, we solve it together. In essence, a bank is an organization that brings two groups of people together. People who have money to spare and people who need it; a bank then adds its knowledge and expertise. If you move away from that basic principle, and into a more abstract world, you lose sight of what is imaginary and what is real.

Peter Blom is CEO of Triodos Bank.

Ethical Positioning: Who Sets His Limits Where?

Financial service providers will soon distinguish themselves based on ethical and moral choices, rather than financial return. This will become a long-term qualifier: a necessary condition for doing business at all, and for attracting and retaining top talent. As an overall "container concept," this will need to be defined individually, in order to be distinguishable and appealing to the chosen target-groups.

The questions then will no longer be who is the cheapest, or who promises the highest return. They will be specific questions about how, where, and when – for example, wether you would like to know which diseases you might get in twenty years' time. Then you would choose an insurer who can provide you with that DNA profile. If you don't want your children to be implanted with a chip that lets big brother know if they happen to be hanging out in dangerous neighborhoods, then you choose an insurer who thinks like you. Do you want to make stem-cells available for your future protection? And so on…

Some service providers will take pride in never having been involved in sub-prime mortgages (before or now, because it would be appalling to think of getting their customers into trouble) or choose to stay away from intransparant derivatives. Others will indicate that their top investors and executives definitely do not receive huge bonuses (thus rejecting the culture of greed). Still others will truly commit to some specific problem or goal and the solidarity of their own vision. No matter what ethical position is chosen, it is essential to honor that promise, which must become an integral part of the company's "genes." Otherwise, and quite rightly, consumers and associates will see through it.

More than ever, the sequence should be: first "be good," then "tell it."

part 3

Back to The Roots

Management Agenda 2010-2015

In the next ten to twenty years, a number of fundamental developments will take place with regard to of globalization, technology, demography, and ethics. They have, in fact, already begun. Globalization is leading to a fast-changing playing field, with new competitors competing by a new set of rules.

Demographic shifts have resulted in a need to look at things differently – to look differently at target-groups, and search for deeper consumer insights. When it comes to innovation, there is a need to look for new concepts of service, and not just new products. Additionally, backward and forward integration must be seriously taken up.

Technological developments have shifted power to the consumer, resulting in shifts in the supply chain, and shifts to new, previously unknown paths of purchase. This is the true impact of technology.

Ethics are increasingly important. This introduces new demands on financial service providers, on products, on organization, and culture. This megatrend also offers the financial sector the chance to take on a completely new role, thus shaping a new future.

Looking Beyond the Crisis

Now is not the most opportune moment, however, to start fulfilling this role. For consumers and other stakeholders, it would be incomprehensible if financial service providers were to begin developing such a position right now. Naturally, the present crisis, with all its problem solving – and anticipation and prevention of problems that might still arise – has to have the highest priority. Damage control is at the top of the agenda for the time being. But doing what's necessary to curb the crisis doesn't detract from the fact that financial service providers must start building for the future. Normally, this might be done with a mass communications offensive: perhaps advertising the fact that we, as a financial institution, are certainly and thoroughly reliable. But this kind of approach will not work in the present climate. Words like "reliable" have been completely perverted by a constant stream of negative coverage in recent years. A much more fundamental approach is needed. Parallel to curbing the crisis and preventing future excesses, financial service providers must envisage the social role they want to play in ten years' time. This vision will determine the changes necessary in organization and culture, products, and service provision. To expand this further, ask questions such as these: What key subjects must the financial industry address to reinvent itself? What should leaders in the financial industry do now, to anticipate the future of the sector?

Firstly, it is absolutely essential for the financial world (banks, insurance companies, and pension funds) to organize themselves better. Governments will certainly stress supervision at various levels – seen, for example, in the initiatives of the Basel Committee on Banking Supervision. But this only sets the boundaries for what will be allowed.

The banks, insurance companies, and pension funds, themselves, will have to invest heavily in self-regulation. Here we are talking about ethical codes of conduct, and strict enforcement of these codes, founded on a deep understanding of the social significance of the industry.

Besides self-regulation, the industry needs to clarify just who, or what institution, can speak on behalf of the sector. This is similar to the eight most important countries, which have organized themselves in the G8 and give their combined opinion on a regular basis. What has come clearly to light in connection with the credit crisis is that the financial world lacks this central platform, which speaks on behalf of the industry and gives a certain amount of direction. Recently, the world has been bombarded almost constantly with yet more "setbacks," popping up from a different angle every time. This creates an impression of a sector in total chaos without any vision, solutions, and above all, direction.

Additionally, we see three areas in which every financial service provider will have to launch an enormous catching-up offensive over the next five years, just to be able to face up to the challenges of the megatrends we signal in this book: talent, innovation, and simplicity.

Next to solving the current crisis, these three critical success factors, which spring up in every megatrend, combined with the management agenda for the next five years, will form a new foundation for the financial sector.

Winning The War for Talent

Why is Talent Such a Crucial Success Factor for The Future of The Financial Sector?

Globalization of financial services has also affected the labor market: globalization and internationalization require different skill sets. The playing field for talent hunters is no longer the local market; it's the entire world. And the talent sought by financial service providers is also attractive to multinationals from other industries. This means the competitive arena will look entirely different in the labor market of the future.

The success of financial service providers will depend on whether or not they are able to retain the really good people. The most important asset for banks, insurance companies, and pension funds is talent.

The demand for top talent is increasing worldwide, while demographics are causing the supply to decrease, as we have already seen in Megatrend 2. In the United States, the sought-after group of 35- to 45-year-olds will shrink by 15% in the next few years. This trend is manifest in almost all Western countries. As new technologies change business, they demand new competencies from financial service providers and different skills from employees. As we saw in Megatrend 3, concerning technology, service is one of the most important themes in the future of finance. Services, in turn, depend on the quality of the person delivering them. Once again, it is a matter of the right people in the right place.

The same applies to ethics. Ethics are intrinsic to us. If you as a financial service provider want to grow on an ethical level, you must invest in ethics and attract the kind of people who put words into actions. Living the brand is key.

Moving With the Times

Banks, insurance companies, and pension funds must move with the times. It is apparent from a number of studies that the vast majority of CEOs and managers regard finding top talent as one of their companies' gravest problems. But in practice, it is apparent that only a small minority give real priority to this problem.

A glance at the top 100 of the Fortune 500 annual ranking of America's largest corporations shows that no fewer than 27 financial service providers form part of this list – more than a quarter! Percentages like this are a measure of the need for talent in these companies and the required attractiveness as an employer brand. Now, the renowned *Fortune* magazine also keeps another list, the "Fortune 100 Best Companies to Work for." If we compare the two lists, the conclusion is bewildering. Of the 27 largest American financial service providers, only two are in the top 100 best companies to work for: Goldman Sachs and American Express.

The various crises in recent decades have not done the image of banks, insurance companies, and pension funds much good. Not a single financial service provider has been at the top of the 100 strongest world brands reported in the newspaper *BusinessWeek* for years.

How this strong awareness of standards affects a company's image in the labor market is shown by the relatively small QuickenLoans, which had a turnover of €400 million in 2006. In 2008 QuickenLoans raced into second place in Fortune's 100 best companies to work for. The reason? The company always kept away from sub-prime mortgages. They could not give their support to such products, and top talent appreciates that. The battle for talent begins by setting ambitious targets. Make it a goal to go higher up the "best companies to work for" list every year.

What Should Your Skill Set Be Five Years from Now?

In five years time, what will your skill set need to be? Financial service providers, like every employer, want the best people they can get. But their idea of these "best people" is still too traditional. They still perceive them from the point of view of their current organograms and management development programs – which in practice is like extrapolating answers to future questions from the past. This results in great candidates, graduates from the right business schools, and people with years of experience, competing in the financial world. But do they also have the skills that will be needed to be successful in five years' time?

The four megatrends presented in *The Future of Finance* point to the new competencies that must be developed by financial service providers: an international scope and mentality, a capacity for innovation, entrepreneurship, a feeling for consumers, forward and backward integration (preventing problems and providing solutions), the ability to find solutions instead of paying out, a pioneering mentality, partnerships, integrating new parties, online and mobile, and so on.

What new competencies do we need? What is still lacking in our company? These are the key questions in the search for talent. The goal is to attract talent with mission-critical skills.

Benchmarks Outside the Industry

The battle for talent is not just fought out among banks, insurance companies, and pension funds. Anyone wishing to be a world-class employer must compete in the labor market with world-class companies from other industries. So don't just compare your organization with those of your competitors. Also look at the well-known ranking lists of most sought-after employers, and then in particular look at those competencies needed in the future of finance.

If online service provision is crucial for your future, then model yourself on companies like Google and eBay. If you need to be just as good in this area, then they are precisely the right benchmark. And there are probably many more interesting candidates working at these companies than at the competing banks X, Y, and Z.

If simplicity is the heart of the enterprise you have in mind, then compare yourself with a company like Apple. Take your inspiration from companies that are higher on the ranking lists.

What Are You Offering?

The next question, of course, is how you persuade top talent to switch to your enterprise. What arguments would you make for your company to a personalization expert from Amazon, for example? Finding the right drivers of choice calls for the same investigative skills as tapping into the deep desires of consumers. Only in this way will you develop an attractive and distinctive offer. Apart from that, research by VODW shows, among others things, the following three trends:

1. Top talent is looking for international career options. This is not adequately recognized by most employers. Companies with good possibilities for continued international growth are more successful in the battle for talent than companies with limited international opportunities for high potentials. The fact that American Express is one of the two large financial service providers that also appear on the "Fortune 100 Best Companies to Work for" is due to its wealth of opportunities for changing careers internally, and especially internationally.

2. Business and marketing talent prefers to work in concerns that are aware of the latest consumer and technology trends. The extent to which a concern actively capitalizes on these trends is extremely important to young potentials in the selection of an employer. This explains, for example, the high position of the relatively small Umpqua Bank in the "Fortune 100 Best Companies to Work for."

3. The present and future generations of high potentials not only want to excel personally, they also want to help alleviate social issues. In their choice of employer, they increasingly allow themselves to be guided by corporate social responsibility. A powerful corporate social responsibility program is a definite plus in the search for new talent.

Be Good – Then Tell It

A strong employer brand is indispensable in the battle for talent. Companies with a strong employer brand get more and better candidates and it costs them less.

From a typically administrative organization, financial services are going to develop into a creative industry. Do we think that ethics are important? If so, we must make that obvious and attract people who feel the same way. This contributes to a strong "DNA," an inherently strong business culture. It creates pride in one's own concern, which in turn creates a better motivated, more energetic, more loyal staff. It is employees like these who become "employer brand ambassadors," happy to tell their peers about their compatible work environment.

Innovation: Making a Difference

Why is Innovation Crucial to the Future Success of the Financial Sector? Consolidation and internationalization are making innovation more crucial. On the one hand, it leads to new international concepts and new ways of leveraging international knowledge and skills, and enables the realization of new growth. On the other hand, we can see that consolidation also creates new space – space that can be used by new players, wether these are known niche players or large players exploiting a specific concept. With market consolidation, innovation means the difference between growth based solely on acquisitions and the realization of real growth in turnover.

Demographic landslides – from an aging population to the emergence of tribes – create new consumer needs. Innovation is the answer to these needs. Furthermore, as we've just seen, a company's innovative image is an increasingly important choice criterion for top talent in a shrinking labor market.

Rapid developments in technology facilitate all kinds of new products, new types of services, and new ways of communicating with the target-group. Consumers are coming to expect this, because providers from other industries are setting the bar pretty high. Constant innovation is necessary to keep surprising customers.

The increasing importance of ethics makes it necessary to look critically at your current offerings and current organization. It also opens up a new vista and new lines of approach for linking up with the spirit of the age of today and tomorrow.

To break free from the everyday grind and inject new energy into an organization, innovation is essential. It frees the industry from the current sad state of affairs and forces it to look further than the present crisis. It provides consumers with a new perspective and attracts new talent. It is, in other words, a shot of inspiration.

Innovation: the Future of Finance

In discussing the four megatrends, we have repeatedly pointed out that innovation in financial services will look very different from the development of yet another car insurance policy or mortgage. Here are six points to keep in mind:

1. Product development is still driven mainly by the capabilities of the product systems, and therefore still takes place mainly at the product level. In contrast, the most important point of departure is the customer, and the best basis for innovation is the deep consumer insights that reveal customers' true desires. On that basis, new propositions can be made. In Megatrend 2 we described how to find out about consumer insights.
2. As an extension of this, we must think about target-group concepts that tailor products, services, and market manipulation to the target-group.
3. Service is at the core of financial services. And with services the proof of the pudding is in the eating. Whereas the traditional focus of financial companies lies in product innovation, the focus must shift to innovation in services – since this is the terrain on which the battle among competitors is being fought.
4. It is essential to create new competencies. Banks, insurance companies, and pension funds should already be starting to develop concepts where partnerships, forward integration (prevention) and/or backward integration (providing a solution instead of paying out) play a role. Such concepts require new competencies and a different business model. New competencies need to be developed, so the main thing now is to start learning.

5. We must bring innovation to market manipulation. Consumer insights relate not only to products and services, but also to new paths of purchase, in other words to new ways for consumers to orient themselves online or offline, and decide to buy. Mass communication may be particularly easy and cheap, but it is no longer very effective in the present climate. The question is how to dominate each step on the paths of purchase.
6. Internationalization is also essential for innovation. Truly successful international concepts work because much thought has been given in advance to how to grow internationally.

Questioning Conventional Wisdom

In view of these six points, the customary use of SWOT (Strength, Weaknesses, Opportunities, and Threats) analyses for creating innovation is almost counterproductive. They take into account only existing competencies, and not those that are required. Indeed, SWOT can deflect from the most important opportunities for real change. A genuine market innovation will take a step back from conventional wisdom from the industry.

Conventional thinking within financial services can be seen in the competencies used by all current players in a number of markets: almost all use similar cost structures, the same distribution channels, apply similar market segmentation, and offer similar products. Some even make price agreements with each other.

Another example of conventional wisdom is taking fundamental imperfections for granted. Even when these are revealed, the conviction that there is no other way remains powerful: "This is how it works in our industry" is a typical reaction. Major market imperfections usually include: the product is too expensive; the product is too complex; experience with the product is minimal; clients have to jump through too many hoops to acquire the product or service; service is sub-standard. For truly pioneering market innovation to be realized, this kind of entrenched, conventional thinking in the sector must disappear.

Take new competencies as your starting point, and use existing competencies with a different intensity from your competitors. Throughout this book, there are numerous examples that show it really is possible to be different.

Introducing New Wisdom

Do you as a financial institution want to play a far more active social role in the medium term? If so, this role, too, must be learned. It is not just a question of employing ethical criteria as preconditions: "We will/will not invest in this," or "Is this in our client's interest in both the short and long-term?" It is about seeing the financial service providers' social role, per se, as a source of inspiration. This means asking certain questions: "What significance do we have and to whom? What assets and competencies can we deploy to help resolve specific social issues?" That's how you make a difference.

Creating a Culture of Innovation

These guidelines may look like quick boxes to tick, but ultimately, success depends on the culture within the company. Is it open to innovation, or is a new concept seen mainly as a disruption of existing processes? How many people have innovation on their list of KPIs? What incentives and inspiration are employees given to venture off the beaten track? What if an innovation fails? Is the employee a hero or has he just made a serious career-limiting move? A culture in which innovation is encouraged to the utmost is the environment for success.

Simplicity is The Key

Why is Simplicity a Key Success Factor for the Future of Finance?

For one thing, simplicity is essential to secure a manageable organization. Consolidation and internationalization require a certain amount of standardization to achieve the advantages of scale – tailor concepts quickly to different target-groups, and to achieve a fast roll-out. But that's thinking from the company's point of view. More important, of course, is the point of view of the consumer.

Simplicity is one of the most important consumer trends. As the world becomes ever more complex, consumers are looking for calm. They are looking for things they can have an overall sense of, the workings of which they immediately and intuitively understand; things that allow them to easily find their way – and don't take up too much of their time.

Technology has seduced many companies into making products and services too complex. Now we have reached a point where we can employ technology specifically to make products and services simpler. Products and services not only need to be easy to understand, they must also be easy for the customer to buy, and easy for sales executives and middlemen to sell.

Ethics requires an open and honest attitude and an outspoken opinion. It requires transparency and authenticity, both of which are impossible to achieve without simplicity. These require total insight, clarity, comprehensibility, and unambiguity.

Financial institutions that can implement simplicity in every vein of their organization lay the basis for transparency and authenticity – and with this, the basis for the future.

We have seen a development toward simplicity among financial service providers. Initially, this meant simply bringing convenient products and services to the market: products not just convenient for the customer but, above all, for suppliers. Simplicity subsequently came to mean specifically self-service – making it easier for customers to do things for themselves and, less costly for banks and insurance companies. Now the focus is shifting to products and services that are easy to understand and use, at any point in the customer process.

The next step toward greater simplicity must be even more fundamental. This is not just important for the future. In the short-term, prompt implementation of simplicity is essential to demonstrate to the market advances in the area of transparency.

The credit crisis makes it clear that complexity leads to risks, lack of control, and dwindling consumer confidence in the industry and the economy as a whole. Transparency is therefore a must – and simplicity is the best way to achieve that transparency.

Advancing Transparency

When the need for transparency is recognized, solutions are usually first sought by adapting products – after all, if product complexity has led to the problems, this is where we should look for solutions. But this view is far too limited, especially if we want to see further than the present crisis.

With an increasing emphasis on ethics, the fourth megatrend, consumers are looking not only at the quality of products, but also the behavior and attitude of the provider. They want to be able to see where their money is going – not just the investment fund it's going into, but what exactly the financial service provider is investing in.

The same applies to investments in the social role and to marketing and distribution. Take, for example the transparency of the reward structure for intermediairies, agents and brokers; their independence, and the cross-subsidizing of products.

An overwhelming majority of consumers view financial service providers as large, inaccessible institutions. Transparency definitely relates to the way a company is organized, from the division structure up to and including the organogram. It relates to how obvious it is to see who is responsible for what, who the consumer can call for what, and where they might go to sort out a dispute.

Putting Simplicity Into Practice

These examples of transparency make it clear that to implement simplicity (the basis of transparency), it is essential to have an overall view. Simplicity must not just apply to the organization, products, service provision, processes, systems, distribution, marketing, touch points, and so on. Simplicity must also apply to, for example, compiling reports. How many days does it take to report on quarterly or annual figures? The best companies can do it in five days; the world's top companies do it in three. Being able to report quickly (and correctly) says a great deal about the degree of simplicity in a company.

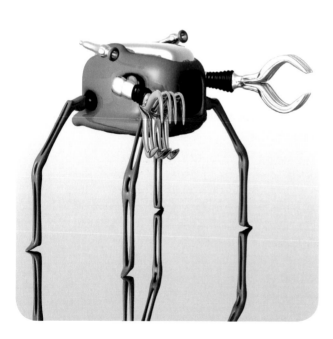

Especially in financial services, it is vital for customers to be able to buy and use services easily. Just put yourself in the customer's place and see what it is like to open an account. How many bureaucratic hoops do you have to jump through? How many offices does an application go through, and how many forms are involved?

Get managers to fill in their own application forms for once, and give them a maximum of five minutes to do it. They probably won't succeed, because everyone from the salesperson to the legal department has a hand in those forms. Customers are not usually asked for their opinions when these forms are drawn up. But in telecommunications and other fast-moving sectors, it has long been the custom to indulge in some mystery shopping, or to "adopt" a customer.

Dare to be different. Many things we said earlier about innovation also hold true for putting simplicity into practice. Make it a rule to recognize damage claims, for example, and only randomly check whether the request is appropriate. This is not only far easier for the customer, it ultimately makes a difference in costs.

Show guts in the way the company positions itself. ING Direct, for example, explicitly chooses to be someone's "second bank." As a result, the bank can concentrate on a limited number of products and services. And the customer knows precisely where he or she stands.

The Laws of Simplicity

A must-read on simplicity is *The Laws of Simplicity*, written by MIT professor John Maeda. In our opinion, this little book is a true bible – in spite of the fact that it is only one hundred pages long. Maeda distinguishes the following ten laws and three keys for making products, services, companies, and life easier, simpler, and more agreeable.

The Ten Laws are:

-   Reduce: The simplest way to achieve simplicity is through thoughtful reduction.
-   Organize: Organization makes a system of many appear fewer.
-   Time: Time savings feel like simplicity.
-   Learn: Knowledge makes everything simpler.
-   Differences: The more complexity there is, the more something simple stands out.
-   Context: The context influences the perception of simplicity, and should be included.
-   Emotion: More emotions are better than fewer.
-   Trust: In simplicity we trust.
-   Failure: Some things can never be made simple.
-   The One: Simplicity is about subtracting the obvious and adding the meaningful.

The Three Keys are:

- Away: More appears less by simply moving it far, far away.
- Open: Openness simplifies complexity.
- Power: Sustainability – use less, earn more.

Simplicity is Pragmatism

At present, financial service providers possess, due to the consolidation wave, countless divisions and subsidiaries, which themselves may operate separately, in a large number of locations. With their different procedures, products, and cultures, they often belong to the same concern in name only. But the customer doesn't make these distinctions, and expects the same convenience in every contact with a bank or insurance company.

Globalization means that banks and insurance companies are active far beyond their national borders. Cultural and working differences often complicate the introduction of simplicity. At the same time, it is specifically the multinationals that can learn from the various best practices of their branches and subsidiaries. As an organization, know what you have under your own roof and use it smartly. Chart how successful departments or branches have organized things. More sharing will make it possible to combine the successes of the various forms into "the optimal solution."

It takes time to achieve simplicity in every cell of an organization' – and in the behavior of every employee. Therefore, keep it pragmatic and look out for long-lasting strategic projects. In essence, simplicity revolves around pragmatism. The implementation of simplicity must therefore also be pragmatic. Extend simplicity through small successes, be it on the national or departmental level. Internally, such successes demonstrate that simplicity works. They also serve as examples for the rest of the organization.

Measuring Success

Simplicity is not a goal in itself, of course. With a limitless budget, all products, services, and processes could be simplified. It is a matter of balance, and it is a matter of investments with maximum results. Each step toward simplicity must therefore be translated into quantifiable targets, such as more solid sales growth, greater efficiency, and more confidence shown from customers or the Net Promotor Score (which shows the extent to which customers would recommend the company to family, friends, acquaintances, and colleagues). Solid results are also necessary to keep the organization enthusiastic and involved. But be honest, too: communicate clearly when goals haven't been met. And in any case, communicate about simplicity only when you can make it a reality.

The Ongoing Challenge of Simplicity

Simplicity is a catchy concept about which everyone has his or her own idea. It promises to make life easier and to focus attention on the customer. In recent years the number of companies promising simplicity has greatly increased. "Get things done and get on with life! It's easier and faster than ever before," Microsoft promised at the launch of the Vista operating system. This was a promise the software company was completely unable to fulfill. It perfectly illustrates that simplicity does not begin – but often ends – with communication. Customers first have to experience products and services becoming genuinely simpler.

"It ain't easy being easy." Implementing simplicity is a process that never ends. It therefore requires an open mind. Encourage the "troublemakers" in your organization. Do what the life insurer Zurich does: they recruited the "challengers" among their staff to be critics whose task it was to keep asking annoying questions. Google allows its employees one day a week to think about new solutions. These are then quickly developed, tested, and, if successful, launched on a large scale. Philips set up a Simplicity Board, which tests new products for simplicity and convenience of use – and if necessary, sends them back to the drawing board.

The Future of Finance

Conclusion:
The Future of Finance is
Back to the Roots

We realize that the picture we paint in *The Future of Finance* is inspiring, certainly with regard to the projected more active role that financial service providers can play in solving the greater world issues, and certainly at this point in time definitely a few bridges too far. But it is the financial service providers in particular that are in an excellent position to make a real contribution towards solving the fundamental challenges they face. This really isn't anything new. Once financial service providers arose as a catalyst to bring the world more wealth and prosperity. The essence, the *raison d' être*, the real deeper meaning of banks, insurance companies, and pension funds, lies in their great social usefulness. By organizing and facilitating money currents, they brought safety, or at least a reduction of insecurity, mutual support in times of need, a carefree attitude and peace of mind. Those are the roots of financial services. And that is how they brought about an enormous acceleration of wealth and prosperity for the human race – for centuries.

This essence has, putting it mildly, been completely lost track of over the past twenty years, but it's to these roots the industry has to return – any which way. At the present moment in history, we are at a crossroads. The only positive aspect of the current misery is the

opportunity it presents for financial service providers to step out from under their own shadow of those past twenty years and to take up their original role again.

Money makes the world go around, but now in the most literal sense. Money oils the wheels of society, no matter what. That realization implies a responsibility. Financial service providers can make themselves useful in solving the great challenges we face as a human race. If they seriously take up that gauntlet, they will also regain some integrity in the eyes of their customers. The financial industry is about to become far more involved with the real economy again. It is going to exert itself to make possible important functions in society, such as care, education, quality of life, and food supply. From the unreal economy, that is artificial, remote from users, non-transparent, and shadowy, the industry is moving toward its original role, as an active participant in a real economy – transparent, authentic, and simple.

In this new time and context, with so many new opportunities, financial service providers must position and organize themselves in a very different way. At the moment, they have the reputation of being a cumbersome, reactive, not very transparent administrative bureaucracy. Instead, they must become pioneers, turning an old bureaucracy into a creative industry, close to the market. They have to listen to what is going on in the market, show entrepreneurship, humility, come up with real solutions, and be transparent, flexible, and open. They must be more than socially responsible. They must make themselves subservient to society.

The future of finance lies in going where it came from in the first place: back to its roots.

sources

Books

Anderson, C., *The Long Tail*, New York, 2006.

Archer, S. and Karim, R.A.A., *Islamic Finance*, 2007.

Armstrong, K., *The Battle for God*, New York, 2000.

Armstrong, K., *Holy War*, New York, 2001.

Bakas, A., *Megatrends Nederland*, Schiedam, Netherlands, 2005.

Bakas, A., *Megatrends Europe*. London, 2006.

Bakas, A. and Buwalda, M., *De Toekomst van God*, Scriptum, Schiedam, Netherlands 2006.

Beck, D., *Spiral Dynamics*. Blackwell, Oxford, 2004.

Bloem, J., van Doorn, M. and Duivestein, S., *Me the Media*, VINT/Sogeti, Netherlands, 2008.

Bolkestein, F., *The Limits of Europe*. Tielt, Belgium, 2004.

Büchel, B., Leleux, B. and Moncef, A., *Anticipating the Future*, 2007.

Chan Kim, W. and Mauborgne, R., *Blue Ocean Strategy*, Harvard Business School Press, Watertown MA, 2005.

Cleveland, H., *Nobody in Charge: Essays on the Future of Leadership*. 2002.

Collier, P., *The Bottom Billion*, Oxford, Oxford University Press, 2007.

Darby, M., *Alliance Brand*, John Wiley and Sons, 2006.

Das, R. and Das, R., *Future Flashes*, Baarn, Netherlands, 2004.

Davies, G., *A History of Money from Ancient Times to the Present Day*, University of Wales Press, Cardiff, 2002.

Ferraresi, P.M. et al., *Unequal Welfare States: Distributive Consequences of Population Ageing in Six European Countries*, Rome, 2005.

Friedman, T., *The World is Flat*, New York, 2005.

Fukuyama, F., The End of History and the Last Man. Washington, D.C. 2003.

Gladwell, M., *The Tipping Point*, New York, 2002.

Godin, S., *All Marketeers Are Liars*, London, 2005.

Greenfield, S., *Tomorrow's People: How 21st-century Technology is Changing the Way We Think and Feel*, London, 2003.

Greenfield, S., *ID: The Quest for Identity in the 21st Century*, London, 2008.

Heath, C. and Heath, D., *Made to Stick*, New York, 2007.

Huntington, S.P., *The Clash of Civilizations and the Remaking of World Order*. New York, 1998.

Huntington, S.P., *Who are We?*, New York, 2004.

Kapferer, J.N., *Rumors*, 1990.

Kapferer, J.N., *The New Strategic Brand Management*, New York, 2008.

Leonard, M. *Why Europe will Run the 21st Century*. London, 2004.

Lutz, P. and Obersteiner, E., *Megatrends Osteuropa*. Vienna, 2004

McDonough, W. and Braungart, M., *Cradle to Cradle*, 2002.

Maeda, J., *The Laws of Simplicity*, 2006.

Mahbubani, K., *The New Asian Hemisphere*, 2008.

Menzies, G., *1421: The Year China Discovered the World*, New York, 2004.

Morgan, A., *The Pirate Inside*, 2004.

Naisbitt, J., *Megatrends 2000*. New York, 2000.

Nieuwkerk, M. and Kroeze, C., *Bubbles*, 2007.

Peverelli, P.J., *Chinese Corporate Identity*, 2006.

Pilny, K., *Das Asiatische Jahrhundert: China und Japan auf dem Weg zur neuen Weltmacht*, Frankfurt, 2005.

Pine II, B.J. and Gilmore, J.H., *The Experience Economy*, 1999.

Pine II, B.J. and Gilmore, J.H., *Authenticity*, 2007.

Prahalad, C.K. and Ramaswamy, V. *The Future of Competition*, 2004.

Reichheld, F., *The Ultimate Question*, 2006.

Ridder, W. de, *Koers 2020: Een gouden decennium in het verschiet*. The Hague, 2004.

Roberts, K., *Lovemarks*, powerHouse Books, New York, 2005.

Ruijs, P. and Sonnemans, M., *Dutch Magic – How Dutch Companies Challenge Global Markets*, 2008

Sinha, A., *Sweet Spot*, Wiley, 2007.

Steyn, M., *America Alone*, Washington, D.C., 2006.

Wilson, D. and Purushothaman, R., *Dreaming with BRIC's: The Path to 2050*. Goldman Sachs, 2003.

Yunus, M., *Banker to the Poor*, 1999.

Articles

Amelio, W.J., 'Interconnected we Prosper', *International Herald Tribune*, June 27, 2008.

Battes, P. and van Wijnen, J.F., 'Alles wordt service', interview with Jean-Paul Votron, *FD Strategie*, May 2008.

Coy, P., 'First Housing, Now Oil', *BusinessWeek*, May 29, 2008.

Dapice, D., 'Inflation Promises a Belt-Tightening Era', *YaleGlobal*, June 18, 2008.

Delta Lloyd Group, 'Over eenvoud', 2007/2008.

Dervis, K., 'Irrational Exuberance to Bust: Financial Bubbles Demand Regulation', *YaleGlobal*, April 23, 2008.

Drake, P., 'En Portada: Santander, "Aquí se trabaja con corbata...roja"', *Actualidad Económica*, July 25 2008.

Einhorn, B., 'Outsourcing the Patients', *BusinessWeek*, March 14, 2008.

Eizenstat, S. 'The Sovereign Wealth Explosion', *Wall Street Journal*, November 9, 2007.

Iyer, B. and Davenport, T.H., 'Reverse Engineering, Google's Innovation Machine', *Harvard Business Review*, April 2008.

Mero, J., 'Power Shift', *Fortune*, July 21, 2008.

Müller, M., 'Over Genen en Genieten' (speech), 6 June 2002.

Nods, R. 'Bank wordt heus gered', *Elsevier* (magazine), 19 April 2008.

Nods, R. and Stellinga, M., 'Kredietcrisis? Er is nog steeds een overvloed aan geld', Interview with Onno Ruding, *Elsevier* (magazine), July 5, 2008.

Oostveen, J. and Stergiou, S. 'Four drivers to improve the sales of advice sensitive products', *Time To Market*, VODW Marketing, 2008.

Peverelli, R., 'Corporate Sustainability', *Time To Market*, VODW Marketing, 2004.

Rehman, A. and Nazim A, 'Islamic Finance: The New Global Player', *Harvard Business Review*, January 2008.

Rohde, M. and de Feniks, R., 'Easy Does It', *Time To Market*, VODW Marketing, 2008.

Rothkopf, D.J., 'Superclass and the Inequity of Globalisation', *YaleGlobal*,

May 14, 2008.

Ruijs, P. and Sonnemans, M., 'ING Direct – Simple Saving', Interview with Dick Harryvan, Board member ING Groep, in *Dutch Magic – How Dutch companies challenge global markets*, 2008.

Ruijs, P. and Sonnemans, M., 'Philips – Multinational Makes House Calls', Interview with Geert van Kuijck, Chief Marketing Officer Philips, in *Dutch Magic – How Dutch Companies Challenge Global Markets*, 2008.

Sachs, J.D., Kiviat, B., Corliss, R., *et.al.*, '10 Ideas That are Changing the World', *Time*, March 24, 2008.

Semanario Philanthropy in Europe, Issue 25

Sonnemans, M. 'The nine features of a smash hit', *Time To Market*, VODW Marketing, 2008.

Struijs, A., 'DNB: Kredietcrisis strekt tot lering', Rabobank Themabericht 2008/14.

van Leeuwen-Fontein, M. and Vulink, M., 'From consumer to prosumer', *Time To Market*, VODW Marketing, 2008.

van Oosterhout, B., 'Laat ze Bloeden!', *Intermediair*, April 17 2008.

van Roekel, E. 'Finovate 2008: 40 financial startups op één dag', *Marketing Facts*, 2008.

Vanheste, T., 'Veel mensen denken dat ik stapelgek ben', interview with Susan Greenfield *Vrij Nederland*, July 12, 2008.

World Wealth Report 2007, Merrill Lynch & Cap Gemini, June 2008.

'Bernacke's Bubble Laboratory', *Wall Street Journal*, May 16, 2008.

'El secreto del éxito de "tu otro banco" en España', interview with Sofía Rodríquez-Sahagún, Director of ING Direct, *Time To Market*, VODW Marketing, 2007.

'Germans Fear Meltdown of Financial System', *Der Spiegel*, March 26, 2008.

'Germans know something about business', *Der Spiegel*, May 28, 2008.

'Globalized Inflation', *Wall Street Journal*, June 21, 2008.

'How Speculators are Causing the Cost of Living to Skyrocket', *Der Spiegel*, June 13, 2008.

'¿Incremento de las ventas de seguros en un 40%? ¡Es posible!', Interview with Luis Badrinas, Reggy de Feniks and Julián López, *Time To*

Market, VODW Marketing, 2007.

'Informe de Responsabilidad Corporativa', *La Caixa*, 2007.

'la Caixa contributes 4m to Gavi vaccination programme', *Money Market*, August 2008.

'Queremos ser el banco privado más recomendado a nivel mundial', Interview with Ellen Kousen, Senior Vice President at ABN-Amro Private Banking, *Time To Market*, VODW Marketing, 2007.

'Reconnecting Brands to Business', interview with Jean-Noël Kapferer and Roger Peverelli, *Time to Market*, VODW Marketing, 2007.

'The Decoupling Debate', *The Economist*, March 6, 2008.

'The high price of free accounts', *The Economist*, July 12, 2008.

'Twin twisters. Fannie Mae, Freddie Mac and the market chaos', *The Economist*, July 19, 2008.

'US Slump Takes Toll Across Globe', *Wall Street Journal*, April 3, 2008.

'What the Fed Could Learn from Europe's Central Bank', *Der Spiegel*, April 29, 2008.

Online sources / archives Trend Office Bakas and VODW Marketing

Blogs, online databases, and online archives of newspapers and business magazines
Actualidad Económica, BrickMeetsByte.com, *Business 2.0*, *BusinessWeek*, CNN, *Corriere della Sera*, Datamonitor, *The Economist*, *The Economist Intelligent Life*, Efma(g), *Elsevier*, *Emerce*, The Globalist, *the Guardian*, *Harvard Business Review*, *Le Figaro*, *Het Financieele Dagblad*, *Financial Times*, *Focus*, *Forbes*, Forrester, *Fortune*, *Frankfurter Allgemeine Zeitung*, the *Independent*, *Le Monde*, *Newsweek*, *New York Times*, *NRC Handelsblad*, Money Market, Marketingfacts.nl, *El País*, *Der Spiegel*, Springwise.com, *Süddeutsche Zeitung*, *Stern*, *Time*, *The Times*, Trendwatching.com, VODW FuturEyes, *De Volkskrant*, *Vrij Nederland*, *Wall Street Journal*, *Washington Post*, *Die Welt*, *Wired* YaleGlobal.

Corporate websites, annual reports, and press archives
ABN-Amro, AEGON, Allianz, American Express, Assicurazioni Generali, Atradius, Aviva, AXA, Banco de Chile, Banco Real, Banco Sabadell, Bank of America, Barclays, BNP Paribas, BBVA, La Caixa, CitiGroup, Commerzbank, Crédit Agricole, Credit Suisse, Deutsche Bank, Dexia Group, easyMoney, Fannie Mae, Fortis, Freddie Mac, Gazprombank, General Electric, GMAC, Goldman Sachs, Grupo Santander, HBOS, HSBC, ING Group, Intesa SanPaolo, KBC Group, Kookmin Bank, Korea Exchange Bank, Lehman Brothers, Mapfre, Merrill Lynch, JPMorgan Chase & Co., Morgan Stanley, Munich Re, Quicken Loans, New China Life, Nordea Bank, Ping An, Rabobank, Raiffeisen Bank Austria, Royal Bank of Canada, Royal Bank of Scotland, Shell, Société Générale, Standard Chartered Bank, Sumitomo Mitsui Banking Corporation, Swiss Life, Swiss Re, Umpqua Bank, UBS, UniCredit Group, Virgin Money, Wachovia Corporation, Washington Mutual, World Bank, Zurich Financial Services.

index